"No people have ever poured out their blood more freely in defense of their liberties and independence."
— *Judah P. Benjamin, Secretary of State*

Plymouth's Civil War:

The Destruction of a North Carolina Town

John Bernhard Thuersam

Wake Forest, NC
www.scuppernongpress.com

Dedication

James Isaac Metts
Fellow Plymouth Reenactor and Proud Descendant of Captain James Isaac Metts, 3rd North Carolina Regiment and Col. Robert H. Cowan, 18th North Carolina Regiment.

Plymouth's Civil War:
The Destruction of a North Carolina Town

By John Bernhard Thuersam

©2024 John Bernhard Thuersam

First Printing

The Scuppernong Press
PO Box 1724
Wake Forest, NC 27588
www.scuppernongpress.com

Cover design by Bill Hunter, Wilmington Design Company

Book design by Frank B. Powell, III

All rights reserved

Printed in the United States of America

No part of this book may be reproduced or transmitted in any form or by any means, electronic or mechanical, including photocopying, recording, or by any information and storage and retrieval system, without written permission from the editor and/or publisher.

International Standard Book Number ISBN 978-1-942806-65-3

Library of Congress Control Number: 2024909368

Contents

Preface v

Acknowledgments vii

Chapter One - Before Plymouth 1

Chapter Two — Town Settlement, Growth and Population 13

Chapter Three - A Political Summary 29

Chapter Four — The Path to War 55

Chapter Five — Independence and Invasion 75

Chapter Six — Loyalty, Treason and Contrabands 93

Chapter Seven — Descent into Total War 115

Chapter Eight — Marauding Terrorists in North Carolina 137

Chapter Nine — Fortress on the Roanoke 151

Chapter Ten — "Three Cheers for North Carolina!" 167

Chapter Eleven — After the Carnage and Ruination 193

Chapter Twelve — Epilogue 207

Appendix A 213

Appendix B 215

About the Author 219

Bibliography 221

Index 231

Preface

The small trading town of Plymouth emerged on the Roanoke River in the early 1790s and one of the most convincing theories of the town name was its brisk shipping trade with New England as well as the West Indies. These commercial ties were strong and it was during the brutally cold Valley Forge winter of 1777 that North Carolinians freely provided the bulk of foodstuffs for New England's starving troops. Ironically, many of the troops invading northeastern North Carolina in 1862-1864 were New Englanders joined by New Yorkers and Pennsylvanians.

Word traveled quickly that northern troops would protect those professing "unionism" and loyalty to "the Union," but in reality practiced unrestrained looting and destruction. By the time the enemy arrived at Plymouth in late 1862, most residents had left to refugee in safer locales. The town itself was devastated on Wednesday, December 10th 1862 when the 17th North Carolina surprised and routed enemy troops occupying the town, the artillery from both sides left many buildings burning hulks. The victorious 17th regiment soon withdrew to nearby winter quarters but any returning residents were to find little remaining. While it may be accurate to state that Plymouth was liberated from the invader, there was precious little that remained post-battle. What remained of the town at Christmas 1862 were only half-wrecked and burnt buildings in addition to a few miraculously left untouched. Today only five pre-Civil War buildings remain as symbols of the town's past.

The enemy was to return a few months later to begin establishing a more permanent base for raids up the Roanoke River toward the important rail bridge near the town of Weldon.

But perhaps the most illuminating aspect of this early war invasion of northeastern North Carolina of 1862-1863 was the "total war" devastation it visited upon civilians. Not only was this reminiscent of Banastre Tarleton's brutality during the Revolution, but also New York's militia in mid-December 1813 ordering Canadian civilians out into the cold while burning their homes on the Niagara River. The reader will discover an indiscriminate "total war" against American civilians as commonplace from the initial landing of Burnside's Expedition at Hatteras Inlet in early 1862 onward. This is well-documented by the commanders of the marauding troops.

John Bernhard Thuersam

Additionally, a deplorable part of the war was the fomenting of hatred between white and black North Carolinians not seen since the Revolution, plus the derogatory word "Tory" was once again in common parlance. To suppress the Virginia colonists' "secession" in November 1775, Virginia's Royal Governor, Lord Dunmore, threatened a violent race war by arming the African slaves and enlisting them in his military as colored troops. They joined Dunmore's British soldiers in "burning houses, ravaging plantations and carrying off slaves" while posting his proclamation emancipating slaves joining British forces to defeat the colonists. Ironically, this would be in evidence again 87 years later but this time with Northern armies invading Virginia, North Carolina and other States.

The 1864 Battle

When compared to the pantheon of well-known American Civil War battlefields, Plymouth, North Carolina does not come quickly to mind as does Gettysburg, Sharpsburg and Shiloh. Too often overlooked in the shade of late-war battles in North Carolina such as Fort Fisher and Bentonville, the epic battle fought here in mid-April 1864 was a much-needed triumph of mostly North Carolina forces led by Brigadier General Robert F. Hoke. President Jefferson Davis was so elated by Hoke's signal victory he immediately promoted him to Major-General.

It was clearly General Hoke's quiet demeanor, secretive Stonewall Jackson-like planning, and the intense loyalty of his chosen subordinates and troops which left little to pure chance. The last was felt in the nervous moments when Hoke's land assault needed the CSS *Albemarle's* arrival to neutralize the enemy's gunboats protecting the fortress. Once the enemy troops became aware of the ironclad behind them, it was simply a matter of time.

It should be pointed out that several valuable volumes exist which describe the mid-April 1864 Plymouth battle and no doubt the foremost is Hampton Newsome's 2019 book, *The Fight for the Old North State* which examines the wider context in which Plymouth and the April 1864 battle occurred. Nonetheless, I remain hopeful the reader will appreciate this honest effort to visualize the town and its people from a 1790s river town to a busy river port to the carnage and destruction of April 1864. And admittedly, this is done from a decidedly local and regional point of view.

Acknowledgments

Many thanks are owed to those who inspired and helped guide me with this project.

Foremost is friend Wayne Newnam who encouraged my first visit to Plymouth in 2014 as a fellow reenactor. This led to two more exhilarating experiences amid the smoke of non-deadly battle and "assaulting" Fort Compher on the same ground as General Ransom's North Carolinians. Another to recognize is friend and reenactor Jim Metts who trod that ground in 2017. None will ever forget the Roanoke River's peaceful and enchanting beauty at morning's first light.

Special thanks go to Steve McAllister for his part in helping me assemble much of the research library from which this book springs, as well as good friend Howard Talley, III for his invaluable assistance with proofreading and final manuscript editing. And certainly my wife Song Suk whose wisdom, patience and understanding always seems limitless.

Lastly, those brave men who fought and died to liberate Plymouth twice were motivated by something very difficult to define but we know what it is, and it's one of the reasons we study the past. That "we stand on the shoulders of giants" as said by French philosopher Bernard de Chartres long ago cannot be stressed enough as we study those of the past.

If we elevate our minds high enough, we can embrace the past as well as foresee the future.

— *John Bernhard Thuersam*

Before Plymouth

Before the arrival of Europeans, the Roanoke River region was inhabited by Indian tribes who archaeologists understand had migrated from the west. Word of mouth tales of the Tuscarora's and Cherokees relate a long, eastward migration with a high probability of them displacing earlier inhabitants through wars. Tribes then inhabiting the Albemarle region were primarily Croatoan with Tuscarora, Catawba and Carolina Siouan to the interior. The Croatoans first contact with Europeans was likely Giovanni de Verrazano in 1524. He anchored off Ocracoke Island to obtain water, convinced he had found the route to Cathay and India though it was actually the Pamlico Sound. There is the mysterious tale of the word "Croatoan" carved into a tree where the Lost Colony settlers were to be when John White returned from England with needed supplies in 1590.[1]

By 1665 the royally-appointed Proprietor George Monck, Duke of Albemarle, held authority in the northernmost county which bordered the Albemarle Sound. Established by New Englanders in 1662, Clarendon County was to the south on the Cape Fear River. It flourished briefly but was abandoned a year later. Given their limited understanding of the globe, from the beginning of settlement and the original charter of 1633, Carolinas western limit was the South Seas as England then referred to the Pacific Ocean — but later realized to be the Mississippi.[2] The colony itself was one until 1729 — Carolinas — named in honor of Charles IX of France and then Charles I and Charles II of England. The word "Carolina" is rooted in Latin and originates in the word "Caroliinus" derived from "Carolus" and translated as Charles.[3]

---

1 Powell, p10-11
2 Ibid p24
3 Wiki, 8.24.23

John Bernhard Thuersam

Though the soil of the northeastern counties was found to be generally more adaptable to grain crops than cotton and tobacco, that of Tyrrell and its contiguous counties contained some large areas of infertile sandy soil. But further inland the land was more clayey topped with sandy loam of remarkable fertility for farming.[4]

Tobacco crops soon became an Albemarle staple with New England smugglers using shallow-draft ships to load the product while operating an illegal trade to Scotland, Ireland, Holland, France and Spain. After a crackdown by the Proprietor who feared retaliation by the Crown, the New England opportunists were driven off and business dropped dramatically. The Revolution itself would be triggered by New England's merchant fleet and smuggling operations that Britain's Navigation Acts tried to stifle.

The late 1600s witnessed a rejuvenated government which strengthened the provincial administration and French Huguenots from Virginia settling on lands south of the Albemarle Sound.[5] About 1704 the first town in North Carolina, Port Bath was established on a bluff overlooking the Pamlico River. This was also the first recorded port of entry in the province. Steady growth in this region continued and by 1710 new settlements extended from the Virginia border to the Albemarle Sound, and along the banks of the Roanoke, Pamlico and Neuse. Noting the growing exodus southward, Virginia officials complained of losing many residents in search of land to plant and cultivate.

Though North Carolina wanted more residents, the newcomers desire for religious freedom clashed with the British determination to establish the Anglican church in their colony. An Anglican missionary stated in 1704 that the Quakers, despite being only one-seventh the population, constituted "the most powerful enemies to Church government." Another missionary viewed the Quakers as "very numerous, extremely ignorant, insufferably proud and consequently ungovernable." Other newcomers under suspicion were those without religion, in addition to Presbyterians who "preach and baptize" throughout the country. In 1704 an Anglican missionary wrote that a minority were truly zealous for the Anglican church but were undermined by the other sects.[6]

---

4 Sitterson, p4
5 Lefler, p49
6 Ibid, p53

The settlement of New Bern by German Palatine, Swiss, and some Englishmen in 1710 added to the mix of newcomers to the colony. Its Swiss promoters wisely sought about 650 healthy and "laborious young people of all avocations" to help guarantee the town's success. The settlement grew quickly with many new homes constructed, but disaster struck in September of 1711 when the Tuscarora's attacked and nearly demolished everything. This brief "Cary Rebellion" had weakened settler defenses and gave the Tuscarora's an opportunity to strike at the European intruders.[7]

The Indians of course resented encroachments on what they believed was theirs and feared the newcomers would take all of their land. The settlers had already reneged on payment for lands purchased from the Tuscarora and complained of Indians hunting too close to their land. Interestingly, in 1711 the Tuscarora petitioned the Governor of Pennsylvania to protest the seizure of their lands and the enslavement of their people.

There existed then a practice of kidnapping Tuscarora, especially women and children, and selling them in the Pennsylvania colony. The Indian slaves were apparently not as desirable as African slaves after the Legislature in 1705 enacted a law against the further importation of Indians. William Penn was a slaveholder himself when his Pennsylvania colony was established, and Delaware as well when created a year later. Penn preferred Africans "for a man then owns them while they live," since white indentured servants departed after their period of servitude. The original Quakers had no misgivings about slaveholding and by 1758 some 70 percent of Philadelphia and Chester County Quaker families actively imported slave cargoes from Barbados and Jamaica. There did exist free black people in Pennsylvania who "led severely circumscribed lives" and could be returned to slavery for laziness or petty crimes. Slavery post-Revolution was on the decline as abolition debates began after 1778 and Quakers realized that keeping Africans seemed an exorbitant expense. As with other northern States, Pennsylvania passed a gradual emancipation law in 1780 which technically maintained slavery until 1848, though black residents were denied the vote and not permitted to serve in the militia. Quakers, like other northern slaveholders, then sold off their African slaves to Delaware or other Southern States for a handsome profit.[8]

---

7 Ibid, p52
8 Harper: www.slaverynorth.com

Historian Lefler writes of "almost every writer of the time mentioning the sharp and irregular practices" of Carolina traders who very often cheated the Indians, with the latter learning to repay the lesson themselves. The Tuscarora decided they would endure the tyranny no longer and rose against the newcomers. The colonists war against the Tuscarora was waged with troops raised in both Virginia and Carolina, who swiftly defeated them in two battles near New Bern in January 1712. The ensuing truce forced the Tuscarora to renounce claims to their land and agree to not plant, fish or hunt on all lands lying between the Neuse and Cape Fear Rivers. This broke the power of the tribe and any Tuscarora fortunate to escape death or enslavement migrated northward to join the Iroquois in New York, completely by 1802.[9]

The continued settlement of the colony included indentured servants; the Proprietors offering plantation masters eighty acres of land for each male servant imported and forty acres for each woman, child and slave.[10] The Lords of Trade ruled that the proprietary colonies be brought under closer supervision of the Crown after what they saw as the ineffectiveness of provincial administration. The "royalization" of North Carolina began a new and significant era in settlement and development. Emphasis was now on the province's value as a source of naval stores and other commercial activities which better aligned with Britain's important mercantile system.[11]

This was paralleled with Parliament approving the important Naval Stores Bounty Act in 1705. At that time England was at the mercy of the Swedish Tar Company for naval stores which were absolutely necessary for maintaining its navy and merchant marine. Given North Carolina's dense forests of pine for turpentine, tar and pitch, the northern Carolina became a material provider for the ready customers of shipbuilding centers up the Atlantic coast, and England.

---

9 Lefler, p57-60
10 Ibid, p115
11 Ibid, p69

North Carolina never became a center of shipbuilding, though some did occur but never a major industry. The colony did see about 25 ships constructed between 1769 and 1772 of moderate tonnage, with Port Roanoke (Edenton) recording 21 of 146 ships clearing its port from April 1771 to April 1772 that were North Carolina-built.[12]

Shipbuilding in the colonial period was primarily a New England affair and its ships were heavily-engaged in smuggling goods to the other colonies and West Indies in violation of British law. This traffic left little for British merchants to export to the colonies and led Parliament to keep a more watchful eye on its New England colonies. Author Reese Wolfe wrote of New England's pre-Revolution stake in what was becoming a profitable transatlantic trade:

"Shipbuilding, especially for New England's triangular trade for African slaves, was sufficiently profitable for the shipbuilders of the Thames district to meet in London in the winter of 1724-1725 and formally complain to the Lords of Trade: "… the New England trade, by the tender of extraordinary inducements, has drawn over so many working shipwrights that there are not enough left to carry on [our] work.""[13]

New England's merchant fleet found a brisk West Indies trade in rum and "black ivory." This was a triangular trade involving rum, slaves and molasses. Wolfe continues:

"Like so many momentous occasions in history, the start of the slave trade had been an offhand sort of occurrence. A Dutch privateer found itself with twenty Negroes taken from a Spanish ship and, not knowing what to do with them, dropped anchor in the river at Jamestown in 1619, a year before Plymouth Rock. The Negroes were offered cheaply as laborers and the Virginia settlers decided to trade tobacco for them. The swap was made and the Dutch sailed away, leaving behind them a cancerous growth that was to bring the parent body close to death before the disease was arrested."[14]

These were laborers — indentured servants as Virginia court records as late as 1660 referred to Negroes. But further north the New Englanders captured Indians along Maine's Kennebec River as early as 1637 and sold them as slaves on the coast. The Pequot War of 1636-1638 ended with some 700 of the tribe killed or taken prisoner, the

---

12 Ibid, p93
13 Wolfe, p42
14 Ibid. p44

John Bernhard Thuersam

latter — including women and children — were sold into slavery at Bermuda or the West Indies.[15] The war virtually erased the tribe from that region.

It was the availability of black slaves from Africa, argues Wolfe, which attracted New England's merchant fleet there and the West Indies, and entrenched slavery in America's southern colonies. The large plantations needed cheap labor, New England had the ships, and African tribes willingly sold their captured brethren to the Yankee traders.

Wolfe concludes: "The mechanics of the all-important trade worked like this: Molasses was brought to New England and made into rum; the rum, highly-prized among the native Negroes on the west coast of Africa, brought its own price among the drinkers, a price that included any of their relatives or friends who might have the bad judgment to be lying about, and the resultant human cargoes were disposed of profitably in Boston, Newport and on south. Or most of the way south. Foreign ships for the most part maintained the supply in the deep South.

Not all the West Indies rum was drunk by Negroes. A flourishing local trade in fur was conducted with the Indians by the extremely profitable exchange of a few bottles of cheap rum or whiskey for the entire season's catch of its drunken owner. New England rum, it is generally agreed, had more to do with the destruction of the Indian tribes on the eastern seaboard than all the wars in which they were engaged put together.[16]

The period 1724-1729 witnessed a large increase in immigration to North Carolina as a result of the Tuscarora defeat, the suppression of pirates and the new administration of Royal Gov. George Burrington. In hindsight, Burrington's government was less than successful but he did build roads and improve harbors in addition to attracting 1000 settlers between 1724 and 1725. Four new counties were added between 1722 and 1730 as "testimony to the increase in population" with Bertie and Carteret in 1722, Tyrrell (from which Washington was formed in 1799) in 1729, and New Hanover in the same year.[17] A decade earlier the land on what would become the town of Plymouth began with the Thomas Long Patent granted by the crown on March 15, 1717.

---

15 Wiki, accessed 12.4.23
16 Ibid, p44
17 Lefler, pp64-65

In 1766 the General Assembly agreed upon New Bern as the seat of government and appropriated funds to erect a fitting residence for the Royal Governor. This was an irritant to the western Scotch-Irish farmers who saw no need for the splendor of Tryon's "palace". The Albemarle Sound advanced rapidly from brisk trade with Virginia ports and lower land rents, half of those in the Neuse-Pamlico and Cape Fear sections. The latter had little contact with the Albemarle region as its trade was focused elsewhere. With the counties of Pasquotank, Chowan, Perquimans, Currituck and Tyrrell having five Assembly delegates each, and Bertie three, the Albemarle had a virtual monopoly in colonial government — the Cape Fear counties had only two delegates each. Prior to 1736 every Assembly had met in the Albemarle region, usually at Edenton, which became known then as the unofficial capital of the colony — every speaker of the House a resident of the Albemarle. But the population and economic growth of the Neuse-Pamlico saw it surpass the Albemarle, but these northern counties remained in a dominant Assembly representation position — thirty-one compared to twenty-three for other counties.[18]

In the realm of religion, the Anglican Church was established by law in the colony though it was never very strong or popular, suggesting this was due to it being a royal decree. Non-Anglicans resented its control of education and being taxed to support the Church, as well as the requirement that Anglican clergy perform marriages. This led to the growth of dissenting sects of Quakers, Presbyterians, Baptists, Moravians, Lutherans and Methodists in the colony after 1730. The Kehukee Baptists of William Sojourner had a congregation in Tyrrell/Washington County, and on the eve of the Revolution this sect had sixty-one churches and some 5,000 members in the colony.[19]

The citizenry of North Carolina in the first half of the nineteenth century was for the most part rural and agricultural with most engaged in land cultivation, and the architecture of their small towns were modest frame or log dwellings, barns and gristmills. The farmers, their families and farmhands all worked the land from sunup to sunset with breaks only for morning breakfast, dinner about 2 o'clock and supper in the early evening.

---

18 Ibid, p162
19 Ibid, pp123-128

Farms such as David Davenport's just north of the Scuppernong River near today's Creswell grew cotton, wheat, flax and tobacco, plus the usual assortment of livestock to be a self-sufficient family community. A Revolutionary veteran, Davenport was elected in 1800 to represent the newly-formed Washington County in the North Carolina Senate.

A much larger nearby property was Somerset Place, the creation of 1773 British emigrant Josiah Collins of Edenton. In 1785 Collins became principal of a corporation which acquired title to vast land tracts near Lake Phelps, just west of 1799's eastern border of the new Washington county with Tyrrell. A large body of water — twelve miles long and eight miles wide — it is believed to have been formed by a prehistorical meteor strike and filled by underground spring waters.

The corporation's intent was to develop the region into productive plantations of marketable produce for export. Collins planned to excavate a twenty-foot-wide by six-mile-long canal connecting Lake Phelps with the Scuppernong River (while draining adjacent swamplands), augmented by small connecting ditches for better flood control, irrigation, and water power for machinery. Once completed, their farm products would be conveyed down the canal to the small port of Columbia on the Albemarle Sound.

This innovative improvement — "a virtual Nile River to the inhabitants" — not only fed the workers and their families with ample produce, but also exported large amounts of corn, wheat, rice and vegetables to distant ports. The on-site sawmill produced dressed lumber, barrel staves, shingles, posts and ship building products which were sold through agents in Charleston, Baltimore, Norfolk & New York, as well as several small North Carolina ports. This elaborate and extensive farming operation so greatly impressed noted agriculturalist Edmund Ruffin that he published an account of Collins' far-seeing operation in 1838.[20]

Another early nineteenth-century eastern North Carolina agriculturalist of note was Ebenezer Pettigrew, the descendant of French Huguenot immigrants who by way of Scotland and Pennsylvania had established themselves in the Carolinas by the 1760s. Ebenezer inherited his land and thirty slaves from his father Charles and became "one of the ablest planters to appear in the three centuries of that American

---

20 Wilson, p3-4

vocation."[21]

The center of Ebenezer's plantation was his home, Bonarva, where despite the hard work of overseeing planting and harvest operations, there was still time to cultivate hobbies, read, conduct agricultural experiments. His father served in the Legislature and Congress — the latter greatly benefiting his State and home population.[22] Ebenezer's hard work, intelligent farming practices and success so impressed the farmers of the region that he received the votes of all but three of the seven hundred free men of Tyrrell County when standing for a congressional seat in 1834. Being a man without interest in political life, he accepted the seat most reluctantly. Being a Whig politically, Ebenezer had become a friend and supporter of Henry Clay during the former's congressional term.[23]

On area farms the men worked the field while their wives were responsible for domestic labors which included making apple jacks, sweet potato pies and jelly cakes, and planning their regular social events. In the evenings the husband often entertained friends at the fireside where they would "smoke corn-cob pipes, spit tobacco juice in the fire, and pass a mug of brandy around." After polite conversation they turned to news of the region: the weather, their crops and, of course politics. The ladies were usually behind them on benches knitting and discussing the latest social news. The young were not left out of weekend social gatherings where courting and "frolicking" predominated while consuming persimmon beer and roasted sweet potatoes.[24]

Smaller-acreage farmers of the region were politically Jeffersonian anti-Federalists distrustful of any centralized government, such as the one fought against in the Revolution, and opposed to any federal taxation. These farmers of the agricultural backcountry, referred to as "yeoman" by those viewing history as Marxist class warfare, truly determined the political alignment of their district. The commercial trading centers were Federalist enclaves.[25] The politics of the region are covered in more detail in Chapter 3.

From the Roanoke River came a bounty of nature which contributed greatly to the farm family diet with shad and herring being

---

21 Ibid, p2
22 Johnson, p81
23 Wilson, pp5-6
24 Johnson, pp90-91
25 Gilpatrick, p86

especially prized at springtime. This bounty also attracted store owners from as far west as Guilford County who arrived in wagons to load with salted fish to take back to market. While there was much improvised gaiety on the farms and plantations, there was also the dark cloud of high infant mortality in the low country. The birth of a child was accompanied by a learned detachment since both mother and child might not survive the ordeal. Ebenezer's wife Ann Shepard Pettigrew, died at age thirty-five after severe complications at childbirth — a tragic loss which brought him melancholia for the remainder of his life. Another threat to life were the seasonal fevers which disabled many for part of the year if not killing those infected.[26]

A dependable source of political news was the local tavern which normally subscribed to at least one newspaper, perhaps from Edenton or New Bern. This was eagerly read by those stopping for a cup of whiskey, West Indian rum or Madeira, to play at all fours, bet on chances and spread rumors. Twice a year militia musters were yet another opportunity for obtaining political news and spreading local gossip. All free white men between eighteen and forty-five years of age were enrolled in the units for protection of the community and State. These musters also provided ample opportunity for petitioning the Legislature on important local and State matters.[27]

Education in the colony was primarily for the planter class though teachers were scarce. In 1716 Governor Charles Eden encouraged England to procure teachers for the colony and planters would underwrite their salaries. The children of farmers rarely had any formal education as they were too busy working with their parents clearing and tilling the land. But very often planters made provisions in their will instructions for the training of poor and underprivileged children: for boys training in the trades and professions — girls in the feminine arts. For example, in 1744 James Winwright provided in his will funds for a qualified man to teach "at least reading, writing and arithmetic."[28]

Wealthier young men like James Johnston Pettigrew of Bonarva Plantation, born in 1828, benefited from private schooling in New Bern and at Hillsborough's Bingham Academy. The latter's classical curriculum taught that wealth and social position brought with them imperatives of duty and responsibility. This instilled character,

---

26 Wilson, pp5-7
27 Johnson, pp96-102
28 Lefler, p133

humility, self-will and the understanding that in his case, his position resulted from the labor and self-denial of his father and grandfather. A highly intelligent young man, Pettigrew easily passed the University of North Carolina's entrance examination a month before his fifteenth birthday in 1843. Post-bellum president of the University, Kemp Battle and a young resident during Pettigrew's time at UNC, said in 1907 that Pettigrew's scholarship had never been excelled, if equaled, at the university. He also noted he had never met a man with a more penetrating mind and Pettigrew being the ablest man he had ever met.[29] Pettigrew went on to become a Charleston attorney and was elected to represent that city in the South Carolina legislature. It is notable that Pettigrew, a future Southern brigadier-general, attracted national attention by leading the effort against a proposal to reopen the slave trade.[30] Suffering an abdominal wound a week after Gettysburg in July 1863, he passed away near the town of Bunker Hill in western Virginia.

---

29 Wilson, p9
30 Tucker, p204

Town Settlement, Growth & Population

"The ancient Greeks were for the most part a rural, not urban society." — *Plato*

In the year 1777 the low bluff which would grow to become a prosperous Roanoke River town after the Revolution was only a small part of the Thomas Long Patent of sixty years earlier. Only four years after the Treaty of Paris was signed in 1783 a grid-pattern of streets was laid out which would become the river town of "Plymouth."

In the year 1777 as well, Pennsylvania-born and medically-trained Hugh Williamson established a trading base at Edenton with his younger brother of imported medicines and other scarcities brought from the West Indies. As the region's population increased to include the emergence of Plymouth on the Roanoke River, Dr. Williamson's medical practice was greatly appreciated by area merchants and planters. And being a businessman who prospered from the region's foreign trade, he was also a staunch Federalist before and after 1789.[1]

HUGH WILLIAMSON

About the same time the doctor established his trading base at Edenton, nineteen-year-old Elkanah Watson of Plymouth, Massachusetts met Williamson with investment money from Providence, Rhode Island businessman Joseph Brown. The latter was part of the most successful mercantile houses in America which financed slaving voyages to Africa and made Rhode Island a center of that nefarious trade. Williamson advised young Elkanah "of the fortunes waiting to be made in this unexploited region" and encouraged his business ventures. The emigration of young Watson from that "Plymouth" may offer a clue as to the naming of the future town on the lower Roanoke.

---

1 Wiki, accessed 9.9.23

John Bernhard Thuersam

Elkanah Watson

Elkanah first established mercantile contacts in France in 1779, and after five years in Europe returned to America. Upon his return he first visited General Washington, gifting him with books from his travels and listening to the General's ideas on opening a canal around the Potomac River falls to better attract commerce from the Northwest to the Atlantic. Washington heartily endorsed opening a canal through the Dismal Swamp to Hampton Roads which would open the fertile northeastern region of North Carolina to ocean commerce.[2]

Elkanah would meet another proponent of canals, Major Hardy Murfree of "Melrose" plantation 50 miles north of Edenton. The Major envisioned a canal from the falls of the Roanoke River to the Chowan River and Edenton, and foresaw this becoming "the nexus of a great avenue of commerce." Watson himself bought land at the junction of the Meherrin and Chowan rivers naming it "Mount Sion" and aligned with Murfree's expected trade route. There he opened a store and being a New Englander was familiar with African slave labor and held three of his own. The *Edenton Intelligencer* of June 4, 1788 announced that his store carried "imported pewter of all kinds" which could be purchased for cash tar or tobacco.[3]

The Thomas Long Patent land and others bordering the Roanoke were considered extremely fertile. This attracted numerous farmers and plantations, with the river being their direct route for produce to easily reach the busy trade centers at Edenton and New Bern. Further up the Roanoke was the town of Halifax, described in 1783 by General Nathanael Greene as a small village of some 60 little homes. President George Washington passed through Halifax on his 1791 Southern Tour and wrote of its polished and cultivated society of some 1000 residents.[4] In August 1787 planter Arthur Rhodes purchased his large tract of low, rich land along the Roanoke, originally part of the Thomas Long Patent of March 1717.

---

2 Parramore, p449
3 Ibid, pp451-453
4 Gilpatrick, pp13-16

Rhodes named his land acquisition "Brick House Plantation" and wisely set aside 100 riverfront acres for an anticipated commercial landing which became known as "Brick House Landing." This acreage was the higher and better-drained topography between Welch's Creek to the west and Conaby Creek to the east, as well as being only several miles upriver from the Albemarle Sound. With the Roanoke River continuing past the landing in a northeasterly direction up to and beyond Halifax, the opportunity for commercial opportunities seemed limitless.

The region's economic development was already well under way with Edenton as a hub and a new town on the Roanoke would enable nearby and upriver farmers, such as large property owners like Daniel Davenport, to transport their products to market. There commission merchants arranged for shipping to distant buyers as well as the import of needed goods to the town and region. Davenport was to become Washington County's first representative to the North Carolina Senate.[5]

The new town center at Brick House Landing quickly attracted trade in naval stores including timber, shingles, tar, pitch and turpentine from the area's forests. Additionally, valuable crops of tobacco and cotton were shipped from this point, which would become the fifth-largest port in the State. This strong commercial activity would make the region attractive to New England shipbuilders in all its seaboard towns. Their ships were built for the whale, cod and mackerel fisheries, inland, coastwise and foreign commerce such as their African slave trade. So many ships were constructed in 1727 that "ship-carpenters in the Thames complained that their trade was hurt" as many of their workmen emigrated to New England. Constructed and launched at Marblehead in 1636, the Desire was that region's first built for "that inhuman traffic which was kept up till May, 1862."[6]

The 172 lots Rhode's established at his set-aside "Landing" were fashioned into a formal grid of streets parallel to and perpendicular to the Roanoke. As was common to period waterfront North Carolina towns, the first river-parallel street was Water [First], then Main Street [Second], then Third and Fourth Streets. The main perpendicular street to the river was named in honor of George Washington, with Jefferson and Monroe Streets to the west and Adams and Madison

---

5 Wiki, accessed 9.14.23
6 Grady, pp71-72

John Bernhard Thuersam

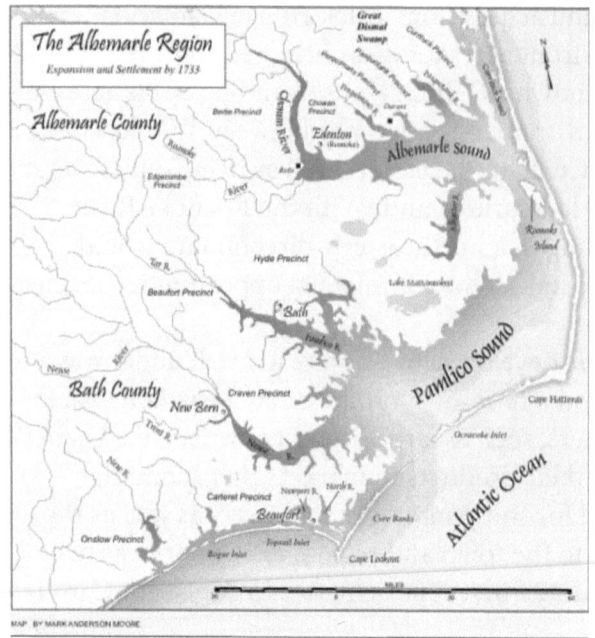

streets to the east. Rhodes initially sold 16 lots before transferring the remainder to nine trustees for 860 pounds. Perhaps for future income, Rhodes and his wife kept a few lots for themselves. Afterward, the trustees erected street-signs and planted street trees to improve and better market the town to potential investors and buyers.

The how and why the town became known as "Plymouth" is subject to several theories. One is that the seven "trustees," to whom Rhodes sold the 100 acres, were New England businessmen from Plymouth who wanted to differentiate it from the rest of Brick House Plantation. Another theory suggests that sailors on ships from Massachusetts made regularly stops there for cargo and perhaps named it Plymouth Landing, later shortened to Plymouth. Another is the previously-mentioned Elkanah Watson whose home was Plymouth, Massachusetts.

The New Englanders were attracted by the area's Longleaf pine and hardwood forests to supply their native region's shipyard needs and profiting from the brisk West Indies trade through Plymouth. The 1790s were a busy boom-time for American-made ships with every sixth vessel launched being sold to foreign interests.[7] In that year the General Assembly designated the town a port of delivery, and by 1808 an official port of entry. Many ships filled with cargoes of corn, rice, peas, pork, hams, tongues, tobacco, ship masts & spars, red & white oak plus barrels of tar, pitch and turpentine departed Plymouth in the 1790s bound for the West Indies. The foodstuffs of these cargoes were destined for the African slaves working sugar plantations and their return ladings often included rum, molasses and sugar, as well as coffee,

---

7 Wolfe, p87

ginger cotton, pimento, mahogany, and indigo.

This brisk trade with Northern ports and the West Indies brought the need for a custom house in town as well as a post office, which opened on March 20, 1793. More changes came in December 1799 when a new Washington County was carved from Tyrrell County, with a new county seat at Lee's Mill (later Roper) where a courthouse was built in late 1801. After being incorporated as a town in 1807, Plymouth's growth as a trade center for the next fifteen years made it a more logical location for the county's official seat of governance, which was moved there in January 1823. Two years later, in November 1824, the new courthouse was completed in Plymouth and would stand until mid-December 1862 when cannon and musket fire during the town's initial liberation ignited it.[8] As Plymouth developed during the first decade of the 1800s it was like others which had taken no serious steps toward fire protection. Twice in 1808, the *Edenton Gazette* reported on attempts to set Plymouth on fire which resulted in residents establishing a patrol which walked the streets nightly. To assure residents of their safety in sleep the patrol would cry out on the hour.[9]

The population of Plymouth as recorded in the 1800 federal census was 257 white persons male and female, 49 free blacks and 645 black slaves. By 1810 this increased to 2,255 white persons male and female, 63 free blacks and 1,287 slaves; and the 1820 the census revealed a great reduction to only 257 total white; 83 free black and 1,675 slaves. In 1830 there were many free black owners of slaves living in the northeastern section of the State including Nancy Boston of Washington County who owned one slave; in adjacent Martin County three free black persons owned 26 slaves between them.[10] The federal census 1850 indicates a population of 951 persons, which included 15 paupers and three who could neither read nor write and living in the Christian charity-supported poorhouse. The population decrease is likely explained by a fever epidemic brought by a ship docked at the wharf which took the lives of many residents. At that time any port towns doing business with the West Indies and other tropical climes had to fear yellow fever coming with the cargo.[11] An epidemic possibly affecting Plymouth as well was the yellow fever which killed 26 resi-

---

8 Washington County Genealogical Society, 7-93
9 *Edenton Gazette*, Feb. 3; Oct. 5.
10 Franklin, p236-237
11 Carolana.com (accessed 10.13.23

John Bernhard Thuersam

dents, both white and black, of Little Washington between the end of August and the 4th of October, 1843. This was reported by the Washington Republican which also indicated 55 families had already left to refugee at a distance.[12]

"At no time during the antebellum period were free Negroes in North Carolina without some slaves"

— *John Hope Franklin*

Those early nineteenth-century census figures record the main occupation of residents as primarily farmers, followed by overseers, millers, carpenters, shinglers, laborers, brick masons, wheelwrights, harness-makers, fishermen, shoemaker, coach trimmer, preachers, weavers, spinners, schoolteachers, housekeepers and students. The town provided enough business for one attorney, 33-year-old Thomas Beckwith. Mulatto residents George and Emma Cooper of Plymouth took in laundry, and Mary Cooper was a seamstress. Free blacks Mary Lee and Harrison Tann were listed as bakers.[13]

In 1860's federal census there were nearly 900 souls living in Plymouth and the town was one of North Carolina's most active ports served by a federal customs house. Washington County's population was nearly 5,500 people with most engaged in farming, of which about 60 percent were white and the remainder black residents — nearly 250 free blacks and 2,100 slaves. The 1860 census also identified 13 free-black persons in Washington County who owned real estate worth $5,843, and another 50 holding personal property totaling $5,077. In that year free-black bake-shop proprietor Mary Alee of Plymouth reported a net worth of $2,750, a very substantial sum at the time.[14]

In nearby Little Washington, free black people were required to register with the town clerk and wear a cloth badge on their shoulder stating "free." Town patrolmen were required to stop all black people on the streets after 10PM and ensure that either they were free or carried a pass from the master.[15] The many free-black persons in northeastern part of the State included Samuel Johnston of Bertie County who held 11 slaves in 1790. This was also the case in Bertie,

---

12 Johnson, pp278-279
13 1850 federal census
14 Franklin, p231
15 Johnson, p128

Northampton, Currituck and Craven counties where free-black owners held as many as five slaves each. By 1830 free-black ownership of slaves had increased with nearby Martin County's Jonathan Critchion owning 24 slaves; both Larry James and Martha James there owned one slave each.[16] Craven County had 12 free-black slaveowners led by John S. Stanly holding 18 slaves, followed by Halifax County's 13 free-black slaveholders then owning one-three slaves each. That black ownership of slaves existed primarily to advance the well-being of the owners, rather than out of sympathy.[17]

"Humanity is divided into two: the masters and the slaves."
— Aristotle, Politics

Human enslavement begins with the dawn of time and not specific to one geographic region, yet oddly the African continent has become synonymous with the word. The word itself is derived from white-skinned Slavic people enslaved by Arab Muslims, with the latter also trading for Africans enslaved by their own people through incessant tribal wars. One African monarch boasted that slaves were Africa's valuable "gold" to trade for goods with other lands.[18]

Europeans did not penetrate very far inland from the sea as the interior was far too dangerous and few if any white men returned from the interior. Inland treks were unnecessary as slaves were readily available from warlike tribes like the Ashanti on the Gold Coast who brought their captured brethren to the coast for sale. Though the "middle passage" sea voyage was described as brutal, it is reported that an equal amount of barbarity accompanied each slave's initial capture and then marched in shackles to the coast.[19]

The slave coast of West Africa as we know it lies between the river Senegal and the Congo River, just south of the equator. At least 20 years before Columbus sailed to the New World a slave market had been established at Lisbon at which Negroes from the Guinea coast were sold to any who would buy. The Moors had told the Portuguese of black-skinned people living in great numbers to the south of the desert — "a race cursed of God and predestined as slaves." In 1502 the

---

16 Franklin, p236
17 Ibid, p159
18 Gunther, p753
19 Ibid, pp753-755

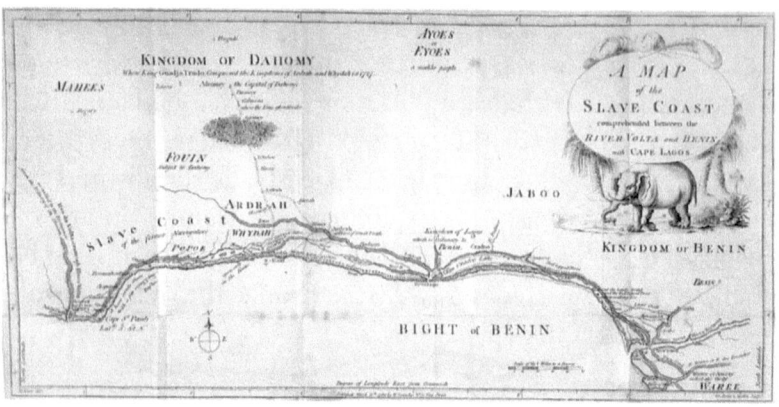

first shipload of Africans had been landed at Hispaniola to work the mines, with this trade continuing until the abolition of Brazilian slavery in 1888. By 1790, the number of "forts and factories" established on the slave coast was about forty: fourteen belonged to the British, fifteen were Dutch; three were French; four were Portuguese; and four were Danish.

The primary traffickers, after the Africans themselves, were the Portuguese and English. Several other nationalities became involved with Britain later gaining a European monopoly of the business via the Treaty of Utrecht in 1712. The King of Dahomey subjugated vast areas and kept his captives in barracoons to await brokers and buyers in vessels.[20] The purchase of a slave in the Cameroons was "two measures of Spanish wine" and he could be sold for a thousand ducats, the profit being some 5,000 percent. As late as 1786, a Nigerian slave would cost two pounds, and bring 65 pounds in America. In that period, 100,000 slaves or more were being shipped across the Atlantic each year in New England and British bottoms.[21]

Africa was not the only source of slaves as Portuguese ships had been exploring the Brazilian coast as early as 1494. There they found brazilwood which yielded valuable red and ochre dyes. The records of the ship *Bertoa* survive and tell of its 1511 voyage to Brazil — returning with brazilwood logs, birds, animals and thirty-five Indian slaves. Human slavery there was already long-practiced by Brazilian tribes including the brutal Tupinikin and Aimore' — the latter of which fed upon its slaves. The Portuguese feared them as they "are so barbarous and intractable that we have never been able to tame them or force any

---

20 Dow, pp1,5,12
21 Gunther, 752

into servitude like other Indians of this land, who accept submission to captivity."[22]

The European's need for laborers led them to begin purchasing slaves from tribes on Africa's west coast, just as Arabs were doing in the north and east, selling this human property on the Arabian Peninsula, Turkey and the Middle East.[23] The persistence of slavery on the Dark Continent was still in evident in the 1950s with central Africa's Tuareg tribe still holding slaves; it is often reported human slavery continues today in the Sudan.[24]

The origin of this trade which later affected North Carolina was the discovery of America and consequent development of sugar plantations in the West Indies. After the aborigines were decimated by English, French, Portuguese and Spanish colonization, Africa became a very dependable source of labor. But most emigrants coming to early colonial British America were under contracts of limited indentured servitude and indenture for life was not unusual. Once a limited contract expired or was bought out, the servant, white or black, would receive land and farming equipment. As demand for labor grew for the indigo, rice and tobacco plantations the Proprietors began importing slaves purchased from African kings.

The Puritan settlers of Massachusetts warred upon the Pequot tribe in what became known as New England as settlements spread on Indian lands. All natives were considered non-religious "strangers" to the Puritans, with conquered and captive Pequots — especially women and children — often sent to a life slavery on West Indian sugar plantations. While this colony was in an inhospitable latitude for large-tract agriculture, large numbers of African workers were unnecessary, though they could be utilized as domestic servants and great profits brought by the slave trade. Their attitude toward colored people is revealed in an act in March of 1788 which made it illegal for a person of African descent to "tarry within this Commonwealth for a longer time than two months" with punishment "not exceeding ten stripes and ordered to depart out of this Commonwealth." Two black persons from North Carolina, James Jurden, Janus Crage and also Polly Johnson, were identified in a *Massachusetts Mercury* (Boston) advertisement of September 16, 1800 and "hereby warned and directed to

---

22 Hemming, p95
23 Gunther, p11
24 Maugham, p164

depart out of this Commonwealth before the 10th day of October next ... so ordered by Superintendent Charles Bullfinch, by direction of the Selectmen." It was certainly possible that both colored men above were residents of Edenton, Plymouth or New Bern.[25] With this in mind one can understand North Carolina's Zebulon Vance caustically referring to New England's Puritans as "men who burnt witches, banished or enslaved Quakers, and had made fortunes from the horrors of the middle passage."[26]

It was not until 1715 that an act of the North Carolina Assembly provided legal sanction to the institution of slavery in the colony; prior to that the actual status of colored people was murky. The first evidence of Africans in North Carolina was in 1709 and 1710 when Rev. James Adams recorded in Currituck parish 97 negroes out of 539 souls; in Pasquotank parish there were 211 negroes in a total population of 1,332. The early concentration of African slaves between the Virginia border and Albemarle region in the 18th century was the logical result of that upper colony's tobacco production which eventually crept into North Carolina. The same was true for the Lower Cape Fear tidewater area with slaves used for rice cultivation. The slaves were later to be more economically employed in the collection of naval stores in the forests.[27]

New England's transatlantic slave trade become so lucrative that its merchant fleet became dominant and by 1750 had surpassed Liverpool as the center of slave-ship construction and outfitting for the transatlantic slave trade. The names of Providence, Rhode Island, Marblehead and other New England coastal towns became synonymous with African slavery. After the post-Revolution ban of the institution within a New England which had regained its moral compass, Massachusetts tinkerer Eli Whitney's 1793 gin changed cotton production from a laborious, time-consuming task into an industry requiring large numbers of field laborers and factory workers. Whitney's invention begat hungry New England textile mills which consumed more and more raw cotton from the South which in turn perpetuated African slavery. It also created a new form of wage-slavery with women and children working long hours in poorly-ventilated, lint-filled factories in Massachusetts in the early 19th century. Nonetheless, New

---

25 Moore, p228-231
26 Dowd, pp240-241
27 Taylor, pp9-12

England's anti-slavery voices increased in the mid-1820s which led to the abolition movement causing sufficient civil strife by the 1850s to fracture the country. This is what inspired Congressman Vance to state in Congress on March 26, 1884:

"Massachusetts is a State more responsible under heaven than any other community in this land for the introduction of African slavery on this continent, and all the curses which have followed it. That State was the nursing mother of the horrors of the middle passage, and after slavery there was found not to pay, her slaves were sold down South for a consideration with their former masters claiming they were no longer responsible for the sin of human slavery."[28]

"The slaves of the South are better off than the servile laboring class of the North."
— *William H. Seward, February 9, 1859*

William H. Seward

The early development of coastal North Carolina was strongly linked to both British and New England merchant fleets which sought timber and naval products from North Carolina's vast pine forests. It was found that slaves could be more economically utilized in the collection of naval stores than tobacco growing, curing and harvesting. Historian Taylor notes that it was common for early planters to send tar and pitch to New England and invest their profits in slaves brought from Virginia because of North Carolina's treacherous coast. For this reason, "ships engaged in the slave trade seldom, if ever, brought their cargoes direct to the colony." Since the Albemarle section was dependent upon Virginia for marketing facilities, and supplies as well, the planters incurred additional costs for all to safely reach their plantations.[29]

---

28 Congressional Record, 6.26.1884; p.2284
29 Taylor, pp20-21

Prior to the American Revolution both Virginia and North Carolina petitioned the Crown to stop the importation of Africans, aware of their growing numbers and greatly fearing insurrection. Though the Founders deemed slavery an abomination and morally wrong, they believed they had no hand in its beginning. Many of North Carolina's constitutional delegates believed slavery would disappear with the end of British colonial trade, with some interestingly seeing little difference between slavery and wage labor. One must keep in mind that this was an era of indentured servitude which is how many immigrants paid for their transatlantic passage on leaky and decrepit ships. It should also be realized that in the postwar both of the Carolinas and Georgia had lost many plantations to British depredations and black agricultural workers were carried off by departing British forces and Tories. The now-United States pressed on with their colonial-derived economies, greatly in need of agricultural workers which could be supplied by those slave-trading States of Rhode Island and Massachusetts, despite any illegalities. Both of those former-colonies remained heavily-invested in the slave trade as financiers, merchants, shippers, shipbuilders and seamen.

Author Benjamin Franklin Grady points out the "compromise" made during the constitutional debates in 1789 regarding non-interference with the slave trade until 1808. He wrote "the Southern States retained the power to purchase Africans imported by New England's slave traders with the proviso lodged somewhere (nobody knows where) that the Northern States could later liberate and enfranchise them. …" [30]

After the close of the American Revolution, New England's slave trade rebounded to the point where it was noticed by the governor of Sierra Leone. In 1797 he reported: "During the last year, the number of American slavers on the African coast has increased to an unprecedented degree."[31] British traders noted this as well. A Bristol, England shipowner complained to his government in 1789 that, since the restrictions were laid upon the slave trade by Parliament, no less than 40 slave vessels had been fitted out in the New England States.

A great change came in the form of a brutal San-Domingue (now Haiti) slave insurrection of 1791 which brought North Carolinians to realize the danger existing within their own large slave population.

---

30 Grady, p80
31 Mannix, p186

This had an effect on reducing new slave arrivals and heavy fines being imposed on slave importations in 1794. As it was feared that rebellious slaves from the Bahamian or West Indian islands might be brought in, this was made unlawful and subject to heavy fines. In addition, in 1798 Governor Samuel Ashe instructed the people of the State to prevent the landing of slaves or free people of color, though smuggling continued.[32]

Though many in North Carolina considered slave importation as "productive of evil consequences and highly impolitic," the lack of available labor allowed the slave trade to reluctantly resume and was not taxed by the General Assembly until 1787. If done legally the Africans would cost a duty of 10 pounds per head if between 12 and 30 years of age. If smuggled, the fine was 100 pounds for each slave imported and the informant was rewarded with one-half the fine.[33] To North Carolina's credit, its citizens' opposition toward the slave trade and pitiful condition of the bondsman were highest during and after the Revolution, and many were concerned about the large number of slaves in their midst even prior to that. Nonetheless, North Carolina's participation in the trade was negligible with virtually no financial incentive to continue it.[34]

The aforementioned Lake Phelps corporation project needed workers but faced serious post-Revolution labor shortage problems. Author Wayne Durrill writes that Josiah Collins in 1787 "sent two ships to western Africa to purchase slaves who, when they landed at Edenton in June, were sent to Lake Phelps."[35] A strong possibility exists that Collins may have contracted with Port Roanoke (Edenton) mariners Henry Hill and John Fitch who in 1786 sailed for Africa and returned with a cargo of slaves, perhaps for Collins or others. Another possibility was the Port of Brunswick on the Cape Fear River to the south, whose customhouse records from 1783-1789 show 290 slaves entering there. Of that number 128 were brought from the West Indies and the others from Boston, New York, Savannah, Charleston Virginia and Maryland.[36] In the first decade of the 19th-century Boston underwriters still insured slave voyages as evidenced by the San Francisco de

---

32 Taylor, pp25-27
33 Ibid, p23
34 Ibid, p29
35 Durrill, p11
36 Taylor, pp23-24

Asis and schooner *Carlota*. At the same time Rhode Island's de Wolf family business skirted around patrols while running slaves into Cuba. As late as 1809 the Africa Institution of London noted the coast of West Africa to be "swarming" with Spanish-flagged ships sailing from the United States."[37]

Given the continued fear of a San Domingue slave insurrection, evening slave patrols became established across the South with North Carolina being no exception. In 1808 "Meteor" wrote in the *Edenton Gazette* that the residents of the town "roused by a sense of their danger, had established a nightly patrol" of the streets. This force was to announce its "all is well" on the hour.[38] Street lights were to decrease the need for patrols, though these came with a fire hazard. By the later 1850s gas lamps became more prevalent in northeastern North Carolina.

American abolitionists fueled by the anti-slavery rhetoric of England's William Wilberforce, greatly stoked fears of insurrection in eastern North Carolina. While the British ended slavery in most of its empire in August 1834 while claiming the mantle of humanity, one who saw them as "hypocritically attacking slavery while at the same time conducting the Chinese coolie trade" was former-Lake Phelps resident James Johnston Pettigrew, who in 1858 had become a member of South Carolina's General Assembly.[39] Many remained unconvinced as this was the same Britain known for its cruel opium trade with the Orient.

This "abolitionism" was deeply disconcerting for Washington county which by 1860 was a region of cotton and tobacco production with an African population constituting a third to one-half the total. The counties of Bertie, Chowan, Northampton, Edgecombe, Pitt, Halifax, Warren, Franklin counties in the northeastern part of the State had over fifty percent African population.[40]

One of the first shocks came in 1829 when free-black David Walker, originally of Wilmington, North Carolina, but then living in Boston, published his "Appeal in Four Articles." His tract was seen as encouraging slave insurrection and Governor John Owen notified police in the State's principal towns to intercept any of Walker's pam-

---

37 Thomas, p569
38 Johnson, p129
39 Wilson, p100
40 Lefler, pp398-399

phlets, including Washington and surrounding counties.[41]

Of the abolitionist class, Joshua Giddings of Ohio represented the most virulent who advocated bloody slave uprisings as occurred in San Domingue in the 1790s. He and others who led opposition to the Fugitive Slave Act of 1850 helped drive the American South to recalculate the value of its political union with the north. Just prior to the war one Virginia newspaper offered $10,000 bringing him as a captive to Richmond — or $5,000 for his head.[42]

As a post-script to the northern trade was the brig *Putnam* of New York City, purchased by Portuguese slave traders in 1857 and renamed *Echo*. After bribing corrupt port officials, the ship was sent to Cuba for fitting out as a slaver, then to Africa to purchase available slaves from tribal chiefs. Once boarded they were off to Brazil and sold to waiting plantation owners. In that year alone at least 15 slavers departed New York harbor on similar voyages.[43] African slaves seemed to be a Southern institution by 1860, but it was New England who had been responsible for creating and sustaining it.

It seemed this traffic in slaves seemed to defy all legislation brought to bear and simply could not be suppressed. As late as March 20, 1861 the *Nightingale* of Boston with Francis Bowen, master, with 961 Negroes on board "and expecting more" was captured on the coast of Africa. The American vessels *Triton* and *Falmouth* were captured off the African coast in May 1861; had the enforcing officer been there one month earlier it was said he would have captured nine more slavers.[44]

---

41 Franklin, pp66-67
42 Wiki, accessed 12.19.23
43 EchoSlaveTraders.cofc.edu (accessed 12.22.23
44 Grady, p223

A Political Summary: 1789-1861

"The State of North Carolina — truly republican without ostentation."

— *4th of July 1809 toast to Nathaniel Macon*

As other Royal Governors did when the colonial revolt spread, Josiah Martin fled to the protection of a British man-of-war, this one at Wilmington in April 1775. On May 2, the colony "seceded" and thus declared independence from the British Crown. In November, a third provincial congress created a constitution for the now-independent State, choosing as president the victor of the Moore's Creek battle near Wilmington, Richard Caswell.

Among the provincial congress's actions, it enumerated the normal guarantees of English liberty and declared the people the sole and exclusive source of government. In addition, this congress adopted an oath of allegiance with strong enforcement provisions to discourage Tories.[1] Though believed to be the beginning of democratic government in the State, rule by the poor, uneducated masses — i.e., democracy — was greatly feared and property ownership made a requirement for holding office. North Carolina's delegates soon joined the Continental Congress of July 1776 in Philadelphia to coordinate and press war against the British. This was prior to any federation being formed, and as the individual colonies voluntarily "seceded" from England to assert their individual sovereignty.

It is recalled that the reasoning behind the action of the colonies which was not initially independence. When General Burgoyne asked a colonist in 1775 what the aim of their revolt against the Crown was, the reply was "to remain masters of their own property, and be

Nathaniel Macon

---

1 Wagstaff, Vol I, p454

John Bernhard Thuersam

governed by the same equitable laws which they had enjoyed since becoming British colonies."[2] Most colonial leaders in British America expected the King and Parliament to reduce what were considered oppressive tariffs, and when this was not forthcoming the drive for independence commenced. The unmistakable parallel by 1850 saw several Southern States recalculating the value of political union with the North. By 1860 this became more widespread and another drive for independence was in the making.

Since the beginning of war with the British, the political leadership of the northeastern tidewater through 1789 was conservative and included Samuel Johnston, James Iredell, Joseph Hewes, Thomas Jones and Hugh Williamson of Edenton and Allen Jones of Northampton. While William R. Davie of Halifax was conservative, Willie Jones of the same town became a voice "implacably opposed to the 1789 Constitution." Though few newspapers existed in the State, New Bern's *North Carolina Gazette* and Edenton's *State Gazette of North Carolina* kept residents politically well-informed.[3]

While framing a government for North Carolina, conservatives were intent upon keeping what was best in the British system such as restricted suffrage and an independent judiciary. These men understandably valued the advantages enjoyed by the conservative colonial ruling classes and sought their continuation.[4] An irony of the American Revolution was that it was fought by the American colonists "to defend the ancient liberties of Englishmen" — as would be the fundamental reason for the American South fighting against the invasion of their soil. Both constitutional liberty and the maintenance of rights were at the bottom of the Revolution as it would be in 1861.[5]

---

2 Wood, p20
3 Gilpatrick, p20-21
4 Jensen, p163
5 McRee, p152

The oddly-named "radicals" — who were in truth conservatives — hated all things British and desired a simplistic new government subservient to the popular will. They feared parting with their newly-acquired personal liberties and were suspicious of any system with excessive authority over them.[6] They pointed to the Revolution as a revolt against a centralized, coercive power and had no intention of re-creating in their America the same system they had fought to overthrow in 1776. Anti-federalists like North Carolinian Thomas Burke were firm in their conviction "that unlimited power cannot safely trusted to any man or set of men on Earth."[7]

In the Continental Congress of early June 1776, Virginia's Richard Henry Lee moved that "these United Colonies are, and of right ought to be, free and independent States, absolved from all allegiance to the British Crown and that all political connections ... are totally dissolved." All American colonies were now independent States.[8]

The broadly-recognized sovereignty of these now-independent States was heard from John Adams in 1774 referring to Massachusetts Bay as "our country" and the Massachusetts delegation in Congress being "our embassy." Adams further wrote Patrick Henry in June 1776 that "the colonies then had the choice before them of declaring themselves "a sovereign State" or a number of confederated sovereign States."[9] Robert E. Lee of Virginia was echoing Adams in the 1860s.

The following year Henry proclaimed that every legislature of every colony "is and ought to be the sovereign and uncontrollable Power within its own limits of Territory." Historian Merrill Jensen who wrote of a peoples' nationalism for their own State is often overlooked.[10] And it is significant that Adam's words "our embassy" were changed in later books to "our people" after the Civil War — with the justification that those words "required softening in 1876."[11]

Though post-Revolution conservatives tried often to institute "a new nation" with subservient States, the radicals expected Congress to create and maintain a federation of independent States, not to install a national government."[12] The fear of creating another all-powerful

---

6 Gilpatrick, p23;29
7 Jensen, p174
8 Ibid, p103
9 Ibid, p167
10 Ibid, pp195-196
11 Ibid, p164n
12 Ibid, p169

central government such as the American colonists had recently freed themselves from — with French help — guided the independent States as they warily formed a common agent to administer certain delegated functions.

This new doctrine of the right of revolution and self-government — the right to create and destroy upon the will of the majority — was a shock to what had come before in the usual form of top-down governing. It was also recognized that those conservatives who supported the Revolution against the Crown and still pleaded for a supreme authority over the new States, had to unwillingly accept the new reality of sovereignty existing in the people of each individual State. By 1787 the conservatives were claiming a fiction that sovereignty existed in the people organized in a nation known as the "United States." But ultimately, historian Jensen notes that "the dispute between State sovereignty versus federal sovereignty began with the first Continental Congress rather than Webster and Calhoun.[13] But one may take the ultra-conservative Alexander Hamilton at his word when testifying in *Federalist* that, under the Articles of Confederation, the States remained sovereign and independent. He underscored this by writing in *Federalist 15* that "the concurrence of thirteen distinct sovereign wills is requisite, under the Articles of Confederation, to a complete execution of every important measure …"[14] As one proceeds to 1861 and constitutional relations between North and South, this is important to keep in mind.

What were the true meaning of the terms "Federalist" and "antifederalist" in that time? The first really meant "nationalist" and very much like the British Crown and Parliament just departed from. Jefferson referred to them as "monarchy men." The antifederalists were really "perfecters" of the Constitution rather than opponents of it, for without them there would have been no Bill of Rights" nor reserved rights to the individual States which created a true federation.[15]

The first constitution of the United States was the Articles of Confederation and it was not until April 25, 1778 that North Carolina's legislature agreed to ratification. Maryland was last to ratify and on March 1, 1781 the Confederation began.[16] While under the Articles

---

13 Ibid, pp163-165
14 Ibid, p175
15 Wood, p xiv
16 Ibid, pp186;238

the State's political leadership paid little interest to its operation with delegates to Congress being more conspicuous in their absence than in attendance. Their political energy was consumed with affairs of their region and State.

In 1787 North Carolina was invited to send delegates to Philadelphia as some States desired revising the Articles with an aim of providing more authority to the central agent of the thirteen member States. North Carolinians in general had no interest in recreating a far-off supreme authority and their only motivation in attending was to create a more workable framework for solving common issues under the Articles. It was clear that the delegates had no intention of North Carolina losing its sovereignty.[17]

The most prominent anti-Federalist in 1787 was Willie Jones from Halifax, some 75 miles upriver from the emerging town of Plymouth. Though active in efforts to secure a majority at the State Convention charged with adopting the proposed US Constitution, Jones was apprehensive that a federal judiciary would play havoc with the authority of the State courts. He additionally detected no protections for freedom of conscience and feared that the State's poor would be ruined by federal taxes. Jones' concerns resonated with the many North Carolinians who again feared losing their dearly-bought liberties to an untried theory of government. It was the influential Jones who urged North Carolina to remain out of the new federation for five or six years to observe how federal judiciary behaved.[18]

Willie Jones

For the above reasons the proposed Constitution was in general opposed in the western part of the State, those in the middle east were divided, and the extreme east, especially the commercial interests, in favor of it. Wilmington's antifederalist delegate Timothy Bloodworth expressed fears that the proposed Constitution would negate State constitutions and abolish all State governments. The Federalist proponents responded that it was a compact between the States which would protect the doctrine of State sovereignty. Some 70 years later

---

17 Sitterson, p23
18 Wagstaff, pp465-428

Southern statesmen would remind their Northern counterparts of this original "compact between independent States" definition.

Despite the anti-Federalist concerns throughout the United States, the new political arrangement went into effect in early 1789 with all States except Rhode Island and North Carolina "seceding" from the Articles of Confederation — originally adopted as a "perpetual" union. These two States continued on as a reduced-member federation continued under the Articles.[19]

The federalists in the State continued their pressure to ratify as the *State Gazette of North Carolina*, now a federalist Edenton paper, frequently wrote of serious commercial disadvantages of remaining outside of the new federation.[20] Other newspapers voicing strong support for this viewpoint was the *Roanoke Advocate* of Halifax. Another was the *North Carolina Journal* of Halifax active in the mid-1790s and the New Bern's *State Gazette of North Carolina*.[21]

It is accurate to state that North Carolina finally acceded to the 1789 Constitution as a matter of economic necessity and with little enthusiasm. It was a State with a predominantly agrarian economy and little interest in commercial development and a healthy distrust of that, though there existed a moderate maritime trade with the West indies from Edenton, Washington and New Bern. The United States Navy was now under a different government and shipping from North Carolina was no longer under its protection. The seizure of ships in the 1790s by French privateers would cause a war scare which led to a temporary increase in Federalist support in the State.[22]

When the anti-Federalists brought forth an amendment requiring a Bill of Rights be added to the Constitution and suggested 26 amendments, one of which guaranteed the reserved rights of the States (Tenth Amendment), the resolution carried by a vote of 184 to 84. Despite this wide margin, the Federalists then attempted to pass a ratifying resolution that was defeated by a 100-vote majority. Those who cast votes in favor included the northeastern counties of Currituck, Chowan, Camden, Gates, Hyde, Perquimans, Pasquotank, Carteret, Bertie, Sumner and Tyrrell — the latter reduced to create Washington county in 1799. Again, and in general, the large landholders of the east

---

19 Sitterson, pp23-25
20 Gilpatrick, p35
21 Ibid, p67
22 Ibid, pp80-82

were Federalists, and the small farmers of the interior and west were the anti-Federalists. The propertied groups sought to curb democracy which they saw as mob rule which would seize their property; they wanted to maintain order with government in the hands of the educated upper class.

Those who claim that the 1789 Constitution formed an American "republic" often cite the alleged words of Benjamin Franklin following the convention: "You have a republic if you can keep it." What was actually formed was "a federation of States, each of which, in the words of Article IV of the Constitution, is guaranteed a republican form of government." The federation of States, the "Union," is a service agency and not a republic in itself.[23]

Those sent to represent North Carolina in the Legislature and federal government were men of means and property. An axiom of that period was that independent men would act in the public interest, and the protection liberty depended upon the protection of property.[24] Historian Wagstaff notes that North Carolina ratified the new governing document "only after hesitancy and mature deliberation, and her subsequent history proved her loyalty to it as long as the Constitution represented her interpretation of its provisions."[25]

Despite assurances the new document was not a "consolidated" government which would trample upon State authority, the average North Carolinian was greatly concerned about the lack of a bill of rights and surrendering their liberties to an untried form of government. In mid-June the commission delegates wrote Governor Caswell noting the singularity of the government being proposed. "A union of Sovereign States, preserving their individual liberties and connected by such ties as to preserve permanent and effective Governments … is a circumstance that has not occurred in the history of man." This letter rather conclusively indicates that North Carolina's delegates were convinced that North Carolina would ever divest herself of sovereignty in the process of political union with the other States.[26]

An important illustration of North Carolinians holding the federation's agent to the letter of the Constitution is Hugh Williamson, a Federalist member of Congress. In 1790 he railed against Alexander

---

23 Livingston, p18
24 Kruman, pp11-12
25 Wagstaff, p31; 475
26 Ibid, p18

Hamilton's plan for the federal government to assume the debts of States, holding that this would be an invasion of those rights reserved to the States and that North Carolina intended no such broad delegation of powers when it ratified the Constitution. Governor Alexander Martin also saw this assumption as inconsistent with the "independence and internal sovereignty of the State." Even fellow-Federalist Archibald Maclaine, disgusted with the idea advanced by Hamilton, threatened "secession" as he stated that "North Carolina will be North Carolina still, in or out of the union."[27] This was 71 years before May 20, 1861.

Moreover, the question of sovereignty being retained by the individual States was reiterated in the 1792-93 case of *Chisholm vs. Georgia*, where the issue was whether a State could be sued by a resident of another State. Though the Court decided in favor of Chisholm, Justice James Iredell of North Carolina dissented, arguing that the States were successors to the sovereignty wrenched from England and being so, could not be sued by individuals. The State of Georgia stood behind Iredell's stand; it was not until 1798 when the Eleventh Amendment was ratified that such questions were removed from the cognizance of the Court. Soon afterward, Justice Iredell's stand was underscored by Jefferson's Kentucky Resolutions of 1798 in response to John Adam's Alien & Sedition Acts. The Resolutions reiterated that each State was declared to be its own final judge as to infractions of the Constitution by the federal government. In short, when undelegated powers were assumed by the federal agent, its powers were "unauthoritative, void and of no force." The concern over President John Adam's drift toward monarchical government so concerned Virginia leaders that they spoke of an overthrow of the federal government, by war if necessary.[28]

Political sentiment in the early 1790s was evident in North Carolina's strong criticism of President Washington's Jay Treaty with England, negotiated in 1794 and ratified in 1795. Both North Carolina Senators voted against John Jay's confirmation as peace commissioner and both opposed ratifying the completed treaty. Edenton's voters protested against provisions of the treaty, and as it required an appropriation of money, every US House delegation from the State voted against it. Many congressmen saw the treaty as a "manifestation of executive usurpation of power" and others feared it would return half

---

27 Sitterson, p26
28 Wagstaff, p480-481

the State to the Granville heirs in England. There was also fear that the treaty's commercial clauses would cut northeastern North Carolina ports off from the lucrative British West Indies trade.[29] In the first ten years of the State being part of the new political federation, it is clear that North Carolinians accepted it without enthusiasm and as a matter of necessity."[30]

In keeping with the general anti-Federalist feeling there was seen but little idolatry of George Washington in the region as Thomas Blount of Little Washington openly criticized the president's last message to Congress and opposed the adoption of his Farewell Address. He was joined by Congressmen Nathaniel Macon, Matthew Locke and James Holland — all Jeffersonian Republicans" — on the ground it was "too adulatory."[31] George Washington received no votes for president as North Carolina entered the current federation after his election.[32]

George Washington

Thomas Jefferson viewed the antagonism between Hamiltonian Federalists and Republicans simply antagonistic theories of government. The former, in his mind, as feared and distrusted the people, and the latter cherished and protected the people. The Jeffersonian commitment to republicanism meant opposition to an artificial aristocracy, political corruption and an insistence on public virtue. In their eyes a republic's citizens were a plain folk of small farmers and planters, who distrusted the elitism of merchants, bankers and manufacturers. These same antagonisms could be said to have continued through the 1850s with the American South actively detaching itself from the "corrupt squadron of stock-jobbers in Congress" representing their own personal interests rather than the mass of voters."[33] Abraham Lincoln's political heritage was Hamiltonian, an admirer of Henry Clay Whigs before morphing into a sectional, high-protective tariff Republican.

---

29 Lefler, pp278-279
30 Gilpatrick, p80
31 Lefler, p280
32 Ibid, p74n
33 Beard, 283

John Adams

"Where annual elections end, there slavery begins."

— *John Adams*

The Jeffersonians in North Carolina were unenthusiastic about a national bank and opposed liberal expenditures of the federal government. In short, no other State legislature was "quite so violent in denunciation of the federal government." The funding and assumption measures of Alexander Hamilton of the early 1790s made the federal agent unpopular and outright obnoxious in this State.[34]

A prime example of northeastern North Carolina's Jeffersonian political leanings in 1796 was a *State Gazette of North Carolina* announcement of electoral candidate John Hamilton of the Edenton District, published in October of that year. Hamilton, who won election, loudly condemned the "foreign and aristocratic principles" of John Adams while pledging himself to Thomas Jefferson.[35]

In the legal realm, the federal judiciary was held in such low esteem in the State that the Superior Court of the Edenton District refused to obey a writ of certiorari from the US District Court, on the ground that being a court of "original, general, supreme and unlimited jurisdiction" it was not answerable to any other judiciary." The State legislature applauded the State court's decision.[36]

But while most of the State was politically anti-Federalist, Federalist sympathies were dominant in the trade-dependent Albemarle and Pamlico Sound region including Edenton, Halifax and somewhat Wilmington, though the latter was mainly anti-Federalist. Though the State voted for Jefferson in 1796, the threat of war two years later brought a temporary resurgence of Federalism until the hated Alien and Sedition Acts of John Adams brought voters back to Jefferson. The effect upon Federalist newspapers was severe as the Halifax *North Carolina Journal* paper published in Halifax was sold in 1807 and brought into a more politically-neutral stance. Also supporting the Federalists

---

34 Gilpatrick, p78
35 Ibid, pp74-75
36 Ibid, p51

was the *Edenton Gazette* which was forced to accept pork and corn for payment at times, and was regularly attacked by the Republican *Elizabeth City Gazette*.[37]

Other Federalist newspapers suffered as well as Thomas Jefferson's election to the presidency caused the party to fall into disarray in the State.[38] To emphasize the State's aversion to Federalists, in 1796 John Adams received but one district vote to Jefferson's eleven. In 1800 Adams received four votes to Jefferson's eight. In 1804 Jefferson received the entire electoral vote of North Carolina; in 1808 James Madison garnered eleven votes to the Federalists three. Since 1789 the Federalists were seen as embracing a government of a favored few, liberal expenditures, loose interpretation of the Constitution and siding with commercial interests rather than the common man.[39]

What would later be called "States' Rights" had been asserting itself strongly in the State since 1789 as voters regularly countered Federalist ambitions. The earliest seeds of States seeking independence from the new federal experiment came in 1798 when John Taylor of Caroline suggested to Thomas Jefferson that Virginia and North Carolina "secede" from the 1789 federation and form a new one. Jefferson disagreed and suggested that only strong protest against what they deemed "hated laws" be pursued. At the end of that year both the Virginia and Kentucky legislatures adopted resolutions prepared by Jefferson which reaffirmed that the American federation of 1789 was a compact between the States, and should the agent at Washington create a law which the States deemed contrary to the Constitution they had ratified, "a nullification by those [State] sovereignties ... is the rightful remedy." Though North Carolina was left out of the above assertion of State sovereignty after its Federalist upsurge in recent elections, the legislature refused to give its formal approval when the State Senate voted to table the Kentucky Resolutions. And though the legislature was then in the hands of Federalists, State voters elected anti-Federalist Benjamin Williams as governor.[40]

Historian Hermann von Holst argued that the Kentucky Resolutions formed the basis of New England's Hartford Convention of 1814, formed by three Federalist enclaves: Massachusetts, Rhode Island and

---

37 Ibid, pp173-174
38 Ibid, p82
39 Ibid, pp231-234
40 Lefler, p281

Connecticut. The Convention proposed "secession" from the United States while Massachusetts Governor Caleb Strong sent a secret mission to Britain to discuss separate peace terms and future trade. Von Holst asserts that the New Englanders had learned from James Madison that a State had a right and duty to "interpose its authority" between its citizens and the federal government. Jefferson's Kentucky Resolutions underscored the States being the final authority on questions of sovereignty.[41]

Distrust and suspicion of the federal apparatus — especially the judiciary — continued in North Carolina through the 1790s unabated with the States' Rights doctrine holding firm. This was underscored in 1792 when anti-Federalist George Clinton of New York ran unsuccessfully as the Democratic-Republican vice-presidential candidate while receiving editorial support from Halifax's *North Carolina Journal* as well as the unanimous vote of North Carolinians. At that time the political and social capital of the Roanoke country was the town of Halifax.[42]

No discussion of early North Carolina political life is complete without mentioning Warren County tobacco farmer Nathaniel Macon, the outspoken and influential representative of his region in the early 1800s. Serving in the State Senate from 1781 to 1784, he sat in Congress for thirty-seven years, 1801 through 1828, in both the US House and Senate. A strong defender of State autonomy, he resisted encroachments of federal powers and supported Thomas Jefferson's Virginia and Kentucky Resolutions of 1799. Jefferson greatly respected and admired Macon's integrity, referring to him as "*ultimas Romanorum*" — the last of the Romans. Macon contended that the public treasury should border upon parsimony; he opposed coastal fortifications and a national military establishment — a standing army. Thomas Blount of the combined Halifax and Tar River District was a willing partner of Macon, believing that a permanent naval establishment would only "plunge us into fresh difficulties." Both encouraged reliance upon the militia rather than a permanent military.[43] After retirement Macon responded to Andrew Jackson's threat of force against South Carolina in 1832 with a well-considered opinion that the American compact of States "cannot be maintained by force." Macon

---

41 vonHolst, V I, pp268-269
42 Gilpatrick, p55
43 Ibid, p87

later served in 1835 as president of the convention to reform the State's Constitution to allow greater democracy in elections.

The Embargo Act of 1807 was a general ban on trade with any foreign nations who harassed or interfered with American ships on the high seas. Though it received general compliance, starving captains were illegally departing North Carolina harbors. The *Edenton Gazette* of April 14, 1809 reported a ship seized at Plymouth and four more at other North Carolina ports. Edenton District Congressman Lemuel Sawyer urged in 1808 a reopening of trade with the West Indies so area merchants could sell the vast lumber stocks they had accumulated. Nathaniel Macon also supported this measure. It was fortunate that Virginia and South Carolina absorbed most of North Carolina's surplus agricultural production during the embargo as this eased the trade deficit. But infuriated by the Embargo, and pressured by his shipping trade constituents in 1810, Sawyer advocated war with England and an invasion of Canada.[44]

Speaking in Congress in 1809 on an issue that would lead to war 52 years later, Macon said "the people where he lived wanted no protective duties to encourage manufacturing." North Carolina's agricultural economy was so dominant that the State's delegation to Congress, both Federalists and Republicans, voted against the tariff of 1816 and against the interests of New England.[45]

Thomas Jefferson

"The acquisition of Canada will [be] the final expulsion of England from the American continent."
— *Thomas Jefferson*

North Carolina's defenseless coastline was of great concern once the War of 1812 commenced, as the army and navy were considered weak due to the Republican's frugal economy. Fortunately for North Carolina and the rest of the United States, Bonaparte was England's primary concern until 1814. State troops were volunteers in 1812 and an additional

---

44 Ibid, pp180-182
45 Ibid, p184

call for 7,000 North Carolina men two years later was met mostly by conscription. With the federal government too poor to supply clothing and blankets, North Carolinians themselves provided these for their troops. "

> Are we the titled Slaves of George the Third? No!
> — *Andrew Jackson*

Andrew Jackson

Though North Carolina was not a military objective of England, the arrival of a British fleet under Admiral Sir George Cockburn with troop transports in mid-July 1813 caused consternation when they disembarked at Ocracoke and captured Portsmouth. This invasion attracted a modest number of slaves who were taken aboard to deprive the colonists of their labor. This raid was sufficiently concerning as to transfer all specie in the State Bank at Edenton to Tarboro and Raleigh. Perhaps considering the shock-value the landing accomplished as sufficient, the Redcoats reboarded their ships and sailed off several weeks later.[46] The British established a full blockade of the Atlantic coast in November 1813, which eliminated any coastal trade except by English collusion. What did prosper was trade via wagons which predictably increased the cost of goods.[47]

Worthy of mention at this time was New England's Hartford Convention in the summer of 1814 as the war was going against the Americans. President James Madison approved a more restrictive embargo act in late 1813 which prohibited trade between American ports, and infuriated New Englanders who were actively trading with the British enemy. Additionally, the Maine district of Massachusetts was British-occupied and Boston was threatened with imminent attack. The Federalist governors of New England refused to supply troops as Madison requested as those States were once again bent upon independence from the United States — the first time being over the Louisiana

---

46 Lefler, p295
47 Mahon, pp102; 122

Purchase as new States could upset New England's power in Congress. New England would threaten secession again over the Mexican War.[48]

The War of 1812 offers an interesting parallel to 1860-1861 when northern Democrats accused newly-elected Republican president Abraham Lincoln of leading the country to dissolution, ruin and destruction. In 1812, North Carolina's Federalist State Senator Archibald Murphey of Orange County strongly criticized President James Madison's conduct of the war with Britain. He charged the "incompetent men" in control of the federal administration of leading the government to the "brink of dissolution" and the nation to "ruin and desolation." Recognizing the reasons why New England sought independence with its Hartford Convention and without condemning it, North Carolina's Federalist Gov. William R. Davie was "astonished at the monstrous strides toward despotism made by the party in power," predicting that "Madison will finish his career amidst the ruins of this country."[49]

The war marked a critical turning point for the United States. Its immediate aftermath witnessed Congress, the executive and judiciary promote highly "nationalistic" and broadly constructionist policies, including "expanded and implied powers" of the Constitution. From 1812 through the Missouri Compromise of 1820, Nullification in 1832, to the Compromise of 1850, the South's spokesmen and elected representatives fought strenuously to control the federal government and insisted upon strict interpretation of the United States Constitution.

One North Carolinian calling for strict interpretation was Halifax planter John Branch, a lawyer who later became State representative for his county in 1811 and rose to Speaker of the House in 1815-1817. In late 1817 Branch was elected governor. He advanced the political temper of his people as a Jeffersonian "Old Republican" opposed to a national bank, internal improvements and protective tariffs. His demand for strict adherence to the letter of the Constitution led him to become one of New England's most vitriolic opponents. These Jeffersonian views could be termed "States' rights" and defined as vigilance regarding any expansion of federal power not expressly warranted by the United States Constitution.[50]

---

48 Lefler, p295
49 Ibid, p297
50 Hoffman, p300

The acquisition of the new territories west of the Mississippi began the descent into sectional quarrel as the South was denied equal access in the new States created. After the Missouri Compromise, the South could only block dangerous federal interference with equal voting power in the Senate. The division along Mason and Dixon's Ohio River line would have assured Southern veto power in the Senate if territories west of the Mississippi had not been acquired.

Businessmen in Plymouth received good news in 1815 with Archibald D. Murphey's internal improvement plans for the State, which included enhanced navigation on the Roanoke River and ensuring well-maintained roads for access to it. Murphey also envisioned a great port near the head of Albemarle Sound as a distribution center "for rich produce brought down the Roanoke," rivaling Norfolk. Given excellent agricultural conditions and its temperate climate, the Albemarle region could ship its products of corn, beans, peas, pork, lumber, tobacco and naval stores to eastern towns and across the sea. His vision was well-received and North Carolina's delegations to Congress were encouraged to press for government funding to open a direct outlet from the Albemarle Sound to the Atlantic.[51]

The relatively-young country entered a difficult period on February 26, 1819. The *American Recorder* of Little Washington wrote of the recent deliberations regarding admitting Missouri as a state, a question quickly becoming a serious issue. The article stated that if the House of Representatives conformed to the decision of the committee of the whole, "[It] may be expected to have an important bearing on the political relations of the several States."[52] From these deliberations and eventual compromise flowed the sectional divide that would in thirty years cause Southern States to reevaluate political union with the Northern States, and begin establishing their own political alliances. Though adherence to a strict interpretation of the Constitution was losing prominence since 1812, the Missouri Compromise debates were bringing them into prominence once again.

Nathaniel Macon, now in the United States Senate, opposed the entire plan of the Compromise, which if passed, it meant that the States, particularly in the South, were admitting that Congress could interfere with private labor contracts within individual States.[53] Ad-

---

51 Gilpatrick, p225
52 Wagstaff, p484/40
53 Ibid, p486/42

ditionally, Congress would then be free to interfere with private labor contracts in new States created from territories west of the Mississippi.[54]

The Jeffersonian Democrats of North Carolina were rightfully perplexed. They were motivated by a sincere belief that government should be nearly invisible, doing little beyond protecting life, liberty and property. The education of children was a parental matter, internal improvements a local concern, and labor contracts personal. The government had no place in these questions.[55]

North Carolina remained an almost entirely rural State by 1820. The population numbers in this year had Edenton with 1,561, Little Washington with 1,034, New Bern with 3,663, Raleigh at 2,674 and Wilmington with 2,633. The state of education was problematic as a third of North Carolinians were illiterate with young people and Negroes be added to these, the number was more than fifty percent. Historian Lefler wrote that of the 177 private academies chartered by the State before 1825, 13 of which were for girls, many were short-lived.[56]

In the 1829 presidential election, North Carolinians helped elect the hero of New Orleans, Andrew Jackson, mostly due to his opposition to the national bank and adherence to "Old Republican" politics. Additionally, Jackson was a Southerner who understood the unique interests of the region far better than New Englander John Quincy Adams who carried only nine counties.[57] This initial support was to change as Jackson later embraced Martin Van Buren as a running mate, who the *New Bern Spectator* of May 16, 1832 wrote of as a "political juggler, father of the American System (protective tariffs), Federalist and abolitionist."[58]

This was also a time of increasing abolitionist agitation coming from northerners who had recently-regained their sense of morality regarding the slave trade and its impact in the United States. The Massachusetts textile mills were busy and growing rich producing fabric from Southern cotton fields, which perpetuated the very slavery denounced by young abolitionists, many of them the offspring of those who had grown rich from slave trade profits. In North Carolina

---

54 Lefler, p409
55 Ibid, p340
56 Ibid, p310
57 Lefler, p327
58 Hoffman, p306

the growing threat of slave revolt from abolitionist agitation was met with more rigid control of its colored population in 1830-1831. In the latter year Nat Turner's murderous rampage occurred in Virginia which killed nearly 70 old men, women and children, resulting in yet more stringent restrictions on the movements and freedom of slaves in North Carolina.[59] The people of the State had not forgotten the San Domingue massacre.

The so-called "nullification crisis" of 1832 came as South Carolina opposed raising tariffs to benefit Northern manufacturers at the expense of an agricultural South. As an original signatory to the Constitution, the State agreed with the other 12 to a strict revenue-only tariff but northern merchants were demanding a protectionist tariff to shield their products from cheaper imported goods. As an agricultural people without manufacturing, the South would pay more as northern producers were protected from foreign competition. This same issue would be repeated in 1860 with the Morrill Tariff, driving the South to seek "a more perfect union."

Though South Carolina threatened to nullify the tariff bill within its own borders, North Carolinians acquiesced while still voicing demands for a tariff reduction by Congress. At this time North Carolinians began hearing threats of independence from the federated union, to be accomplished "from the revolutionary principle" as was done in 1776.[60] Not one to back down, the formerly "Old Republican" Jackson asked Congress to pass a "Force Bill" in 1832 for the purpose of marching troops into South Carolina. The important question was what would Jackson's American troops do once they arrived at the South Carolina border?

This "Force Bill" was opposed by many in North Carolina including former Gov. James Iredell and other "Old Republicans" who voiced approval of their neighbor's resistance to federal coercion. Both North Carolina's Democrat and National Republican parties denounced nullification as "disunionist." Interestingly, the anti-Van Buren forces in North Carolina were supportive of a possible Jackson-Philip P. Barbour national ticket, the latter of Virginia. On October 13, 1832 the *Carolina Watchman* wrote that Barbour had publicly denounced both the protective tariff AND South Carolina's nullification of federal law. Barbour also declared that a State had the authority to declare in-

---

59 Sitterson, p33
60 Sitterson, p31

dependence from the "union" if it wished. But Van Buren showed his Federalist colors by stating his support for protective tariffs which would attract New England votes.

Jackson went on to victory with Van Buren as his running mate, but in the process had altered the political landscape. Many saw this as a personal victory for Jackson and a triumph of "unionism" over Southern nationalism. The *Halifax Free Press* reported in late November 1832 that the General Assembly by a five to one vote declared "nullification as "revolutionary … subversive … and leads to a destruction of the Union." But importantly, a resolution was also adopted stating that a majority of citizens considered the protective tariff unconstitutional and condemned it as "unjust and oppressive." This indicated that though North Carolinians thought the hated protective tariff was no reason to disrupt the federation, they still deemed it unwarranted.[61]

Martin van Buren

US Representative and Democrat Jesse Speight of Greene County was one of the few North Carolina congressmen who favored the Force Bill, believing that coercion was necessary in this case, though oddly declaring it wrong in principle. In the US Senate, Bedford Brown attacked nullification as "unsound Federalist doctrine" but stated that his constituents desired that he work for reconciliation with South Carolina. He further believed that Jackson's "Force Bill" would make bloodshed likely.

There were still many who believed the union was a good political system, but others feared the increasingly "imperial" nature of the federal agent in Washington — a reminder of John Adams reign — and that the proposed "Force Bill" would alter State and federal relations. The *Halifax Free Press* quoted Raleigh's *Constitutionalist and Peoples' Advocate* timely editorial of January 1, 1833: "Blood can never cement the Union."[62]

Putting this in proper perspective, the new Whig political party of the early 1830s, which opposed Democrats, was built around Henry Clay's advocacy of a nationalist, protective tariff, internal improve-

---

61 Hoffman, pp307-309
62 Hoffman, p310

ments and a national bank program. All of the above were anathema to the American South, though some eastern North Carolinians like William Gaston, Edward Dudley, Ebenezer Pettigrew, Edward Stanly and Kenneth Rayner remained supportive of nationalist Whigs.[63]

With increasing population by 1835 and with western antifederalists becoming more vocal, the pressure for democratic reform fueled demands for a State constitutional convention in 1835. The 1776 constitution allowed property-holding residents to vote for General Assembly members, who then elected the governor and other State officials. All taxpaying residents could vote for House of Commons members, but only those owning at least 50 acres of land could cast ballots for senators. To be eligible for office, one considered for the position of governor had to own lands worth at least 1,000 pounds, members of the Senate at least 300 acres, and House of Commons members at least 100 acres. The push for reform became louder as western settlement increased to provide a slight advantage in population over the east, though the latter remained dominant in political power.[64] The demands for reform were vocal in the western part of the State as the *Carolina Watchman* of Salisbury reported that should the legislature refuse to pass a convention bill for reform, "we of the West admit that the experiment is dangerous, but cost what it will the experiment will be made …" Thus western North Carolina openly threatened to "revolt and secede."[65]

In 1835 a Statewide referendum to ratify the Constitution's amendments approved them by a vote of 26,771 to 21,606, revealing the sharp sectionalism between east and west. This hampered compromise and statewide economic development as each region focused on their own interests and success.[66] To demonstrate that the State did not overwhelmingly accept Whig leadership, voters in 1836 preferred Martin Van Buren for president while electing Whig Edward B. Dudley of New Hanover County as governor. Voters also preferred a Whig State Senate. It is telling that Dudley, a strong supporter of State aid to railroad development carried the western part of North Carolina as well as fourteen eastern counties.[67]

---

63 Lefler, pp329-330
64 Ibid, pp332-334
65 Ibid, p335
66 Ibid, p338
67 Ibid, p343

Democracy seemed ascendant but the modern reader is cautioned about its meaning then — the founders' saw it as the rule of a mob and this word does not appear in the United States Constitution. Chief Justice John Marshall stated that "between a balanced republic and democracy, the difference is like that between order and chaos." Alexander Hamilton admitted that "we are a republican government and real liberty is never found in despotism or in the extremes of democracy."[68] The United States was founded as a constitutional republic and as Article IV, Section 4 states: The US shall guarantee to every State in the union a republican form of government," though the manner of enforcing the guarantee was left undefined.

Europeans visiting the United States in the latter 1820s wrote of the emerging democracy with several complaining of "vulgarity, lawlessness, mobs, vanity, the love of money-getting, lack of cultivation, and provincialism …" These were seen as the result of "the social and political experimentalism" of the United States.[69] Visiting Frenchman Alexis de Tocqueville was critical of America's emerging democracy, observing that "the majority constituted a force of opinion intolerant" of minority viewpoints. His gloomy view of the "leveling" attributes of democracy, which discouraged higher achievement, recognized the ineluctable evolution toward equality of conditions" which risked a new type of despotism.[70] His traveling companion Beaumont concluded that Americans "are a commercial people consumed by a thirst for riches" and susceptible to the less-honorable passions of cupidity, fraud and bad faith in that pursuit."[71]

In 1840 the State unveiled its new classically-themed capitol building in Raleigh, the work of Scottish architect David Paton. The visual message conveyed by its architecture underscored the foundation of North Carolina's republican governance as it recalled the Parthenon and other famous buildings of ancient Greece, the very underpinning of Western civilization.[72] The year also witnessed the political strength of the new Whig party which carried the State in the presidential contest, and again in 1844 and 1848. The Whig's also dominated congressional delegations and kept its leaders in the Senate about half

---

68 Wiki, accessed 12.15.23
69 Jones, p309
70 Jardin, pp216-217
71 Ibid, p114
72 Lefler, p33

the time, as national rather than State issues were in the forefront of public concerns.⁷³ The two parties by this time were clearly delineated; the Whigs were pro-business and saw corporations as beneficent; the Democrats desired prosperity but were uneasy with special interests and concentrations of power limiting individual freedom and equality.⁷⁴ A political development of this time was the rise of anti-foreign elements in the North which culminated in what became the "American" or "Know-Nothing" party. The military was called in to suppress "the anti-foreign" riots which had erupted in Philadelphia in 1844. The suppression was led by Brigadier-General George Cadwalader, a native Philadelphian who was hung in effigy by the anti-Catholic rioters. Cadwalader would later become a Major-General in the Union army.⁷⁵

In the 1848 national election, North Carolinians voted for Southerner General Zachary Taylor, who they believed would protect their interests in the political federation. Though marginally a Whig who had to be cajoled into the party, Washington County strongly supported the war hero as did adjacent Tyrell and all other counties bordering the Albemarle Sound, excepting Currituck. Interestingly, all counties on the Pamlico Sound supported Taylor as well. Martin county on Washington's western flank overwhelmingly supported the Democratic candidate for president, Lewis Cass.⁷⁶

This was also a time of increasing sectionalism and by 1850 Southern States would begin serious discussions regarding a peaceful path to separation from the North. The State's Whigs were dismayed by their Northern brethren's tendency to interfere with their section's labor system as they did not at the same time condemn the North's dismal mill and factory working conditions, nor their part in bringing the Africans to American shores. They saw Northern mill owners as outright hypocrites who held profits higher than the question of who

---

73 Ibid, pp329-330
74 Kruman, p25
75 Warner, p63
76 Wiki, accessed 10.23.23

was working in the cotton fields; and being aware of "blackbirder" slavers who bribed New York customs officials to clear ships destined for Cuba, then Africa and Brazil.⁷⁷

Many throughout the county and State like James Johnston Pettigrew of Lake Phelps were coming to believe that despite talk of compromise, the subject of independence from the North would be discussed in the halls of Congress and throughout the country until the event itself occurred. In early January, 1850 Pettigrew confided to his diary while traveling in the North:

"I saw something of politics in Washington and am fully convinced that the Union cannot possibly last longer than five or six years, at the most. I am amazed when I see the rapid strides that the spirit of disunion has made in all quarters in the course of a year. No one considers it at all startling to discuss the matter in a calm tone, whereas a few years ago it was necessary to be worked up into a furious passion before the word could be uttered; and the only question seems now to be, the consequences of the act." ⁷⁸

The decade of the 1840s was the zenith of Whig strength in the country, and by 1854 their party candidates, especially in the South, were roundly defeated. The political radicalization of abolitionists, the Nat Turner massacre, the John Brown raid and growth of the purely-sectional Republican party as a Whig alternative initiated serious discussions in the South about recalculating the value of political union with the North. Underscoring the reason for less Whig support in the South was historian Lefler writing that the Whig decline was due to their greater concern for "towns, manufacturers, bankers and merchants rather than lesser concern for the great mass of common people and small farmers in an agrarian State."⁷⁹

North Carolina Whigs like Thomas Clingman were pushed into the Democrat party after the 1846 Wilmot Proviso prohibited African slavery in the acquired territories.⁸⁰ That party suffered a devastating loss with the 1850 election of Rockingham County's David Settle Reid, a Democrat, as governor. In late-January 1850 Rep. Thomas L. Clingman, a conservative Whig of Buncombe County, delivered a fiery speech in the House stating that the South would be in a much better

---

77 McKay, pp14-15
78 Sitterson, p55
79 Lefler, p330
80 Ibid, p417

position economically outside the current political union, but it was willing to remain if justice were granted. He added that "When we ask for justice and to be let alone, we are met by the senseless and insane cry of 'Union, Union!' Sir, I am disgusted with it … We do not love you, people of the North, well enough to become your slaves. God has given us the power and the will to resist." In closing he warned: "Do us justice and we continue to stand with you; attempt to trample on us and we part company."[81]

In the 1852 national election Democrat Franklin Pierce won North Carolina by a narrow majority as the demise of the Whigs accelerated. By 1854 the party was dead in the State with its survivors moving to the new anti-Catholic, nativist American party, also known as the "Know Nothings." Many old Whigs took the party into what became the northern Republican party which was initially composed of a disparate array of factions.

As shown above, the idea of a State's "secession" from the 1789 federation was not new in 1861 as New York, Rhode Island and Virginia included the proviso of withdrawal in their ratifications of the United States Constitution. Others saw no need to do this as it was more than evident that a State could leave when it so desired. New England itself had threatened independence from the federation on several occasions between 1804 and 1848.

South Carolina in 1832 was asserting its opposition to a tariff that was no longer for simple revenue to support the federation's government as originally agreed to, but a shield to protect New England industry from foreign imports. When that State began reevaluating the value of its political union with the North during debates over the Compromise of 1850, North Carolina Democrats believed political independence was then unjustified. But they also held that the federation's agent in Washington had no authority whatsoever to force a State to remain in the political union.[82] Whig party editor William S. Ashe wrote: "when government becomes destructive of the ends for which it was established, we shall be in favor of throwing off such government and establishing news safeguards for our future happiness … we shall call it revolution and make up our minds to abide the consequences." Even in early 1861, North Carolina Whigs who opposed "secession" were supportive of "revolution" given the Republican refusal

---

81 Sitterson, pp65-66
82 Kruman, p127

to help find sectional compromise.[83]

"In contemplating the causes which may disturb our union, it occurs as a matter of serious concern that any ground should have been furnished for characterizing parties by geographic discriminations: Northern and Southern, Atlantic and Western …"
— George Washington, September 17, 1796

The Republican party of Lincoln was a new political organization in 1856 which was fueled by purely sectional considerations. After an electoral victory with 39 percent of the popular vote (the Republican party did not print ballots in the South) Lincoln urged his party's leaders to refuse any compromise with the South in their effort to control what they would consider a "national" government.

Dr. Mary Scrugham wrote of the primary contention between Republicans and Democrats in 1860 in her 1921 "Peaceable Americans."

"It cannot be said that there was a basic antagonism between the Northern and Southern people in regard to the slavery question in the Southern States. If there was any real vital difference between the North and South, it was on what constituted a sectional control of the federal government. Northerners in 1860 failed to realize that the Republican party of 1860 answered perfectly to Washington's definition of a geographical party against the formation of which he solemnly warned his fellow-countrymen in his Farewell Address." [84]

---

83 Ibid, pp128-131
84 Scrugham, p60

The Path to War

"We are not a nation, but a union, a confederacy of equal and sovereign States."

— *John C. Calhoun*

As the year 1860 began Democratic party leadership in the South became more pro-active in response to northern abolitionist agitation, especially after the Harpers Ferry violence in mid-October 1859. This insurrection, and the fact that Brown was financed in his mission by wealthy northern men made it clear that continued political union with the North was a danger to the people of the South. Since 1850 there was increasing popular sentiment in favor of separating from the north and forming a more perfect union of Southern States. The forming of the new and purely sectional Republican party in the early 1850s underscored the widening divide as the 1854 and 1860 Republican presidential candidates were not on the North Carolina ballot.

John C. Calhoun

The State's popular vote tally in the November 1860 national election was: Breckenridge on top with 48,539 votes, Bell with 44,990, and Douglas with 2,401. Given this Breckenridge received a majority of 848 votes in North Carolina. While the votes cast for Bell and Douglas may be classed distinctly as Unionist votes, those for Breckenridge may also be seen as such since the vote by counties indicated a tendency to revert to the old party divisions. The plot is very similar in detail to the gubernatorial vote in August, and both bear close resemblance to pre-1850 Whig and Democratic divisions. The northeast was strongly unionist though planter William Pettigrew of Washington County spoke for both secessionists and conditional unionists.[1]

---

1 Lefler, pp420-421

John Bernhard Thuersam

The counties clustered around the Albemarle and Pamlico Sounds as well as the eastern end of the state from north to south, gave Whig majorities as in former tacit compacts with the non-slave-holding west. Western North Carolina voted Bell majorities except where the alignment had now become permanently broken through special influences. Breckinridge was popular the in eastern slave-holding areas as Democrats held the tier of tobacco-producing counties along the Virginia border and cotton- producing counties of the west which bordered on South Carolina. The latter areas had been wrested from the Whigs only since 1850, but North Carolinians of all parties now suffered common defeat by the new sectional party of the North. Nonetheless, a calm acceptance of the result and acquiescence in the national decision seemed widespread, as evinced in the press.[2]

Nationally, the popular vote result — the Republicans had no party organization in North Carolina to print ballots — was 1,857,610 for Lincoln, 1,365,976 for Douglas, 847,953 for Breckinridge, and 590,631 for Bell. The die was cast — even if all three opponent totals above were joined under one candidate, Lincoln would have won with a majority of seventeen and one-half votes in the Electoral College.[3]

Given the great popularity of Nathaniel Macon in the northeastern region of the State his opinions resonated with the residents, rich and poor. He summed up the question of the individual States when commenting on South Carolina's nullification position. He wrote friend S.P. Person on February 9, 1833:

"I have never believed a State could nullify and stay within the Union, but have always believed that a State might secede when she pleased, provided she would pay her proportion of the public debt; and this right I have considered the best safeguard to public liberty and public justice that could be desired." [4]

The gubernatorial election of 1860 pitted Rowan County-native and Democrat, John W. Ellis against Elizabeth City-native and Whig US Congressman, John Pool. The result was a slender victory for Ellis with county-majorities in Martin, Edgecombe, Halifax, Chowan, Currituck and Hyde counties. John Pool won Washington and Tyrrell

---

2 Wagstaff, p118
3 Dumond, p112
4 Dodd, p385

counties with majorities of 69 and 57 percent respectively. Nearby counties with Pool majorities were Bertie, Hertford, Perquimans, Pasquotank, Camden and Beaufort.[5]

Governor-elect Ellis proved to be a practical, conservative leader who anticipated problems with the radical Republican regime taking power. Fortunately, the legislature was dominated by those like Ellis, who hoped war could be avoided, but feared more violence such as Nat Turner's bloody massacre and the Harpers Ferry insurrection incited by radical Republican abolitionists and their wealthy northern financiers. Anticipating additional abolitionist threats to the State, a month earlier the legislature passed a bill enacting legislation to provide protection and maintain public order during the existing and expected "troublous" times ahead.[6]

As with other Southern States immediately after Harpers Ferry, North Carolina requested a company of US regular troops be detailed to the arsenal at Fayetteville along with sufficient rifled muskets for militia company volunteers. The John Brown insurrection spurred the organization of many militia companies. Gov. Ellis requested 2,000 long-range rifles with bayonets from the War Department to properly equip them. This was oddly refused with the excuse that the State's quota had already been exhausted. This forced militias to order weapons from private dealers and obtain powder from newly-established

---
5 Wiki, accessed 12.15.23
6 Sitterson, p209

John Bernhard Thuersam

private factories in North Carolina.[7]

The State in 1860 was still mostly-rural, and of the twenty-five towns listed in that Census, half had populations under 1,000 each. There existed a general scarcity of money, manufacturing was yet to be developed and the average citizen's income and standard of living was low. It was a time when farm hands earned about $10 a month with board and a common laborer was paid 50 cents per day. Wilmington then was the leading seaport and rail terminus in the State, as well as most populous at nearly 10,000. The largest town near Plymouth was New Bern with a population of 5,432, while Elizabeth City, Kinston, and Tarboro all had residents of more than 1,000.[8]

The town of Plymouth in 1860 was home to 409 white residents, with most employed in mercantile, professional, hotelier, housekeeping and religious pursuits. The colored population totaled 463, of which 62 were free blacks. Washington County's population at the time totaled 3,184 white along with 237 free Negroes and 2,064 Negro slaves. Most of the latter were employed on county farms.[9]

Residents of that time read Plymouth's *Roanoke Cresset*, a paper edited and published by Robert S. Goelet from 1858 to 1861 at his Water Street office adjacent to the post office. Goelet's *Cresset* was described as a leading voice for North Carolina's independence during the convention campaign, as was the *Wilmington Journal* and *Wilmington Herald*; Goldsboro's *Rough Notes and the Tribune*; the Tarboro *Southerner*. The February 9, 1861 issue of the *Cresset* wrote that it "would as soon clasp a hyena in love's embrace as hold fellowship with infernal abolitionists, who steal our Negroes and insult our persons." Lincoln's February 9th speech at Indianapolis in which he revealed extreme nationalistic and threatening views, was denounced by the *State Journal* of February 20th for disclosing "a bloody purpose to coerce States with fire and sword, the people of the seceded States."[10]

Well-respected planter William S. Pettigrew spoke in Plymouth on February 19th with a voice of reason and moderation as he called for a convention of the States as the appropriate constitutional measure to find compromise, a path encouraged by President Buchanan. Petti-

---

7 Hill, p13
8 Lefler, p378-379
9 Durrill, p10
10 Sitterson, pp213-214

grew advocated constitutional solutions and "additional guarantees as the aggressive character now manifested by the North render necessary for our safety." He expressed regret that congressional Republicans refused to support the Crittenden Compromise to ensure the future of the union, and added that if guarantees of political equality not come forth the South would have no political future within the 1789 union.

In a February 26th speech Pettigrew stated:

"If the North continues to trample the Constitution and to laugh at and despise all the dangers & perils by which she is encircling us … North Carolina must either become a conquered province, degraded, despised, her property taken from her and ruled by a tyrant. If we cannot obtain the security of our rights under the Constitution, a convention must determine how we are to take care of ourselves."

Like many others in his State, Pettigrew was a devoted unionist as long as North Carolina was accorded equality in all respects to the other States in the political union voluntarily acceded to in 1789.[11] He echoed Nathaniel Macon's sentiments as he held the individual State's as superior to the federal agent they themselves had created, and understood that each could withdraw from the union at will though responsible for its proper share of the public debt.

Another well-respected citizen was Charles Latham of Plymouth, a committed unionist though his sons would all volunteer to defend North Carolina. He was resolved to see the State remain in the union "provided it could gain guarantees of its constitutional rights."[12] Another voice supporting independence was Judge Asa Biggs of nearby Martin County, who made it clear "that any State had every right, when sufficient cause existed, to withdraw from the 1789 union by the same method by which it entered, and by such a proceeding the citizens were absolved of any allegiance to the United States."[13]

There were many in the South who believed Northern voters would not support a purely sectional president, especially a candidate devoid of qualifications. Lincoln's only political experience was eight years in the Illinois House of Representatives followed by two years of representing Illinois in the US House of Representatives with no national leadership or foreign policy experience. Lincoln gained the

---

11 Sitterson, p2
12 Sitterson, pp216-217
13 McCormick, p20

presidency with a 39.8 percent plurality as the three other candidates garnered more than 2.8 million votes to Lincoln's 1.9 million. Just the shock of his marginal victory prompted seven States to set dates for their election of convention delegates to consider their future status within the 1789 federation of States. Nonetheless, some remained open to dialogue with Republicans and any signs of earnest compromise. North Carolina unionists considered these Republicans simply a Northern minority while favoring remaining in the Union unless Lincoln's administration attempted actions deemed unconstitutional.

Rather than a cohesive party with common vision, the Republicans of December 1860 were an unstable mix of northern Whigs, Transcendentalists, Know-Nothings and radical abolitionists lacking well-considered or defined policies. After its defeat in the 1856 presidential contest after garnering 33 percent of the vote, the party took on a pro-protective tariff plank to attract northeastern votes while quieting the anti-Catholic, Know-Nothing wing to win the immigrant vote, especially Germans. For the latter purpose Lincoln purchased the Springfield, Illinois *Staats Anzeiger* type and press, establishing Dr. Theodore Canisius as editor and stipulating that the weekly "print nothing opposed to or injurious to the Republican party." The doctor honored his instructions and was repaid by Lincoln's 1862 appointment of Canisius as U.S. Consul in Vienna.[14]

Though William Seward was far more qualified for the presidency by virtue of national and foreign policy experience, Lincoln excelled as a shrewd manipulator of public opinion. He was also aware that a national political campaign needed many supportive newspapers given they were the primary opinion molders of that time.[15] After his election Lincoln communicated little and was careful to say nothing that might cause his unstable party of factions to disintegrate. To underscore how little Republican leaders understood the Southern electorate from whom they received no votes, they could only express surprise at the unusual political excitement generated by Lincoln's election. The only manner in which the South could be assured of safety within the old union was through northern State legislatures agreeing to compromise, which being under Republican control, refused. The Republican-controlled States which had helped elect Lincoln also supplied

---

14 Wiki, accessed 12.20.23
15 Taylor, p112

him with troops with which to commence his war.[16]

This northern intransigence forced many, if not all Southern politicians into the "secessionist" camp. An example of this was Georgia's Herschell V. Johnson, the vice-presidential candidate on the Stephen Douglas ticket. Despite being an opponent of immediate independence for his own State, he proclaimed that the great mass of the Southern people supported independence "and would not receive patiently its negation by the federal executive."[17]

"Congress possesses many means of preserving the union by conciliation, but the sword was not placed in their hands to preserve it by force."
— *President James Buchanan*

President James Buchanan

A former diplomat, Buchanan delivered his fourth Annual Message to Congress on December 3, 1860 stressing that the Union could be saved by constitutional and peaceable methods — a convention of States to iron out their difficulties through compromise. He identified the reason for the country's grave peril as the "long continued and intemperate interference of the Northern people with the question of slavery."[18]

While not endorsing States withdrawing from the union, he justified resistance through "the right of revolution, which ought to be the last remedy of a despairing people, after every other constitutional means of conciliation had been exhausted." Buchanan, mindful of Article III, Section 3 of the US Constitution defining treason, denied the right of Congress or himself as President to wage war against any State holding that the federation was based upon public opinion and that "if it cannot live in the affections of the people, it must one day perish."[19]

The question of the federation's agent, the federal government, a

---

16 Dumond, pp148-150
17 Ibid, p151
18 Seward, p480
19 Dumond, p154

creature of the States — acting to coerce a State for whatever reason, was discussed at the convention framing the Constitution. James Madison, known as the "Father of the Constitution," said "the more he reflected on the use of force by the federal government, the more he doubted the practicability, the justice, and the efficiency of it, writing that "a union of the States containing such an ingredient seemed to provide for its own destruction."

To this Alexander Hamilton added: "But how can force be exercised on the States collectively? It is impossible. It amounts to war between the parties. Foreign powers also will not be idle spectators. They will interpose, a dissolution of the union will ensue, and no such right or power can be found anywhere in the Constitution.[20] Additionally, as enshrined in the platform resolution of the Republican party Chicago Convention, on which Lincoln was elected and reaffirmed at his first inaugural, was the following: "we denounce the lawless invasion by armed force of the soil of any State or Territory, no matter under what pretext, as among the gravest of crimes."[21]

The conditional ratifications of New York, Rhode Island and Virginia, the latter stating specifically, as did the others, that "the powers granted under the Constitution … may be resumed by them whensoever the same shall be perverted to their injury or oppression, and that every power not granted thereby remains with them and at their will."[22] It is more than clear that had all thirteen original States been aware that there was no withdrawal from the 1789 compact none would have ratified it.[23]

As a means of conciliation between the sections, in mid-December 1860 a resolution of Virginia's Alexander R. Boteler's was adopted which would create a special committee of one representative from each State to consider methods of settling differences between North and South. Adopted by a vote of 145 to 38, a close inspection reveals that some conservative Republicans voted affirmative, though the 38 in opposition were all Republicans. The committee chairman himself was distrusted by Southerners and wherever possible Republicans were placed in committees rather than Democrats. Republicans were in complete control and thus ensured that it was a graveyard for every

---

20 5th Madison Papers, 140 and 200
21 Christian, pp187-188
22 Ibid, p18
23 Ibid, p187

proposal of compromise and conciliation introduced in the House of Representatives. Importantly, there was no basis for sectional harmony as long as Republicans, at Lincoln's urging, used their now-overwhelming political power in Congress to advance their sectional party interests at the expense of the American South. This was the root cause of Southern States declaring independence and forming a more perfect union.

Historian Dwight L. Dumond summed up resistance to peaceful compromise in early 1861 with: "Had the Republicans deliberately sought the most efficient method of furthering the secession movement they could have found none better than their refusal to listen to methods of conciliation, and the haste with which they threatened violence against South Carolina and other States which might follow her.[24] The willful refusal to find peaceful remedies to solvable sectional issues helped launch a war that claimed the lives of a million Americans and brought an end to the United States Constitution.[25]

The *Star of the West*

With his approval of the Star of the West's *re-supply mission to Fort Sumter in early January 1861, Buchanan lost the confidence of the Southern people and accelerated the independence movement in South.*[26]

---

24 Dumond, p168
25 Ibid, pp156-157
26 Ibid, p178

In late November, 1860 President Buchanan spoke with Secretary of War John B. Floyd, a former governor of Virginia, regarding the strengthening of Fort Sumter with more troops. Floyd replied that "he would risk his own life and honor on the declarations of the South Carolinians" that the forts would not be touched. Buchanan was not satisfied with this Southern point of honor and Floyd agreed to produce orders for the fort's reinforcement, though confident this would bring on conflict.[27]

This conversation so agitated Floyd that he summoned Mississippi Senator Jefferson Davis and Virginia Senators James M. Mason and R.M.T. Hunter "to assure Buchanan there was no danger to the forts." Davis found the President agreeable on some of his views but failed to convince him of the wisdom of withdrawing soldiers from the harbor. Though an able man, James Buchanan was unfortunately timid and lacked the nerve to deal with the Fort Sumter question, as Jefferson Davis later recalled. Davis strongly doubted whether any other States would have followed South Carolina's independence had Buchanan withdrawn the troops from Fort Sumter. In his view such a conspicuous act of conciliation would have defused independence movements in the other States.[28]

Buchanan, in Davis's mind, was the last president of "the old school," opposed to any doctrine of coercing a State into submission to the will of a mass of people in the United States. While discussing the removal of troops at Fort Sumter, Buchanan readily agreed that the initial cession of State land for a fort, "for purposes, lapses, whenever that fort should be employed by the grantee against the State by which the cession was made," on the simple principle that any grant for a specific purpose expires when it ceases use for that purpose. Simply put, the coastal States ceded land to the federal agent for protection from foreign seaborne enemies, never dreaming that a fort's guns would be turned upon a State the fort was built to protect.[29] Following on that point, the three senators advised Buchanan of his attorney-general's error in stating that the government had purchased and owned outright the land beneath Fort Sumter. The only thing owned by the government, they said, were the constructed improvements made upon the site and which South Carolina would negotiate reimbursement for.

---

27 Archampaugh, p150
28 Bancroft, p145
29 Davis, p217

To Buchanan's reply that he viewed State "secession" as a "nullity" and therefore had no reason to give up the forts, the Southern senators asked if they were merely property, then why the need to garrison them in time of peace and frighten the citizens? As it was evident that the very reason the forts existed was to deter foreign aggression alone, the cession never contemplated under any circumstances the federal government using them against the people of South Carolina. But as a Northern Democrat in the now-nationalistic North, Buchanan and his advisors greatly feared the political consequences of evacuating any forts. While still firmly committed to finding a peaceful solution to what he saw as a crisis, Buchanan viewed Congress as the proper forum to settle this question of forts and the States deciding upon political independence.[30]

In mid-December 1860, Francis W. Pickens, grandson of Revolutionary war hero General Andrew Pickens, was elected governor of South Carolina. Events began moving quickly as Gov. Pickens wrote Buchanan on December 17th requesting the transfer of Fort Sumter to South Carolina's control; three days later South Carolina's legislature voted in favor of the State's independence. Apparently without orders, the fort's commander secreted his nearby Fort Moultrie force into a vacant Fort Sumter under cover of darkness the night after Christmas. This was seen as a provocation as it was understood that the commander was under an implied pledge to act on the defensive only.

For Buchanan, this move was fully unexpected. The President could not order the troops back to Fort Moultrie, as he was advised to do by many Southern men, without a majority of his cabinet resigning. In late December he suggested to some his intent to send Anderson back to the mainland but found the northern public mind against such an action. Further complicating his dilemma were the actions of bombastic northern men encouraging politicians to "whip up public opinion" with cannon salutes and parades celebrating Anderson's move to secure Fort Sumter. These inflammatory demonstrations went against the President's determination to find a peaceable solution to the issue, though it only increased the number of his enemies in the North. It was during this unsettled time that threats of an assassination attempt on Buchanan's life surfaced, credited to "a species of propaganda of the Republicans intended to exacerbate North-South

---

30 Auchampaugh. pp151-152

relations."³¹

Buchanan's early January attempt to deceptively reinforce Fort Sumter with the *Star of the West* triggered Wilmington's "Minutemen" militia into seizing Forts Johnston and Caswell at the mouth of the Cape Fear River as the ship neared, fearing government troops would reinforce these forts. Immediately afterward Gov. Ellis instructed that both be returned to their lone caretakers, stating there was no reason for their seizure. Afterward he wrote the War Department for assurance that they would not be garrisoned, which he was assured was not planned, "unless they were threatened."³² This response revealed Lincoln's intentions and Ellis quietly began preparations for North Carolina's coastal defense should things worsen. And to better train the growing militia organizations, the Governor ordered cadets from the North Carolina Military Academy to Raleigh to serve as drillmasters for the militia companies.

In what proved to be the last gasp of the federalism handed down by the Founders, on February 4th the Peace Conference convened in Washington, chaired by former President John Tyler of Virginia. Buchanan endorsed a constitutional convention for the States to find compromise. North Carolina sent delegates but the opportunity had passed as several Southern States had already withdrawn to form a new federation were and not represented. The Conference met for three weeks and proposed a constitutional amendment very similar to the Crittenden Compromise, but Republican intransigence and Lincoln directing his party's delegates to refuse compromise measures ended any hope for peace. Lincoln feared his party's dissolution if a compromise was attained.

George Davis, the well-respected Wilmington unionist appointed to represent North Carolina at the Peace Conference was greatly disappointed with the result. Addressing the residents at Wilmington upon his return he said: "No arrangement had been made — none would be made. The division must be made on the line of slavery. The South must go with the South ... or as the

George Davis

---

31 Burgess, p86
32 Hill, p28

tail-end victim of a Free Soil north." Three other North Carolinians delegates were convinced that hopes of compromise with the north were at an end. Thus, were Southern unionists pushed into joining those promoting secession, though they would refer to it as "revolution" as was done in 1776.[33] To the many North Carolinians who looked to the Peace Conference for final adjustment of the difficulties between the sections, its failure made it clear there was no hope of compromise.[34] In fact, an overwhelming majority of North Carolinians were now in favor of independence and argued only over how it was to be accomplished: be it called revolution or secession.[35] By the end of March, the New Bern *Progress*, Tarboro's *Mercury* and *Southerner*, Goldsboro's *Tribune* and *Rough Notes* and *Washington Times* all called for separation from the North. By now there were few "Tory" voices calling for the State to adhere to what was now a northern Union, one being the editor of Little Washington's Dispatch, a Whig paper.[36]

"If peace cannot be maintained with honor, it is no longer peace."
— *John Russell, 1st Earl, 1853*

Adding fuel to the pyre of the 1789 American political union was Buchanan himself as he signed into law the Morrill Tariff on March 2, 1861 after passage by the now northern-dominated Senate. There still remained a few Southern and western Democrats lingering in Congress, with Rep. Daniel Sickles of New York wryly noting that "our Southern friends will perceive that … you intend … to tax them on the necessaries of life in order to enrich the manufacturing classes of the north."[37] Signing this tariff into law only two days before leaving office, Buchanan helped make clear the economic dominance the north intended. The tariff took effect only days after the Provisional Confederate Congress voted a virtual free tariff of 10 percent on imported goods which would decimate northern commerce.

Still a great mystery is what followed, why Northerners seemed to overwhelmingly want to continue political union with the South — even at the cost of war. Author Kenneth Stampp posed the question

---

33 Wilmington Journal, March 7, 1861
34 Sitterson, p231
35 Ibid, p245
36 Hill, pp36-37
37 Stammp, pp163-164

of why northerners considered the creation of a Southern political federation to "have been such a terrible disaster." Though this followed Andrew Jackson's toast: "Our Federal Union — it must be preserved!" Why it had to be preserved was a question debated throughout the war.[38]

There is no question that Lincoln had to have financial support to initiate his war and this was found in the northern capitalists who endorsed the use of force against the South, however reprehensible, illegal or unconstitutional. The South's departure threatened their future profits, national bonds declined in value and those invested in government securities envisioned financial disaster. Also fearsome to northern merchants, bankers and investors was the possibility of property confiscation of Southern holdings, as well as Southern debts that might very well be repudiated.[39] It is that Lincoln's clever attempt to resupply Sumter in mid-April gave northern businessmen what they wanted, an end to inaction with commerce and profits at a standstill, no matter the cost.[40] Four years later the government in Washington had a two million-man standing army astride a defeated South, a secret service able to arrest any American upon a whim, and northern governors' dependent upon Lincoln. The Founders' federalism was a distant memory.

After an interregnum from the Peace Conference of February to early April 1861, and after Lincoln had dispatched spies to Charleston to observe activity within the city, he sent the steamer *Star of the West* with troops and ammunition below deck to reinforce and resupply Fort Sumter. Despite being strongly advised by Southern unionists to not attempt this and to allow a cooling off period for South Carolina to rethink their actions, the new President chose his party's cohesion rather than peace and conciliation.

Charleston's batteries opened fire once the ultimatum deadline to the fort's commander had passed and soon it was in South Carolina's hands. Soon Gov. Ellis received a request from Lincoln's Secretary of War for two regiments to wage war upon his neighboring State, to which he replied:

"Your dispatch is received, and if genuine (which its extraordinary character leads me to doubt), I have to say in reply that I regard the

---

38 Ibid, p205
39 Ibid, p223
40 Ibid, p269

levy of troops for the purpose of subjugating the States of the South as in violation of the Constitution and a usurpation of power. I can be no party to this wicked violation of the laws of the country, and to this war upon the liberties of the free people. You can get no troops from North Carolina." [41]

The *Raleigh Register* of April 17 wrote:

"Lincoln will wage a war of coercion against the [Southern] States. We shall be found on the side of the section in which we were born and bred, and in which live our kindred, connections and friends. If this makes us secessionists, then let us be so called."

In retrospect, the State's many "unionists" had implored Lincoln to abandon Fort Sumter for two reasons: to allow time for South Carolina to rethink its actions, and assure them that a peaceful path to keep North Carolina within the Founders' federation was possible. This would have been the logical and constitutional course, but it was Lincoln himself who lectured his own party against any and all compromise. These North Carolina "unionists" remained anti-secession but eventually justified the State's course toward independence as a "revolutionary" act which paralleled that of 1776. To the North, the emotional outburst generated by Lincoln's intentional provocation at Fort Sumter was the work of newspaper sensationalism which tagged the action as "an insult to the flag" while ignoring Lincoln's role in a

---

41 Hill, p35

confrontation of his own creation. By way of his stated determination to collect taxes in those States declaring independence, Lincoln had unmistakably made "a declaration of war."[42]

That Lincoln had used the Fort Sumter provocation as a trigger for war was disclosed in his May 1st letter to Gustavus Fox, assuring him that "You and I both anticipated that the cause of the country would be advanced by making the attempt to provision Fort Sumpter (sic) even if it should fail, and it is no consolation now to feel that our anticipation is justified by the result."[43] Additionally, Sen. Orville Browning of Illinois wrote in his diary of July 3rd, 1861 of Lincoln stating that "the plan of sending supplies to Fort Sumter succeeded. They attacked Fort Sumter — it fell and thus did more service than it otherwise could."[44]

Gov. Ellis now put the State on a war footing and issued a call for a special session of the legislature on May 1. Fort Macon had already been seized and he ordered all others on the coast taken at once. Though still a State within the United States, Lincoln ordered a blockade of the North Carolina coast in late April which was an act of war upon the State. The Governor's decisive actions were generally approved by those already independence-minded as well as the Whig unionists. The latter had opposed "secession" but opposed coercion by Lincoln's Republicans while calling it revolution in the spirit of the colonists of 1776 throwing off the yoke of British oppression. Those county representatives notable in the independence convention included Dr. Warren Bagley and Judge Asa Biggs of Martin; R. H. Smith, L.W. Batchelor and C.J. Gee of Halifax; Eli Spruill of Tyrrell; James Bond and S.B. Spruill of Bertie; William S. Pettigrew of Washington; Joseph S. Cannon of Perquimans; Dr. Richard Dillard of Chowan; George Howard and W.S. Battle of Edgecombe; H. M. Shaw, John B. Jones and D. McD. Lindsay of Currituck; Kenneth Rayner of Hertford; Richard H. Smith of Halifax; Rufus K. Speed of Pasquotank; W.J. Ellison, E.J. Warren and R.S. Donnell of Beaufort; and E.N. Mann of Hyde County.[45]

On May 20, 1861 the Legislature passed an Ordinance dissolving the union with the United States, and proclaimed North Carolina in

---

42 Grady, p286
43 Fox, p43f; CW, 4:350-351
44 Browning, O.H. Diary
45 McCormick, pp95-97

full possession of its sovereignty and a free and independent State. Being next to last to join the old union in 1789 after the States had seceded from the Articles of Confederation, it was now last to depart it. Of note, nowhere in the Ordinance was found the word "slavery." Just seven days later North Carolina's ratification of the constitution of the Confederate States of America was proclaimed as the State became part of "a more perfect union."

If one looks retrospectively at the career of the new American Union from 1787, there was a constant suspicion of the central agent of the then-recently independent States creating it, and the steadily-increasing power drawn to that central agent at the expense of those independent States. At the Constitutional Convention of 1787 James Madison regarded a proposal to use military force against errant member States with: "A union of States containing such an ingredient seemed to provide for its own destruction. The use of force against a State would look more like a declaration of war than an infliction of punishment — and considered by the party attacked as a dissolution of all previous compacts by which it might be bound."[46]

From the regal administration of John Adams which imitated European monarchy, to the New England States nearly seceding in its Hartford Convention of 1814, to the Missouri Compromise of 1820 which Jefferson viewed as the "death knell" of the Union, the central agent was steadily increasing its power at the expense of the States. This led to confrontation with South Carolina which resisted a protective tariff and Jackson's blustery threat of waging war against a State. The steady immigration of European immigrants to the north — a new political constituency as they settled westward; increasing abolitionist agitation against the South; a dubious war with Mexico which acquired more territory to argue over; and finally, the Compromise of 1850 which was to end all sectional squabbling, which it did not. The South wanted separation.

Following Jefferson's "death knell" warning came the famous dinner toast of Vice President Calhoun on April 13 1830, the occasion of Jefferson's birthdate. It was in response to President Andrew Jackson's toast: "The Federal Union: It must be preserved!" Calhoun stood and raised his glass: "The Union, next to our liberty the most dear: May we remember that it can only be preserved by respecting the rights of the States."

---

46 FoundersOnline, accessed 12.26.23

Buchanan   *Lincoln*

The aftermath was many States in the South began calculating the value of its political union with the North and open discussion of declaring independence to form a more perfect Union of Southern States.

President James Buchanan conferred with his attorney-general Jeremiah Black for a studied constitutional response to State's declaring independence. Black was a former Chief Justice of Pennsylvania's Supreme Court, Buchanan's nominee for a seat on the US Supreme Court in early 1861, and perhaps his closest official advisor. While both personally disagreed with a State voluntarily withdrawing from the 1789 federation, and not being able to discover a coercive power the President held to hold a State in the federation, he admitted that "it may be safely asserted that the power to make war against a State is at variance with the whole spirit and intent of the Constitution."[47]

Having now convinced himself of holding no authority to attack a State removing itself from the 1789 Constitution it voluntarily ratified, Buchanan said "it may be safely asserted that the power to make war against a State is at variance with the spirit and intent of the Constitution" and the federal government had no authority to prevent a State from seeking independence.[48] Though he disagreed with "secession" — being a diplomat he astutely advised a constitutional convention of the States to solve the issues peaceably. This follows Jefferson's opinion as he wrote to John Cartwright in March 1824 regarding the "common

---

47 Dunning, p164
48 Ibid, p165

umpire" to decide ultimately between them. If urgency is required, Jefferson said that a convention of the States must be called to decide the question.[49] At the same time the editor of the *New York Tribune*, Horace Greeley, wrote "The South has as good a right to secede from the union as the colonies had to secede from Great Britain."[50]

Despite Buchanan's able constitutional research and logic, Republican party leader Lincoln counseled absolutely no compromise with the departing States which would crush any Southern unionist hope for sectional conciliation. This uncompromising policy would cost over a million lives by April of 1865.

After his ill-advised Fort Sumter expedition was predictably fired upon and driven off, Lincoln then claimed to possess a war power necessary to "preserve the nation" amid a "mortal peril of a conscious nationality" in the face of "combinations." No constitutional provision was cited other than his claim that a president possessed a "war power."

Historian Dunning suggests that had Lincoln's view of national supremacy over all States been put to a vote in early 1861 in the north alone, in all probability it would have been defeated. Being a skillful attorney Lincoln needed a *casus belli* which a clash at Fort Sumter provided when his relief expedition received the predictable welcome Thus the new Southern republic could be blamed for initiating hostilities.[51] Lincoln admitted this in a letter of May 1, 1861 to friend G.V. Fox, writing that his administration got what it wanted: "You and I both anticipated that the cause of the [north] would be advanced by the attempt to provision Fort Sumter, even if it should fail; and it is no small consolation now to feel that our anticipation is justified by the result. Very truly, your friend, A. Lincoln." A few days later Lincoln began raising his army which only Congress has the authority to order.[52]

While revisiting events that led to the destruction of the town of Plymouth during the war, it is worth revisiting the US Congress's resolution authorizing Lincoln's invasion. It claimed that the war was forced upon the country and "not waged in any spirit of oppression, or for any purpose of conquest or subjugation, or purpose of overthrow-

---

49 Foley, p836
50 Mitcham, p119
51 Dunning, p170
52 Mitcham, p152

ing or interfering with the rights or established institutions of those [Southern States], but to defend and maintain the supremacy of the Constitution and preserve the union with all the dignity, equality & rights of the several States unimpaired."[53]

According to this the war was to end with the several State's reversing their declarations of independence and returning their representatives to the US Congress. If the "union was preserved," all would revert to as before — including the status of the South's labor system. But in reality, the Constitution had changed under the victorious Republican party with all States subservient to it and threatened with invasion should they resist. This was no longer the Constitution of the Framers.

The rapid concurrence of northern State governments controlled by the Republican party in ignoring the Constitution's intent emphasized the completeness of the revolution's progress. Soon the idea of a government limited by the written instructions of a past generation would grow dim in the smoke of battle.[54]

"What country can preserve its liberties if its rulers are not warned that the people preserve the spirit of resistance?"
— *Thomas Jefferson, 1787*

Thomas Jefferson

---

53 Randall, pp366-367
54 Dunning, p174

Independence & Invasion

"With the Lincoln administration rests the responsibility of precipitating a collision and fearful evils of a cruel war."
— *President Jefferson Davis, 7 April 1861*

To underscore the State's position relative to joining the new Southern Union, a majority of North Carolinians in February 1861 voted against a convention to even consider the question of departing the 1789 federation — a month before Lincoln's inauguration.[1] But Lincoln's refusal to use diplomacy to defuse the crisis, his warlike provocation at Fort Sumter and raising an army without the consent of Congress helped drive North Carolina toward the new nation. Even the foremost opponent of secession, Jonathan Worth, wrote in mid-May that Lincoln had alienated unionist men in the State and left no alternative but "to resist until we repel the invaders or die."[2] And some may have recalled the words of Col. Robert Howe speaking to members of North Carolina's 4th Provincial Congress regarding separation from England in 1775:

Jefferson Davis

"*Independence seems to be the word; I know of not one dissenting voice.*"

In a bold act of war nearly a month prior to North Carolina declaring its independence on May 20th, Lincoln declared a naval blockade of the southeastern coastline which included North Carolina. Once Lincoln announced he would raise an army without the consent of Congress, the State withdrew from the 1789 federation and shortly afterward ratified the Constitution of the new confederation.

Sensing trouble ahead after Buchanan's *Star of the West* affair and

---
1 Hill, p265
2 Hill, p266

John Bernhard Thuersam

apparent Republican disinterest in compromise, Governor John Ellis wisely initiated military preparations for the State's defense. After the collision at Fort Sumter on April 12, 1861, Ellis directed that artillery batteries be constructed along the State's long coastline and manned by North Carolina troops. He ordered as well the strengthening of existing forts — Macon near Beaufort, plus Caswell and Johnston at the mouth of the Cape Fear River. At Federal Point below Wilmington, Battery Bolles was erected facing the Atlantic and later enlarged to become the massive earthen "Malakoff"[3] fortress Fort Fisher fashioned by the capable Colonel William Lamb of Norfolk.

On the Outer Banks two earthen forts with protective plank facings were erected in early 1861 to protect the port of Hatteras from enemy attack. Fort Hatteras was only about 250 feet square armed with twelve 32-pound smoothbores; east of Hatteras and nearer the ocean was Fort Clark with five 32-pound smoothbores. The latter guns were at the end of their career with new rifled cannon surpassing them in range and accuracy.

What initially attracted enemy naval operations against Hatteras was the success of small craft preying upon Northern merchant ships passing offshore, whose operators now demanded government protection from what a Northern officer termed "a depot for rebel privateers." At the same time the State's military board recognized that seizing enemy prizes off the coast would surely attract a military expedition against the poorly-defended northeastern coastline and open the region to enemy pillaging and marauding, thus sealing it off from the rest of the State. Interestingly, New England's penchant for smuggling found Lincoln's early blockade porous; one federal official reported "unscrupulous New England men engaged in a lucrative business, aiding and abetting a contraband trade along the Atlantic coast from Virginia southward." Official papers show their ships loaded with goods bound for the West Indies but "in collusion with the rebels are taken as prizes enroute," then return to their home port "with no cargo and a show of honesty that is surprising."[4]

In late-August 1861 came an enemy expedition whose goal was ending what was referred to as "piracy" with the "ultimate purpose of a permanent occupation of North Carolina soil". This flotilla of some 26 vessels included 7 warships totaling 149 guns and nearly 900 troops

---

3 Massive Russian fortress near Sevastopol. See: Crimean War.
4 Hill, p161. Also see ORN, Vol I, 6, 111

aboard transports. To oppose this menacing flotilla were the 350 men of the hastily-assembled 7th North Carolina Volunteers, soon reinforced to 700 men crowded into Forts Clark and Hatteras with their old smooth-bore guns.[5]

The naval bombardment of Forts Clark and Hatteras witnessed the first instance of the United States Navy using its guns to kill or maim Americans. The fleet's vastly superior firepower took its toll in the attack on Fort Hatteras, though naval commanders chafed at their ineffective landing force of some regulars and a mixed bag of others. The latter were described as "a miserable, thieving set of rascals, terming themselves a "Naval Brigade" but without officers or organization of any kind." These were joined by "a promiscuous crowd of some 150 of Max Weber's German regiment," from New York City. Considered unruly and expendable, they were left on the beach overnight to fend for themselves.[6]

Nonetheless, the loss of both forts so quickly caused great consternation and blame-placing in North Carolina and the Confederate Congress demanding a full accounting of the disaster.[7] But it quickly became clear that the hastily-erected coastal defenses were woefully inadequate to resist the amphibious assault that the northern navy demonstrated it was very capable of so early in the war.

---

5 Hill, pg164
6 Barnes, p80
7 See: Report of the Roanoke Island Investigation Committee, 1862, Richmond

This was not the first instance of an enemy fleet on North Carolina's soil. Eleven British warships with barges of troops had anchored at Ocracoke on July 11, 1813, and for five days landed men there and at Portsmouth while creating a panic in northeastern North Carolina. The enemy captured two American privateers and seized livestock, but made no attempt to attack New Bern as was expected. Likely considering that town not a strategic position to occupy and hold, they were gone a week later.[8]

In the North, the Outer Banks disaster brought rejoicing as it was only the previous month that blue-coated troops were soundly defeated at First Manassas.[9] By mid-October the situation for North Carolina dimmed further as Forts Ocracoke and Oregon were in enemy hands, with the Albemarle and Pamlico Sound inlets patrolled by enemy warships.[10] Historian McCallum asserts that "the short-sighted North Carolina and Confederate leadership had blundered badly" with the loss of the State's northern sounds, all of which paved the way for Northern troops to conquer Washington, Plymouth and other eastern towns in the spring of 1862.

Assigned to the military occupation of Hatteras was the 9th New York regiment whose colonel described the inhabitants he now ruled as "a class of people who subsist from fishing and hunting as well as from cargoes stranded upon the stormy coast … The islanders mingle but little with the world; apparently indifferent to this outside sphere, they constitute a world within themselves."[11] The islanders were told they could remain in their homes if they submitted to an oath of allegiance to the federal government, with about 250 agreeing to the offer in order to be left alone. Other inhabitants unwilling to live under the Northern government abandoned their homes and escaped to the mainland with many joining North Carolina regiments.

The occupiers suffered under two delusions at the time. The first was believing that a majority of the submissive people on the sounds were actually loyal to the North. This was fueled by impressionable young officers writing reports to superiors claiming that thousands of loyal men were there holding Union meetings in secret. They also believed that a thousand Northern troops scattered on the sounds

---

8 Gilpatrick, p206
9 McCallum, p94
10 ORN, I, 6, xvii
11 OR, 4, 610

would prompt the loyalists — or "Tories" — to hold a convention and bring a third of North Carolina back to the North's federation within two weeks.[12]

The second delusion of the invaders was the belief that "Bankers" who felt abandoned by their State were politically-influential people who would make themselves "heard and felt in this struggle." That there was indifference regarding the Confederate States along the coast is undeniable. General Richard C. Gatlin, a Kinston native himself, commented on a statement regarding Washington County that had been made by "two intelligent and worthy citizens" of that county, says: "If I am correctly informed, the feeling is not confined to Washington County, but has its ramifications along the sounds in many directions." The people simply wanted to be left alone and live unmolested. It is equally undeniable that this disaffection was confined largely to a class of persons who never make themselves heard or felt in any struggle. One invading soldier characterizing the "Bankers" offered this: "Their indifference or neutrality was evinced by raising white flags to their roof-tops on the approach of either Confederates or federals."[13] There were also the malcontents that W. E. DeMill of Beaufort County wrote of in a letter to Gov. Henry T. Clark, described as "the lower class of once so-called Unionist party." Nonetheless, Northern officers who had little time and interest in learning the character of these people were under orders to use them as soldiers and as

---

12 Delaney, p353. See also, Hill, pp176-179)
13 Col. Claiborne Snead, Sketch of a Georgia Regiment, p36

framers of what would be a reactionary, Tory State government.[14]

In an effort to raise troops loyal to him, Lincoln requested General Winfield Scott frame an order for recruiting North Carolinians at Fort Hatteras. He suggested that "[Secretary of State William] Seward's nephew Clarence A. Seward would be willing to go and play colonel and assist in raising a force." It was found that "the number of white men who expressed a willingness to enlist was so small that it was not found necessary to convert young Seward into a colonel."[15]

The next effort was to use these dissidents to expedite a convention in which "these counties would vote themselves back into the 1789 federation and take up arms to defend themselves if necessary."[16] One Northern colonel decided to issue an edict assuring the people that his troops had not come to pillage and plunder. "We come," he declared, "to give you back law, order, the Constitution and your rights under it, and to restore peace."[17] This was similar to British Colonel Banastre Tarleton's proclamation in South Carolina some 75 years earlier "offering full rights of citizenship and pardon to all who would take the oath of allegiance to the Crown, and declaring all others as rebels."[18]

Despite the soothing proclamation of non-interference and preserving the antebellum status quo, the invaders had already demonstrated their proclivity for stealing livestock, while looting and burning the homes of civilians, made clear the true intent of the invaders. In addition, an editorial of the expropriated *New Bern Daily Progress* on March 26th assured residents that the invaders had not come to interfere with the South's system of labor, assuring all that "we propose to let the people of the South manage their Negro question as seems best to them."[19]

The colonel reported to his superior that "I regret to be compelled to state that the conduct of the men and some of the officers of the 20th New York Volunteers has been that of vandals. They have plundered and destroyed." After stating how they rifled the boxes and trunks and fired the quarters of the captured Confederates, he said: "The next day they commenced breaking open private houses and stores, and I saw party after party come in, some of them headed by

---

14 Hill, pp177-178
15 OR, 4, 613
16 OR, 4, 608
17 OR, 4, 658
18 Shy, pp231-232
19 Browning, pp 604-605

commissioned officers, loaded down with the result of their plundering. This conduct continued until I was compelled to adopt the most severe and stringent measures." [20]

It was a clear impossibility to bring back loyalty to a federal government that had unleashed an armed occupation which had begun with the looting and destruction of private property. An enemy engineer stated in September that he found "all the inhabitants that I conversed with unite in complaining of the vandalism of our troops, some houses being completely rifled. Such conduct on the part of our soldiers is but little calculated to conciliate those who may be useful to us."[21] The pillaging went far towards working a change in the attitude of even those who had taken the oath of allegiance — which was thought to safeguard private property. This showed the true "unionism" of the islands to be other than loyalty.[22]

If one believes it was Lincoln's intention to re-unite the country into a harmonious federation — which it had not been since 1830 — the alienation of supposedly-unionist civilians by his military would have been studiously avoided. But only a month after the federal invasion commenced a northern lieutenant perceptively wrote:

"The idea of union sentiment which is thought to exist in this state is incorrect, I think. The people are now hostile, if they were not a few weeks since." [23]

From the conflict's beginning the north's Articles of War, established by the United States Ninth Congress in 1806, loosely governed the behavior of its armies. For example, Article 54 stipulated that "All officers and soldiers are to behave themselves orderly in quarters and on the march; and whoever shall commit any waste of spoil … of trees … in houses, gardens, cornfields or meadows, or shall maliciously destroy any property whatsoever belonging to the inhabitants of the United States … shall be punished by a general court martial." The only caveat here was unless the destruction was ordered by the commander-in-chief of the armies.[24]

The soothing words of the invader's proclamation seemed to follow the Articles in spirit, but the behavior of his troops, as described,

---

20 OR, 4, 658
21 OR, IV, 592
22 Delaney, p352
23 ORN, I, 6, 304
24 Lieber, pp15-16

told another tale. A dispirited lieutenant of the New York regiment wrote in September that "all the inhabitants that I have conversed with unite in complaining of the vandalism of our troops, some houses being completely rifled." He added that "Such conduct on the part of our soldiers is but little calculated to conciliate those who may be useful to us."[25] The town of Winton felt the hard hand of war as a New York regiment marched in on February 20th and applied the torch after his Zouaves had sufficiently pilfered the stores and homes. Lost in the flames was the Courthouse with all of its records, and nearly all the private homes of the village.[26]

After the capture of Fort Macon near Beaufort the confident Burnside announced that any further objectives would be accomplished "at his discretion," suggesting a march to seize Goldsboro and Raleigh next, then to Wilmington and Fort Caswell to the south. As he moved inland during mid-March 1862, Burnside, like the British before him, believed a strategy of pacification would gain success.

The enemy-designated "contrabands" did not fare well during the invasion as they were impressed as mess servants or orderlies of common soldiers. Their treatment at the hands of the men in blue was demonstrated in mid-March 1862 by some intoxicated men of the 48th Massachusetts regiment entering a "contraband" shack and

---

25 OR, 4, 592
26 ORN, I, 6, 639

"abused most shamefully with bayonets and knives, cutting several severely." One had a finger cut off, another cut in the stomach "which will undoubtedly prove fatal."[27]

During the occupation, which northeastern North Carolina suffered under for most of the war, civilians intimidated by the military learned to outwardly behave "loyally" (as "Tories") to avoid persecution. An enemy commander conducting a raid with Negro troops in late 1862 lived off the country much of the time, and stated that he "judiciously discriminated in favor of the worst rebels" and their property before reaching Elizabeth City.[28] Some civilians committed illegal and violent acts against neighbors they disliked if they felt protected by the enemy. The latter was true as landowners believed to be pro-Southern were persecuted and/or deprived of their land, with those feigning loyalty to the enemy squatting on their land and stealing movable property.[29]

The State's busiest port at New Bern became the next target of the enemy after the occupation of the Outer Banks. With preparations completed in early March for an attack, enemy gunboats proceeded up the Neuse River early on the 14th along with over 10,000 troops marching onshore until reaching the Croatan works and Fort Thompson six miles below the city. Here they were opposed by some 3800 North Carolina soldiers and a few Marylanders, all under the command of General Lawrence O'Bryan Branch.[30]

From 8AM through noon the defenders fought courageously with the enemy taking severe casualties in their assault, but an unprotected gap in the defensive line with insufficient reserves to seal it was exploited by the enemy. Being driven from their defenses and with some units cut off from retreat amid constant fire from gunboats steaming further upriver to the city, a general retreat was ordered while all State warehouses full of military stores were set afire. The sight of their utterly demoralized troops fleeing the city sent residents into shock, and they took flight as well before the invaders. They had been under the impression that Branch's force and Fort Thompson were more than sufficient to repel the enemy with many wagers made earlier that New Bern would not even be attacked.

---

27 Priest, p9
28 Barrett, p178
29 Shy, p233
30 Hill, p221

One enemy soldier-diarist wrote home of the many triumphant blue-coated soldiers marching into an "almost deserted city" in the afternoon of March 14, 1862. Revealing his abolitionist leanings, he wrote that "scarcely more than two hundred of the ruling-race had dared to face the invader, and so hurried was the departure of the citizens that marks of their haste and fright were everywhere." A piano left on the street was eyed by one soldier to be shipped northward at the first opportunity, and the diarist added that the "colored servitors" of those departed, "to whom "Massa Linkum's" soldiers were angels of delivery, hastened to us to express their delight at the situation." Despite this apparent show of appreciation, the soldiers requisitioned black men to harness horses to carts of looted furnishings from certain homes and taken to camp.[31] One Massachusetts soldier recorded that "The soldiers and sailors had free run for the first twenty-four hours and everything they wanted and much they did not want was looted from homes."[32] Burnside's proclamation had been forgotten.

The enemy now warned homeowners and shopkeepers to return to the city or expect the loss of their property. A young resident who fled in panic expected her beloved volume of *A History of the United States* would surely be pilfered by the invader. Before departing she had inscribed it thus: "If this book should fall to a Yankee's hands fall, remember you forced us to flee from home and friends, a peaceful family — may this memory forever haunt thee."[33] Store owners loyal to the dollar flew US flags to attract northern soldiers with money to spend, but soon came to view them as inveterate and clever thieves. Despite merchant efforts to catch shoplifters, soldiers would enter in groups of twos with one occupying the owner while the other surreptitiously pocketed items.[34]

While the enemy consolidated their capture of New Bern, its fortification began with an intent of holding the position if liberation was later attempted. Daily expeditions were sent out to acquire knowledge of the area's topography, test the strength of the defenders and attract any natives willing to take the oath as "buffaloes." The latter included Southern deserters and those overawed by the free movement of gunboats and troops. Energized by their string of victories after the loss of

---

31 Roe, pp94-95
32 Putnam, p114
33 Roe, p95
34 Mahood, p128

Roanoke Island in early 1862, New Bern fell in mid-March and Fort Macon being occupied the following month, the enemy began fortifying New Bern with outer defensive positions while gunboats patrolled the Pamlico Sound, and the Neuse and Trent Rivers. From this strong base the gunboats were also used to ferry troops to the Albemarle Sound to the north for inland raids.[35]

In both Raleigh and Richmond, news of New Bern's fall, and the relative ease with which the enemy accomplished its capture, caused great concern. It was feared that should the enemy be sufficiently reinforced they could sweep across North Carolina to divide the upper and lower Confederate States. This could be equally devastating after the divide caused by the recent loss of Forts Henry and Donelson, plus New Orleans. General Lee himself warned his government after New Bern's loss that another "disaster [in North Carolina] would be ruinous."[36]

The immediate defensive solution for the new Confederate States was to rush more troops to North Carolina to oppose any further enemy advances, with the view that, had enough troops been in the State prior to invasion, the New Bern disaster would not have occurred. Upper military leadership was bolstered as well with changes in command and centralized around Goldsboro, all of which brought improvements in civilian confidence. The troops were also being equipped with British Enfield rifled-muskets brought by blockade runners to Wilmington.[37]

With their hold on New Bern now secure, the enemy began sending out raids to destroy crops, kill livestock and burn homes and farm buildings of neighboring farms. This not only drove white families further inland to escape the depredations, but also left many colored families homeless, hungry and without shelter. The latter could now only look to the invaders for the food, shelter, health care and employment lost to them.

The earthen fortifications the enemy envisioned around New Bern needed many workers, which meant combing the region for "contraband" men to impress as laborers if they could not prove they belonged to a North Carolinian loyal to Lincoln. It was common for little or nothing to be said about wages or how long they would be worked,

---

35 Hill, p315
36 OR. 108,512
37 Hill, p304

and if any resisted the Provost Marshal would simply arrest as many as possible.³⁸ The enemy built its earthen Fort Totten to defend New Bern with the labor of contrabands, who wore a "mark of distinction — hats with white muslin patches emblazoned with black "U.S." letters." For this backbreaking work they received daily rations, and little more.³⁹ Importantly, the lesson was not lost on those "contrabands" who fled to the enemy and realized they had abandoned their masters only to be re-enslaved by new ones in blue who used them as servants, cooks and hard laborers. Though told they were "free," there was now no return to their old homes and farms which had been destroyed by their new friends offering them a spade and hard labor. That the hard work was dangerous is an understatement as one Massachusetts soldier recorded: "The negro pioneers, in their tree-felling, had the misfortune to kill one of their number. The boxing and burial of his remains were hardly an interruption of their labors." To the colored people at New Bern, "every Yankee soldier is an angel of light."⁴⁰

"Contraband" Wagon

The invaders condescending view of colored people was on display in mid-May 1862 when two mulatto soldiers, John Williams and David Molsen were discovered in the ranks of the Forty-eighth Pennsylvania Regiment, were immediately discharged and sent north.⁴¹

---

38 Maslowski, p101
39 Priest, p23
40 Roe, p132
41 Priest, p36

With an enemy-occupied New Bern a stark reality, defense of the region fell to a mobile defense force known as the 41st Regiment, North Carolina Troops, also known as the 3rd North Carolina Cavalry. Composed of several detached companies of horsemen, this vast picket force protected a great arc of coastline sweeping from below the Cape Fear River at the South Carolina line, to the Blackwater River at the Virginia line. The troopers were local men who knew their areas — roads, fords, swamps and streams — opposing enemy raids, communicating with their spies within enemy forces, and providing intelligence of enemy movements to larger units. Plymouth-area residents in this unit included Sergeant Major Thomas S. Armistead, Color Sergeant Levi J. Fagan and Regimental Surgeon Dr. Benjamin M. Walker.[42]

This protective force attacked enemy patrols emanating from New Bern while protecting isolated farms and plantations. Those colored residents captured in enemy raids and taken to New Bern were often repatriated to their homes, an example of which was a night raid by North Carolina cavalry into nearby Carolina (Morehead) City. After destroying some railroad tracks the horsemen "carried off some 12" colored men who had been impressed as labor gangs by the enemy.[43] Sometimes those like Mary Attamore who lived alone in her farmhouse were strong enough to discourage ransacking Northern soldiers. More than once assaulted by blue-clad "bummers" seeking plunder, she awakened one morning to them digging up graves in the nearby family burial plot. After angrily confronting those seeking valuables who disturbed the final rest of her ancestors, the grave-robbers left empty handed.[44]

The Northern occupation of New Bern followed the usual pattern of controlling the civilian population while discouraging "disloyalty," which would later appear in occupied Plymouth. This included a system of passes and permits, mail censorship, retaliation, oaths of allegiance, forcing men into local "militia," and confiscation.[45] Despite such repressive measures the enemy was confounded by the presence of an underground "rebel mail" that communicated military activities and strength from within New Bern to North Carolina's forces sur-

---

42 Carolana.com, 41st NC Regt online, 10.9.23
43 Priest, p50
44 Anderson, p18
45 Maslowski, p69

rounding the town. An example was Mrs. Elizabeth Howland secretly conveying details of enemy forts being constructed; others like Mrs. A. M. Meekins ran the blockade into New Bern to ascertain enemy strength later in the war for General Robert E. Lee.[46]

As enemy gunboats ascended the Pamlico River to the south, the town of Little Washington was found undefended. The blue-clad troops disembarked to a lukewarm welcome from those who had not yet fled, perhaps a third of the original population. Before their earlier departure, North Carolina soldiers had burned a gunboat under-construction as well as cotton bales and naval stores. Once ashore, the enemy raised their flag at the courthouse as they awaited Massachusetts troops who would garrison the town along with several gunboats.

It was now only a matter of time before Plymouth would also be visited and occupied. To best visualize the invasion and areas of control as it spread further inland, one historian suggested drawing a line on a map from the Virginia line down through Plymouth, Little Washington and New Bern. The areas west of that line from Hamilton southward through Greenville, Kinston, Goldsboro and downward to Wilmington remained free of enemy control. All areas east of that line were under now enemy occupation and would serve as bases from which to conduct their destructive inland raids.[47]

Edward W. Stanly

In what has been termed an impossible mission with the goal of restoring North Carolina to the 1789 federation after Burnside's occupation of the Outer Banks, as well as a small area of northeastern North Carolina, Lincoln appointed as his "proconsul" Edward Stanly on May 19, 1862. He was under the impression that Stanly, a native Whig though resident of California, might foster "a harmonious reconstruction" of the State after Burnside's "the strong military show of force plus benevolence and conciliation." A grand failure in the end, it only created the appearance of a "unionist" government in the State where the enemy's military existed.

---

46 Anderson, pp16-17
47 McCallum, p94

Stanly's instructions were to help reconstitute local self-government and reassure the population of the national government's limited war aims of restoring the union.[48] But so out of touch was Stanly with his native State in 1862 that he was considered a traitor and his mission an absurdity. Stanly wrote to Gov. Zebulon Vance after his inauguration in early September 1862 and the governor's response was frank, noting that the appointment of a military governor for North Carolina "implied its subjugation" and that he had directed that military authorities ignore Stanly's pretensions.[49] Vance continued that the State "had dissolved its connection with the old government, and entered a solemn pact" in a more perfect union with like-minded States. He also advised Stanly of "how his name was execrated and cursed and that "damned atrocities were being committed daily under his own eyes", and asked how as a North Carolinian he could "walk through the smoking ashes of the homes which once greeted you with hospitable welcome" and across farmlands desolated by the enemy he adhered to.[50]

Stanly offended Northern abolitionists when he insisted that he had been brought to New Bern to restore the old order of things, and if he facilitated the opening of colored schools it "would do harm to the union cause" of bringing the State back into the fold as Lincoln wanted. This brought him grief from abolitionists who saw Stanly as "disloyal to the union, inimical to the Negroes and a friend of slave owners."[51]

Agreeing wholeheartedly with New York editor Horace Greeley's published views regarding the north's war aims, Stanly believed "our great civil war was opened on the part of the Union … with a general expectation that it would be prosecuted to a successful end without disturbing the foundations and buttresses of slavery." Though a military governor with Lincoln's blessing, Stanly was opposed by the Republican party's influential radicals in his efforts to protect the property of those considered unionists, opposed when he closed abolitionists schools for Negroes, and opposed when "contrabands" were enlisted against his protestations. Stanly loudly complained that North Carolina's Tories who stoutly opposed independence in 1861 were now convinced that the North envisions "our entire destruction and total

---

48 Browning, p590
49 Hill, p273
50 Vance, p200
51 Hill, p282

desolation of our country, and condemn[s] us to irredeemable misery and hopeless ruin."[52]

Stanly's instructions that "contrabands" be returned to their owners quickly drew fire from abolitionist critics. Northern military commanders realized that many of them belonged to slaveowners considered unionists and reluctant to alienate them if not returned. The infamous Ben Butler began using "contrabands" as army labor since the South was utilizing colored labor for military fortifications as well as their agricultural workers.[53] Perplexed with the number of contrabands in his hands after devastating the countryside, Burnside wrote his superior within a week of his occupation of New Bern that "they are now a very great source of anxiety to us" and the city "was being overrun with fugitives from surrounding towns and plantations." The "contrabands" were being assigned as work gangs constructing fortifications and marched to their hard labor as a pioneer corps under old faded flags with fifes playing.[54] The hard labor did little for the health of those colored men put to this work and housed in crowded quarters, often exposing them to fatal disease.[55]

Stanly recognized as well the plight of loyalist farmers with commodities to sell who were cut off from interior markets and with curing salt all but unavailable. They were preyed upon by sharp Northern shipping agents who reaped enormous profits from those isolated people as they beat them down on price for turpentine, lumber and cotton.[56] Obviously taking Lincoln's assignment seriously, his efforts at conciliating civilians to the Northern union was seriously undermined by his troops "who regularly conducted the most shameful pillaging and robbery that ever disgraced an army in any civilized land."[57]

Stanly wrote of a "regiment of abolitionists" who conveyed more than $40,000 worth of looted property on empty troopships returning north. "They literally robbed the cradle and the grave. Family burial vaults were broken open for robbery; and in one instance (the fact was published in a Boston newspaper and admitted to me by an officer of high position in the army) a vault was entered, its metallic coffin removed, and the remains cast out so that the body of a dead (Northern)

---

52 Ibid, p286
53 Ibid, p278
54 Roe, p128
55 Hill, p279
56 Ibid, p290
57 Barrett, p173. See: Stanly-Charles Sumner Correspondence

soldier might be put in the place." [58]

An increasingly "total war" mindset in the North was led by leading abolitionists in Congress, especially abolitionist Charles Sumner of Massachusetts who demanded Stanly's termination. To this was added a new department commander replacing Burnside who turned a blind eye to the continued pillaging which targeted all civilians, including those identified as pro-union.[59] Historian Barrett tells us that the continued "deplorable conduct of the federal troops" along with Lincoln's emancipation edict" and decision to fight the American South with colored soldiers convinced Stanly of the hopelessness of his situation. In his resignation letter of January 15, 1863, he wrote that could no longer assure North Carolinians "that Lincoln's administration was only trying to secure their rights and to restore the union." Of Lincoln's emancipation scheme he added: "It is enough to say I fear it will do infinite mischief," would crush hopes of finding peace with conciliatory measures. He felt that it would also bring most dire calamities to Negroes themselves."[60]

After his resignation, Stanly wrote radical Senator Sumner: "Had the war in North Carolina been conducted by soldiers who were Christians and gentlemen the State would have long ago ended their rebellion. Instead, what was done? Thousands and thousands of dollars' worth of property were conveyed north. Libraries, pianos, carpets, mirrors, family portraits — everything that could be removed — was stolen by men abusing law-abiding North Carolinians while preaching liberty, justice and civilization." [61]

It is important to note that it was not to be until the third year of war that an official document was issued to guide the conduct of Northern armies in the field. Though the War of 1812's Articles of War remained to guide the US military in 1861, this did not prevent crimes and atrocities against civilians. Despite a new code being issued in May of 1863 prohibiting the above, nothing would change as commanders ignored its provisions while politicians looked the other way.

Sadly, prior to the "Lieber Code" of conduct the north's military, especially in North Carolina, was guided by the sympathy or cruelty of commanders, or how much control they exerted over their soldiers when in contact with civilians.

---

58 Hamilton, p95
59 Hill, p286
60 Ibid, p293
61 Hamilton, pp94-95

Loyalty, Treason & Contrabands

"Patriotism is defensive; nationalism is aggressive. Patriotism is the love of a particular land with its traditions; nationalism a political and ideological substitute for religion, modern and populist."

—*John Lukacs*

For the Greek's, "Patria" meant the place of one's ancestors, the native city and country. This can be said to be the underlying patriotism directing the energies of North Carolinians defending their State after the Fort Sumter provocation of mid-April 1861 and Lincoln's nationalistic demand for troops to wage war upon a sister State. This act of war had driven even the most "unionist" North Carolinians to support political independence and joining the other Southern States in a new political federation. One author estimated that support for North Carolina's independence before Fort Sumter to be 30 percent, and in excess of 95 percent afterward.[1]

"The first object of my heart is my country: my family, my fortune, my own existence."

— *Thomas Jefferson*

The men of Washington County who volunteered for North Carolina's defense were initially known as the "Morris Guards" under Capt. Henry M. Gilliam, later Capt. Stuart L. Johnston. The company name apparently honors Col. Ellwood Morris, a Pennsylvania-born civil engineer who was charged with construction of Forts Clark and Hatteras in late-April of 1861. The Plymouth wharf was then busy with steamers carrying materials, weapons and laborers to Ocracoke and Hatteras.[2] The men enlisted at Plymouth and mustered into the 7th Regiment, North Carolina Troops in mid-July 1861 as Company

---

1 Garren, p3
2 Tolbert, page lxxix, Vol. I. Morris was a distinguished prewar engineer who was employed by the State-owned Cape Fear and Deep River Navigation Company. At the outbreak of war in April 1861 Gov. Ellis gave him the rank of militia colonel and assigned him to the defense of the Outer Banks. Upon his return north in the fall of 1863 to live with his mother, he wrote that the neighbors "gave him a cool reception.

John Bernhard Thuersam

H, then hurried to Ocracoke Inlet with other area units and shortly afterward to Hatteras Inlet. With the fall of Fort Hatteras in late-August, the North Carolina troops surrendered there included the three officers, four NCO's and 59 privates of the "Morris Guards." Most of these men would be captured at Hatteras and exchanged in January and February 1862. Another unit organized at Plymouth in August 1861 was a State Militia company under Capt. William A. Littlejohn and James H. Smith, a home guard which provided local defense through the end of the war.[3]

A Martin County legislator in constant communication with Gov. John W. Ellis in early May 1861 was Asa Biggs. His excited letter to Ellis from Plymouth on May 6th reports Col. Morris being at New Bern in search of materials, laborers and steamer transports to build and equip the Cape Hatteras forts he was in the process of erecting. Biggs informed the governor that he was chartering two schooners and a steamer to Morris and "report to him with such laborers and materials as in my judgment will be necessary." Biggs was recruiting free-black workers and hoping to have 40 to 50 hired soon, and on May 7th Biggs writes Ellis again to report that the Plymouth newspaper carried Col. Morris's advertisement for 300 laborers. Morris was also notifying the people of Washington, Edenton and Elizabeth City to encourage free-black laborers to report to the engineering officer soon arriving in their towns.[4]

The 7th Regiment was reorganized as the 17th North Carolina Regiment in mid-May 1862 with the "Morris Guards" incorporated as Company G, under Capt. Thomas J. Norman. A second Washington county unit was the "Liberty Guards" as Company H, commanded by Capt. Stuart L. Johnston. The 17th Regiment was commanded by Lt. Col. John C. Lamb of Martin County and drew its men from the surrounding counties of Pasquotank, Hyde, Carteret, Pitt, Hertford, Currituck, Camden, Martin, Tyrrell, Gates, Perquimans, Franklin, Washington and Beaufort. Due to the strong enemy forces at New Bern threatening inland counties, the 17th Regiment was assigned picket duty service in eastern North Carolina to observe enemy movements, especially at Plymouth, Little Washington and New Bern.

In that era women would be shunned if their menfolk had not enlisted or volunteered to serve in some capacity in defense of the State.

---

3 Carolana.com. Both 7th and 17th Regiments, NC Troops
4 Tolbert, p723-726

Some young ladies openly refused to marry a man who did not enlist, yet some expressed fear of being alone and unprotected should their men depart for war. This was most often the case in areas with Tories who might adhere to the enemy with the men choosing this to protect his family.[5] As an indication of war preparation, Mrs. Edmondston at Halifax wrote of her husband "teaching me to shoot." She recorded in her diary a short time later that as their men departed for camp "The women of many of them wept, sobbed, nay even shrieked aloud, but I had no tears to shed. … The sentiment of exulted patriotism which filled my heart found no echo in lamentations, no vent in tears." Of the men gone to war she wrote: "they are gone in the exercise of man's highest and holiest duty!"[6]

The men of a community like Washington County were uniformed by ladies who worked feverishly to complete all before their departure for war. They were then usually presented with bouquets and motivated with a speech from the region's most respected lady. And flying above their ranks, the "Morris Guards" had a battle flag lovingly-crafted of donated silk fabric, which would be defended to the last.

Other area communities like Little Washington presented on June 21, 1861 their "Jeff Davis Rifles" flag made from the wedding gown of Mrs. T.H.B. Myers. At Halifax County Mrs. Elizabeth Wiggens, who would send seven sons to war, recorded in her diary: "May 15, 1861, made flag for the Home Guards at Ringwood."[7] The girls

---

5 McKean, Vol I, p24
6 Edmondston, p69
7 McKean, p49

of Chowan Institute presented a flag to the Hertford Light Infantry; and the Edgecombe Guards were presented with their flag from Miss Cornelia Crenshaw at Tarboro.[8] The ladies work would not end with the departure of their men as "soldiers' aid societies" sprang up to knit socks and gloves, make shirts and trousers, and underwear, plus tents, haversacks, blankets and canteen covers. North Carolina troops near occupied towns like Plymouth had packages of food and drink clandestinely delivered by loyal residents.

Once the 17th Regiment assembled it was sent to the Virginia theater of war and assigned to Maj-General D. H. Hill's Division which would participate in 1862's Seven Days, Malvern Hill and Sharpsburg battles. Though held as reserves at the Fredericksburg battle, they suffered greatly under the enemy's heavy enemy artillery bombardment.[9]

After New Bern's occupation the enemy began enticing local men into their "Union Volunteer" units. On June 12th in Plymouth, a colonel of the 9th New York Regiment addressed a meeting exhorting military-age men to enlist and obtained some from nearby Beaufort, Bertie and Washington counties. These men would be committing treason against North Carolina by waging war against it, as well as aiding and abetting an enemy. They would be derisively-referred to as "buffaloes."

Marcus Tullius Cicero

"A nation can survive its fools ... but it cannot survive treason from within."
— *Marcus Tullius Cicero*

King George III declared those British colonists in America who "seceded" in 1776 as guilty of treason, and sent troops to coerce them, violently if necessary. The invading Redcoats ruled towns under martial law and "rebels" wishing to avoid prison and property confiscation were offered royal pardon if an oath of allegiance to the Crown was signed. Many Tories — their allegiance to the Crown real or feigned — served with British forces lest their property and families

---

8 Ibid, p53
9 Manarin, Vol III, p136; Vol IV, p201

be threatened.[10] This would be repeated in the years 1861-1865.

General George Washington issued a proclamation requiring all swearing allegiance to the Crown to either "take an oath of allegiance to the United States" or be treated as common enemies. With this edict he raised the then-interesting question of national citizenship as opposed to that of each individual sovereign State, which each new "State" had declared. The anti-federalists in Congress immediately saw Washington's words as dangerous, insisting that it not be regarded as a precedent.[11]

In that war both sides demanded "loyalty" from the citizenry: in 1861 Lincoln expected North Carolinians to be "loyal" to his government in distant Washington. This was an era when American States, especially in the South, expected supreme loyalty from their citizens. North Carolina was "the country" in the same manner as Robert E. Lee famously viewed his native Virginia as "the country" to which he owed his supreme allegiance. After refusing compromise with the Southern States to continue the fraternal union peacefully, Lincoln's Republicans initiated war against the new Southern "Union" established in March of 1861. After an independent South Carolina used force to oust US troops from its now-sovereign territory, the cry of "treason" was heard in the North.

"Treason" is defined in Article III, Section 3, of the US Constitution and should the reader agree with Lincoln's assertion that States could not withdraw and remained permanently within the United States, then the answer is simple. Lincoln was waging war against "Them," the States, as well as giving aid and comfort to their enemies, and he was clearly guilty of treason as were Northern governors who provided troops for the invasion southward. This is why his predecessor, James Buchanan, ably advised by his attorney general, was constrained. They were both aware that waging war against a State is treason.

North Carolina's Constitution stated the same regarding treason and this applied to all residents including colored laborers. Of course, any remaining "Unionists" (Tories) in the State moved constantly in an atmosphere of scorn and prejudice if their opinions were known to neighbors. As this occurred during Plymouth's occupation, their veil was shed after Northern troops arrived and their favor and protection

---

10 Shy, p191
11 Jensen, p173

John Bernhard Thuersam

sought. The "Tory" motivation was often the result of settling old disputes with neighbors or store owners with inventory to sell to anyone. The reaction of North Carolina's slaves to the invasion of Hatteras and after was mixed, with most remaining faithful to their home and masters. Many of course sensed a change and often deserted their homes with indifference to an uncertain future with absolute strangers. Others remained home but became increasingly insolent and unruly while perplexed masters expected them to disappear at any moment.[12]

Author William A. Blair notes that Northern legal opinion experienced a change in the early stages of the war with the charges to grand juries revealing judges' positions on treason and the legality of the American Confederacy. Through the end of 1861 federal judges commonly denied the right of Southerners to form "a more perfect union" of their own. But from 1862 onward it became common for federal judges to use their grand jury addresses as occasions to denounce the South as traitorous enemies and encourage support of Lincoln's war.[13]

An interesting legal device of Northern politicians was the creation of "implied treason" which provided a flexible tool for Northern politicians who wanted newspapers monitored for any editorials questioning US government policy, or publishing views construed as approving of "secession." One Supreme Court Justice siding with free speech was Samuel Nelson who wrote that oral, written or printed words, "however treasonable, seditious or criminal of themselves, do not constitute an overt act of treason within the definition of the crime." When confronted with official acts of the Confederate States government, Nelson joined the other justices in declining acknowledgment of the war being between two countries. Another justice instructed a jury that the war was "an insurrection or rebellion which grew into a civil war," that the power of the insurgents could not be considered a state, and that "the entire Confederate experiment" consisted of traitors trying to overthrow the US government.[14] While reflecting upon the question of where the "treason" of 1861-65 lay, former soldier and North Carolinian Benjamin Franklin Grady observed in 1899: "The power to punish for treason was destroyed by the federal government 1861-1865; since then, many persons guilty of it have been rewarded for it by that federal government; and it is now proposed to place them on the pension

---

12 Maslowski, p98
13 Blair, p71
14 Blair, p73-76

roles at the expense, in part, of the people of the Southern States."[15]

Democrats in the North were now seeing through the twisted logic of Republicans who preferred calling it a "civil war" now rather than "a rebellion." The latter now viewed the federation's government as a sovereign power subject only to the international rules of warfare, and opposed by Southern States, still within their Union, populated by public enemies, equally belligerents and traitors with their property open to seizure and/or confiscation.

Outspoken Northern Democrat Samuel S. Cox of Ohio wryly noted their adoption of this term "civil war," which he embraced earlier as it asserted a limited conflict shielding one's property from military confiscation. He wrote that "members [of Congress] who a year ago claimed it a rebellion rather than a civil war now find it is so," adding, "when it will answer the purposes of vengeance and emancipation."[16]

Samuel S. Cox

The term "contraband" as used in the Civil War can be traced to a mid-June 1861 Thomas Nast political cartoon which portrayed a colored person clutching a northern general's leg as if to beg for protection from his Southern owner.[17] This term would continue to be used throughout the war to describe uprooted colored refugees from deserted or destroyed plantations at least until Lincoln's January 1863 edict.

As the North's armies invaded the South, they overran farms and plantations while ransacking homes and outbuildings which were afterward destroyed or burned. The owners may have already fled with their workers but those left behind were told by Northern officers, especially of the increasingly-abolitionist wing of the Republican party, that they no longer served their owners. This was very often interpreted as absolute freedom to leave their homes and go anywhere, and many believed this deliverer would provide them with food and shelter. These new mouths to feed caused many Northern commanders to treat them as a labor force paid with rations, as did the infamous

---

15 Grady, p51n
16 Blair, p88
17 Wiki, accessed 10.23.23

REVOLT OF THE NEGROES IN SAN DOMINGO.

Butler at New Orleans in 1862.[18]

Lincoln's edict interfering with the South's labor system where he had no control was by no means original. Salisbury's *Carolina Watchman* of September 30, 1862 explained this "as an example of the fanaticism which has been growing upon the people of the North for years." The *Raleigh Register* called Lincoln's action a "bid for servile insurrection" which imitated the action of Virginia's Royal Governor Dunmore in 1775 who expected the immediate surrender of the colonists should he arm the slaves.[19] Wartime governor and later congressman Zebulon Vance refuted the Northern myth that the South's defense of "slaveholding" was a reason for independence, stating at an 1886 Grand Army of the Republic conclave in Boston that "seven-tenths of our people owned no slaves … and felt no great and enduring enthusiasm for its preservation, especially when it seemed to them that it was in no danger."

The Confederate States Congress's response to Lincoln's edict, i.e., what they saw as encouraging race war, was swift. The Judiciary Committee in early 1862 proposed that enemy military officers, including non-commissioned, be imprisoned at hard labor when captured until Lincoln's "odious proclamation" was repealed. It stipulated that the

---

18 Randall, 478
19 Moser, p55

white officers of black troops (i.e., leaders of slaves in rebellion) would suffer the death penalty if captured.[20] The painful memory of San Domingue's brutal 1791 massacre guided the South's actions regarding the wholesale arming of slaves.[21]

As Republicans moved closer to embracing colored troops to help solve the recruiting dilemma, claims of their existence in the Revolution began to be heard. Ohio Congressman Cox spoke in Congress on January 30, 1863:

"It is incorrect to state that there was a settled policy by American colonists for the employment of Negro troops. The British did so with the actions of Royal Gov. Clinton of New York and Lord Dunmore of Virginia, the latter who in Nov. 1775 emancipated all slaves who "would repair to His Majesty's banners," calculated to deprive the colonists of agricultural labor and "hurl the Negroes into the war as an element of diabolical insurrection" and race war." Cox continued: *"the use of black men under arms was a question of expediency and availability … The Continental Congress records of August 24, 1778 indicate 755 Negroes employed in the Revolution, with 586 reported as present. There was no indication of their use, but doubtless they were bootblacks, servants, teamsters or private soldiers."* [22]

Cox went on to claim no analogy between any colored soldiers in the Revolution and their use at the present since in 1776 colored men were used — when used at all and very rarely — on the side of their loyal masters and with their full consent. They fought to defend colonial independence, not for their own freedom. They "were not sought to become fiends and bring about San Domingue-styled insurrections."[23] Underscoring this he said: "General Washington took command of the army on January 3, 1775, and in regular instructions to recruiters in Massachusetts on July 10th prohibited enrollment of any "Negro" in the army."

Cox related Washington's council of war in early October 1775 attended by Generals Lee, Putnam, Heath, Gates, Greene and others. The question raised was "whether it was advisable to enlist any Negroes in the army; and if so, should there be any distinction between those slaves and free." All agreed to reject slaves and by great major-

---

20 Ibid, p59
21 See Wiki, Saint-Domingue Revolution, 1791.
22 Cox, p318
23 Ibid, p319

ity, to reject Negroes altogether. In his orders of November 12, 1775 Washington states: "Neither Negroes, boys unable to bear arms, nor old men unfit to endure the fatigues of the campaign, are to be enlisted."[24] During that war the British were in the habit of carrying away colored people from colonists for the same reason as Lincoln — to deny colonists their agricultural laborers. Lord Dunmore of Virginia enlisted them in a "Pioneer Corps" primarily as fortification laborers and soldiers if needed. After England's defeat those emancipated departed with the British on ships bound for Canada, Bermuda or the Bahamas.

In an attempt to bring the Border States under his sway, Lincoln asked their congressional leaders in mid-1862 to support his plan of gradual emancipation followed by their colonization to central and South American countries. They overwhelmingly rejected the plan as unconstitutional interference with State prerogatives and questioned the very legality of public money raised for emancipation. They reminded Lincoln that the problem dividing the old union was clearly the Northern States infidelity to the Constitution, and federal powers delegated for the equal protection of all were being used against the private institutions of the South."[25]

Lincoln had the Caribbean in mind for colonizing these "contrabands" which would placate Northerners fearful of freed blacks migrating northward to depress wages and take their jobs. Author Michael J. Douma wrote extensively of Lincoln's colonization ideas and noted that "Historians have long known that in the summer of 1862 Lincoln announced his intention to negotiate with foreign powers concerning the colonization of freedmen abroad." For the next two years federally-funded initiatives arose to settle freedmen in Chiriqui [Panama] and Haiti — in addition to the British Honduras, Guiana, Danish St. Croix and Dutch Surinam. The talks were very serious and continued even after the war, anticipating the transport of freedmen to these islands very much in need of laborers. Many leading men in Lincoln's administration were proponents of colonization including William Seward, Charles Sumner, Francis Blair, Preston King and Benjamin Wade.[26] This attitude would change when enlistments stagnated

---

24 Ibid, p320
25 Message from Border State Congressmen, 14 July 1862, *Lincoln Papers*, Library of Congress.
26 Douma, p2-4

and Northerners responded to conscription with draft riots in major cities. The idea of colored troops had become a realistic alternative.

Lincoln surrendered to the Radical wing of his party who believed a "moral crusade" would remove its appearance as a war of conquest. If Lincoln did not act quickly, said one Northern congressman, the South's desire for European recognition could cause President Jefferson Davis to emancipate all bonded Africans before Republicans could cloak their war in a glorious cause to "free the slaves." Lincoln then issued his proclamation on January 1, 1863 while claiming it as a "war power." Reaction was swift as the former editor of the Nashville Democrat denounced Lincoln's edict as "the crowning act of fanatical folly." In his view as a Tennessee unionist, Lincoln had changed the war aim from one of fighting "secession" to that of subjugating the entire American South. Even the normally unionist *Chicago Times* editor "charged Lincoln with an absolute lack of constitutional authority for such unilateral decision."[27]

Union "contraband" camp

By mid-1862 Lincoln's war effort encountered serious problems as civilians and soldiers alike were weary of war, endless casualty lists and caskets coming northward after battles, especially after the carnage of Second Manassas and Fredericksburg. In addition, many soldiers angered by Lincoln's emancipation schemes were not re-enlisting, or worse, deserting in droves. General Don Carlos Buell reported 14,000 absentees from his army in late 1862, which worsened by early January 1863. General Hooker's Army of the Potomac reported 200 officers

---

27 Marvel, pp236-239

Captured Northern deserter

and men a day deserting, and thousands unaccounted for.[28] In addition, Lincoln's mid-1862 emancipation proclamation caused unrest in his blue ranks as the soldiers in blue who signed on the "save the Union" refused to fight to emancipate anyone.

The desertion problem was so acute that a national conscription bill was put forward by Massachusetts Senator Henry Wilson. The Republican-dominated Congress hurried the bill along as they feared the public's retaliation at the polls and expected the next Congress to not endorse it. Republicans wanted a "national" army raised by the draft and free of State interference which Abram B. Olin of New York said originated in "the accursed doctrine of States Rights and State sovereignty — which has been chiefly instrumental in bringing upon the Republic our present calamity." Democrats retorted that "desertions were increasing and recruiting at a standstill" due to Republican tyranny, and that a national army answerable only to a President would establish an irresponsible despotism.[29]

Many veterans and paid substitutes, attracted by generous reenlistment bonuses, would simply disappear after receiving the bounty money. One Illinois soldier wrote in late February 1863: "I got tired of the war and came off home. This country is full of deserters" … "they are coming home every day." An alarmed Governor David Todd

---

28 Tarbell, Vol 2, p162
29 Hesseltine, p290

of Ohio asked Lincoln to grant amnesty to his soldiers who agreed to return to their regiments in thirty days. Iowa's Governor Kirkwood requested arms for his citizens to defend themselves from roving bands of deserters; Indiana's Republican provost marshal admitted that the southern part of his State was "ripe for revolution, in peril and the sooner a draft comes the better."[30]

At the end of 1862 Lincoln's general-in-chief, Henry Halleck, directed his field commanders to refrain from any large-scale operations through 1863 in an attempt to conserve both land and sea resources, especially the former. This meant that small-theaters such as North Carolina, Georgia, South Carolina and Florida would not receive additional troops, as Halleck grumbled: "Every general is pressing for more troops as though we had a cornucopia of men from which to supply their wants." Since mid-1862 the enlistments had dwindled to near nothing.

Northern commanders, especially Grant whose army lost immense numbers of men to Lee and received the most recruits, complained of the latter's poor quality. At Petersburg in mid-1864 Grant admitted that the majority were pure mercenaries and "many diseased, immoral or cowardly." The War Department informed Grant that they were receiving only half the men that were being discharged after meeting their enlistment terms, and that volunteering had virtually ceased.[31] Meade's Army of the Potomac lost "fully one-half of its veterans who went home rather than face death another day. As veterans, the draft boards could not conscript them."[32]

Foreign governments complained of US government recruiting agents enticing their men into their army with promises of money and land. Prague's *Die Morgen Post* in March 1863 wrote of the Homestead Act being "a common lie, a way to lure Austrians to America to enroll them in the Union army." Prussian minister Baron Grabow complained to Lincoln's Secretary of State that German immigrants seeking land to cultivate were instead enlisted at Boston's wharf upon arrival "under the allurement of $100 in gold," but instead paid in greenbacks.[33] And interestingly, of the nearly 2.8 million men in Lincoln's army, a little more than 950,000 should be referred to as foreign-

---

30 Ibid, pp291
31 Rhodes, p323
32 Montgomery, p96
33 Sideman/Friedman, p123

ers, rather than northern-born; with an additional 179,000 colored men, mostly from the South, in blue uniforms.[34]

Conscription was not a military solution endorsed by all Republicans. *New York Tribune* editor Horace Greeley saw conscription as an anomaly in "a free state" and it "must be reformed out of our system of political economy." The Republican party eventually pushed its "Enrollment Act" through Congress and for the first time in US history the federation's agent in Washington raised and supported its own army. The Act ignored the States except for assigning each a quota of troops, and established assistant provost marshal districts which enforced the quotas of men aged twenty to forty-five. Exemptions required a $300 commutation or providing a substitute, and draftees received the same bounty as voluntary enlistees.[35]

As predicted the draft was highly unpopular with the public as two districts in New Jersey found it necessary to conduct its business with an armed escort. Enrollment officers in Pennsylvania and Delaware had barns and homes set on fire, received anonymous threatening letters, had their homes fired into; in Vermont, marble quarry workers attacked enrollment officers. In Ohio, militia troops sent to protect enrolling officers who were ambushed.

This dearth of white Northern men enlisting meant more coastal raids emanating from occupied Hilton Head to overrun Georgia, South Carolina and Florida plantations for "contrabands"; the same was occurring in North Carolina to fill depleted Northern ranks.

Northern men earning good wages in a booming wartime economy could, if drafted, pay a $300 commutation fee for a substitute to serve in their place. The paid substitute would receive as well the proffered bounty money from the State, town and county and all three received draft-quota credit for him. The conscripted man paying the $300 would avoid service, but his name was placed back into the pool and could be drafted again with the same result. This system naturally generated bounty-jumping as many substitutes took the money and deserted at the first opportunity, often doing the same in another State. To help deter this, heavy guards were posted at draft centers as well as on the rail cars carrying them to training centers and the guards themselves could be bribed for escapes. It was said that "thieves seeded every lot, ready to stomp or stab anyone who resisted their pilfering."

---

34 French, Appendix p354
35 Hesseltine, p292

One brigade expecting 200 conscripts to fill their depleted ranks lost 50 to desertion on the way to join the unit. Those that arrived were locked up by NCO's to prevent their running off; a colonel of artillery was convinced that none wanted to serve and were only after the bounty money offered.[36]

Conscription was a desperate measure by Lincoln to fill his army with men literally rounded up in Northern villages, towns and cities. They were most often poorer men who could not afford the $300 and more for a substitute — which was the total annual income for many families of that era. This also meant that the army consisted of many ill-educated men with little, if any, patriotic fervor, desire to fight and a tendency for indiscriminate looting when in the South.

It was the "contraband" question which triggered much discussion in the North regarding how to utilize them in the war effort while at the same time avoiding any migration northward. The latter was a plank in the Republican party platform whose goal was to restrict colored people to the South. In mid-1862 Lincoln and his Cabinet were in talks with the Danes, Dutch and British who were interested in black laborers for their Caribbean possessions. As the war dragged on and his battlefield casualties caused plummeting enlistments, Lincoln leaked his early emancipation edict he naively believed would bring the Southern States back. Those States understood the limits of presidential authority which did not include edicts interfering with the private labor relations of States.

Before the end of 1862 both Quartermaster General Montgomery Meigs and Secretary of War Stanton advised Lincoln of the desirability of using "contrabands" against the South. Meigs, somehow under the impression that all soldiers in the Southern army owned plantations, wrote in mid-November that 'the labor of the colored man supports the rebel soldier, enables him to leave his plantation to meet our armies, builds his fortifications, cooks his food, and sometimes aids him on picket by rare skill with the rifle."[37] Stanton wrote in a somewhat Marxist vein in early December that "By striking down this system of compulsory labor, which enables the leaders of the rebellion to control the resources of the people, the rebellion would die of itself."[38]

Lincoln's proclamation of emancipation was in essence a decree, or

---

36 Ford, p121
37 OR, III, ii, 809
38 *Lincoln, Complete Works*, vol ii, 242

edict, without the authority of Congress. It was unheard of in America though continental Europe had experienced royal decrees ad infinitum. Further, the decree was an admission by Lincoln that the only available course for continuing the war against the American South was "emancipating" its primary and dependable source of labor.

By the time Lincoln's edict was issued on January 1, 1863, the Northern armies had already acquired thousands of "contrabands" seeking food and shelter after their homes had been overrun and razed. The commanders initially put them to work as fortification and general laborers, cooks and teamsters in return for food and shelter. Often left behind were the wives and children who were forced to fend for themselves.

The new liberty accorded the black man to wander freely caused great concern as both soldiers in blue and northern civilians feared these workers could travel northward to compete with the good-paying jobs held by white men. The solution to this and dwindling northern enlistments was organizing the Bureau of Colored Troops in early 1863, which diminished the need for Lincoln's draft. They were capable of rear echelon operations as guards, supply and general labor, and occasional combat support. This, accompanied by the strong emphasis of reenlisting veterans nearing the end of their terms with exorbitant sums for the time, would allow the Radical Republicans to continue their war through Lincoln. The only concern on the horizon was the latter's reelection in November 1864, which his War Department would deftly manage.

"The Massachusetts Idea" was the brainchild of its wartime Governor John Andrew who solved the problem of officials like him conscripting their constituents and paying the political price at the next election. The Northern men enjoying the higher wages of a booming war economy chafed at the specter of enlistment or conscription, while northern governors at the same time feared electoral defeat at the polls in retaliation if they supported the latter. To solve the dilemma in Massachusetts, in early 1863 Lincoln authorized Governor John Andrew to raise a regiment of colored troops which would be credited to the Massachusetts quota of men. This was applauded by Amos Lawrence and other industrialists who feared the loss of skilled white workers to the draft and also saw blacks as "less costly than paying high enlistment premiums to whites."[39] Andrew and other governors

---

39 Abbott, p117

thought it politically-wise to enlist "contrabands" as colored troops, keep them in the Southern States while assuring their constituents that the "contrabands" will not come northward seeking employment for cheap wages and take the jobs of their constituents.

John Andrew

Andrew expected his regimental officers to be found among the young, white abolition-minded intellectuals of the State, but found few black men to enlist in Massachusetts. He then dispatched agents to other northern States and Canada to entice recruits for his new 54th Massachusetts Colored Regiment, the roster of which included only 13 percent residents of that State. Soon after the 55th Massachusetts Colored Regiment was formed after State agents scoured twenty-five States, plus Africa, Canada, and South Carolina's Sea Islands for able-bodied "contrabands" to fill its ranks.[40] Andrew also sought Lincoln's permission to recruit those "contrabands" in Virginia, North Carolina and the District of Columbia.

Andrew's strategy caused other Northern governors to complain to Lincoln of "the raids on their colored constituents" by Massachusetts and demanded they be given the draft quota credit for those taken from their particular State — regardless of where they were taken. The political practicality of this troop-quota scheme raised the interest of other northern governors who saw colored troops as "a means to an end, and if one more Negro went [to war] another white man could stay at home." Eventually needing to distance itself from northern State governors squabbling over their troop quotas and credits, Lincoln's government decreed that it was the logical agency to recruit colored soldiers who would henceforth be known as "United States Colored Troops."[41]

Andrew also had two civic-minded Massachusetts abolitionists looking elsewhere for recruits, John Murray Forbes and Amos Lawrence. Forbes admitted in January 1863 that "volunteering with and without bounties is nearly played out," but recruiters sent northward found some soldiers willing to desert the Canadian army to collect the

---

40 Daniels, p95
41 Hesseltine, p288

high US bounty payments. Their agents to California bought sufficient men for a company of cavalry, while admitting a practice of "the usual amount of deception."[42] The army needed to continue Lincoln's war would cost an astronomical sum in those days. From 1861 to 1865, enlistment bounties of the federal, State and local governments would reach $750,000,000.[43]

Western leaders critical of Lincoln's endless calls for more and more of their constituents to serve in blue, were scolded by Lincoln in 1863:

"Gentlemen: After Boston, Chicago has been the chief instrument in bringing this war upon the country. The Northwest has opposed the South as well as New England. It is you who are largely responsible for making blood flow as it has. You called for war until we had it; you called for emancipation, and I have given it to you. Whatever you have asked, you have had. Now you come here begging me to not conscript your men. You ought to be ashamed of yourselves." [44]

In the end, the threat of national conscription was Lincoln's whip to force the governors to raise their quotas as Lincoln's recruiting agents — or the unpopular draft would come forth and they would pay the political price. But with only 36,000 men actually conscripted, it was seen as a law to exempt men from service rather than one to acquire needed soldiers.[45]

---

42 Abbott, p114
43 Wiki, accessed 9.23.23
44 Tarbell, Vol II, p149 Lincoln scolding a Chicago delegation complaining of his endless demands for more troops.
45 Hesseltine, p306

> "The bare sight of 50,000 armed and drilled black soldiers … would end this rebellion at once."
> — *Lincoln to Stanton, March 26, 1863*

Advised that only generous bounties or forced conscription were necessary to raise white troops, Lincoln and others saw an alternative in colored troops. Colonization was forgotten.

Since the war's beginning it was common then to see colored seamen, especially pilots, serving aboard Confederate States Navy vessels. The US Navy followed suit by utilizing free-black seamen in late-September 1861 when Navy Secretary Gideon Welles authorized the recruitment of colored men, but only with the rank of "boy" and paid a maximum of $10 per month.

In June of 1863 the Northern military authorities in eastern North Carolina began recruiting colored men and designated them as "Colored Troops." Less than two years later the Confederate States government would begin enlisting colored men though they had served alongside white Southern soldiers since the outbreak of war. An early example of this were the Louisiana Native Guards of New Orleans, an all-black prewar militia mustered into State service by the governor in May, 1861. After New Orlean's enemy occupation in 1862, the unit's black officers were replaced by white appointees, and the rank and file replaced with "contrabands."[46]

That there had existed poor relations between occupation troops and "contrabands" can be surmised from the annual report of Major George J. Carney, Superintendent-General of Negro Affairs for the Department of Virginia and North Carolina. He wrote that after congressional approval "permitting the enlistment in rebel States of soldiers to be counted upon the quota of the loyal States enlisting them, the City of New Bern was flooded with recruiting agents and able-bodied Negroes were in great demand." Carney found of the 250 colored men enlisted there and eligible to receive generous bounty money for doing so, "few presented any appearance of having been thus furnished. Their families are nearly as dependent on the government for food as if no bounty had been offered or paid, suggesting the suspicion that the money found its way into the wrong pocket." While believing "some of the recruiting agents in North Carolina were persons of in-

---

46 Hollandsworth, p2-4

tegrity and honor ... it is not too much to say that others were scoundrels of the deepest dye, who left this District enriched with ill-gotten gains."

His detailed 1863 report strongly-criticized the US military for failing to meet its obligations to the then-dislocated and dispossessed colored population. He reported that after Roanoke Island's occupation, "the Negroes began to be employed by the Quartermasters, Surgeons, Engineers and other government officers "with "verbal promises to pay at rates varying from $8 to $25. per month." Carney found more often than not "the freedmen were never paid and deliberately swindled out of their earnings by some officer leaving the service." He found unsettled accounts amounting to more than $18,500. In the end, fearing the freedmen would never be paid for their labor, Major Carney exhorted them to consider their monetary loss "as one of the sacrifices for freedom; as something that they should willingly bear for the country's good."[47]

An early September 1864 report from North Carolina to General Butler revealed difficulty in procuring colored men for labor battalions. His subordinate wrote that "The Negroes [on Roanoke Island] will not go [to be laborers at Fortress Monroe] voluntarily, so I am obliged to force them. They will not go willingly ... I am aware that this may be a harsh measure but ... we must not stop at trifles."[48]

The initial reaction in the North to colored troops was mixed, as they were as yet untested in battle (except as Southern soldiers) and didn't inspire widespread confidence. White Northern soldiers did not consider them useful for anything but heavy-labor battalions, an "unamusing novelty and social experiment gone too far, and a source of unease and concern."[49]

In late-1863 General Benjamin Butler of 1862 New Orleans notoriety, and promoter of US Colored Troops, was installed as head of the Department of Virginia and northeastern North Carolina. An important order of business for his raising of troops was creating encampments for "contraband" families of colored men who could be pressed into blue uniforms. He saw this as necessary as northern troops regularly destroyed the plantation homes of colored people

---

47 James, p15: Annual Report of the Supt General of Negro Affairs, Dept. of Virginia & North Carolina. Jan. 1, 1865
48 OR, XLII, II, 653-654
49 Longacre, p48

leaving them nowhere to live. Being very much ostracized in official Washington, Butler also saw raising colored troops as a path to power — and during that winter "sent out numerous Negro-collecting raids into the no-man's land beyond his fortified lines." Butler's own general order of December 5, 1863 stated that "the recruitment of Negro colored troops has become the settled purpose of the Government" and reminding his officers and men to assist in this recruiting measure, "irrespective of personal predilection."[50]

Butler instructed his officers that "lazy Negroes were not to be coerced" into uniform but sent to fortification labor details; in addition, officers and men were forbidden to exploit the "contrabands" for private use. The colored would be subject to a draft, or conscription as needed, and paid $10 per month. He had great difficulty obtaining white officers willing to command the colored troops, and those willing had but little military experience and often became alcoholics.[51]

But strong criticism of colored men in blue uniform came from their own commanders like Butler, who saw colored people as "deferential and intellectually inferior" and struggled greatly to overcome this. It is clear that Butler's "Army of the James" was a backwater assignment to keep him militarily occupied as he remained politically potent. He was also aware that if not for his colored army he would have no army at all. An officer instructing colored artillerists believed it impossible to teach the new gunners "how to aim a piece with even tolerable correctness, cut fuses and count." A white colonel of a colored cavalry unit grumbled that his troopers lack pride spirit and the intellectual energy of the whites." Some officers treated their colored soldiers with contempt while others praised their ability to drill.[52] That the colored soldier was fighting "for rights and liberty" came loudly from those resisting Lincoln's draft, insisting that the liberated colored men remain in the South to stop Rebel bullets.

A practical problem in securing this manpower source was that few military-age, colored men lived in the north and should they enlist at the same rate as white men, would total no more than 18,000. The solution then was to entice, seize and carry off Southern agricultural workers for the ranks, which would at the same time cripple the South's food production. This is why northern military raids to

---

50 West, p221
51 Ibid, p222
52 Longacre, p56

the South's interior, especially when accompanied by colored troops, carried with them new uniforms and accoutrements for the new "enlistees." By the end of the war, nearly 179,000 colored soldiers had been taken into the Northern army to defeat the independence of the Southern States, nearly a third of the total troops raised by the latter.[53] These were not all volunteers as General John Logan reported to Grant in late February, 1864. He wrote that "a major of colored troops is [in Huntsville, Alabama] with his party capturing negroes, [and] with or without their consent … They are being conscripted."[54]

If the war prosecuted by Lincoln was indeed to emancipate slaves, then reports reaching Washington in early 1865 that the Confederate States Congress was doing this should have brought an end to the fighting as "slavery" would not be a bar to negotiations for a restored union. In March, upon approving the measure enlisting colored troops, Congress properly required individual slaveowners to first emancipate the colored men so they could enter military service for their country. In the North there remained those like Rep. Cox who preferred the leave the question "to the States individually." "*Slavery is to me the most repugnant of all human institutions,*" but the principle of "*self-government*" by the States over their own affairs was "*even more precious than the end of human bondage*" in the US. "*If the federal government can interfere in this matter, then federal interference could be expected in all domestic matters.*"[55]

---

53 French, Appendix, p353
54 OR, XXXII, II, 477
55 Lindsey, p93

Descent into Total War

"The right of conquest has no foundation other than the right of the strongest."

— Jean-Baptiste Rousseau

Jean-Baptiste Rousseau

After the conquest of New Bern, inland towns like Little Washington became easy targets for enemy gunboat incursions and troop transports. On the Tar River off the Pamlico Sound, this once-bustling town, the first named in the country for George Washington in 1776, was soon occupied though only a third of its people remained. Those who had not fled welcomed the enemy troops in hopes that their "oaths of allegiance" and visible signs of patriotism would save their homes, property and stores from looting and destruction.[1] Impressed with the doubtlessly-disguised "union sentiment" greeting his troops, the Northern commander wisely decided to station a company of Massachusetts troops there along with three gunboats to keep the populace in awe. Nonetheless, town shopkeepers were sure to fly US flags at their establishments to attract the greenbacks of the soldiers.

The wife of the 40th North Carolina Regiment's Lt. Macon Ellison wrote him in early May 1862 of "two thousand 'contrabands' assembled in occupied-Little Washington and led by a local Tory leader calling himself 'the Colonel.' She reported that this "buffaloe" had taken it upon himself to decide which inhabitants would have their slave property returned, who didn't, and what slaves would be retained for US military labor.[2]

The news of Little Washington's occupation caused some at Plymouth, only 35 miles northeast, to clamor for Northern "military

---
1 Barrett, p122
2 Virginia Ellison, Macon Bonner Letters, 1862-1864. UNC Library, Special Collections. Accessed 9.8.23

John Bernhard Thuersam

River Gunboat

protection" to hopefully avoid looting and destruction. This came in early May 1862 when three enemy gunboats docked at the wharf to search the town. Finding nothing suspicious they pressed on upriver to Jamesville to search for any "rebel army stores." Further upriver at Williamston they seized the steamer *Alice* with a considerable cargo of bacon stores and towed the vessel back to Plymouth. While there the Custom House was searched and records inspected to study recent water traffic at the docks.[3] The gunboat officers wanted to know how many town men were of military age, where their homes were, their current whereabouts and whether they serving in North Carolina's forces. An evasive answer could easily expose their families to threats, property seizure, arrest or reprisals.

At mid-month two more gunboats arrived at the Plymouth wharf in an effort to overawe residents who now found large broadsides of "Burnside's Proclamation" posted, advising residents that North Carolina's elected officials were "a few bad men and the worst enemies of the citizens." It further disclaimed any intentions of "destroying your freedom, demolishing your property, injuring your women, liberating your slaves and such like enormities, all of which we assure you, are not only ridiculous, but utterly and willfully false."[4]

After several "Tory" residents claimed of being "disturbed" by their neighbors one gunboat was ordered to remain at Plymouth as a warning. This became common in occupied towns as war brought into prominence people of little importance who seized the opportunity to settle past political or social vendettas, while loud and offensive in their professed loyalty to the Union.

---

3 Barrett, p124
4 Edmondston, p177 (see: www.ncpedia.org/printpdf/13765)

After the mid-April 1862 battle at South Mills in nearby Camden County which decimated the 9th New York Infantry, the enemy expedition returned to New Bern. Within two months Plymouth would receive its first enemy garrison when a New York colonel was authorized "to place a company at Plymouth as a nucleus around which local union men can rally under the protection of the gunboats."[5] This was the same New York regiment which battled their own citizens thirteen months later who were rioting in protest of Lincoln's unpopular draft. This resentment of the unpopular war and conscription led to insufficient recruits for the 9th and forced its consolidation with the 17th New York Regiment.[6]

The men of the 9th New York assigned to Plymouth was the battered remnants of the mostly-German Company "F" of whom many had been killed or wounded at the recent South Mills battle.[7] After being encamped at Plymouth they would begin enticing area men to desert their North Carolina regiments for the protection of their families, regular food rations and pay in US greenbacks. They could also enlist in the so-called First and Second "North Carolina Volunteer" regiments being organized and were known as "buffaloes."

The "buffaloes" served as guides for the coming raids on neighboring farms and plantations, ransacking and looting any suspected of disloyalty while livestock were killed or carried off. When the colored farm workers were informed of their "freedom" they often emulated the men blue. Diarist Edmondston recorded in mid-May 1862 that the servants left in charge of a neighbor's house "have plundered her shamefully and taken what they wanted" … and "Miss Blount's new servants have gone to the Yankees." She added that "Yankees encourage the Negroes to join them … [and] thinks he is as good as a Yankee & is insolent in proportion." While there was initial reluctance by enemy officers to take on more mouths to feed, this changed as the North began impressing "contrabands" into labor battalions.[8]

A young North Carolina cavalryman referring to the Northern enemy as "a godless foe" wrote in August 1862 of the "many fine dwellings" in the Trenton-Pollocksville area that were "mostly all destroyed, the Yankees having knocked to pieces those which they could not

---

5 OR, I, VII, 476
6 Wiki, accessed 9.23.23
7 Graham, p184
8 Edmondston, p173

burn — chairs, sofas, bedsteads, wash-stands, bureaus and all sorts of furniture are broken up and scattered over the streets and fields." Near Pollocksville "we passed several of the finest farmhouses I have ever seen — all ruined." In addition to the physical destruction, the enemy killed all the livestock.[9]

The increase in raids and destruction emanating from Plymouth forced State authorities to act. A small reconnaissance force sent to estimate enemy strength at the town was thwarted by a local Northern sympathizer who warned the enemy of the force nearing the town.[10] Halifax diarist Edmondston then wrote of a company of "buffaloes, so we hear, about Plymouth" and stating that she had not heard of this term before, but was informed that "they are our enemies."[11] These were bands deserters, thieves and murderers from both sides, and including colored men, who took advantage of the chaos of war in northeastern North Carolina. This term would apply as well to the two so-called "North Carolina" regiments the enemy organized and utilized for guides on their raids, as well as for fortification and wharf labor.[12] The "buffaloe" greatly feared capture by North Carolina troops as they would be tried for desertion or treason, with hanging the probable result. For this reason they more often insisted upon behind the lines camp-work.

---

9 W.G. MacRae letter, August 2, 1862. Hugh MacRae Papers, Duke University
10 Jacocks, p8
11 Edmondston, p291
12 Delaney, p364

As enemy troops patrolled the region surrounding Plymouth, they often found farms and plantations occupied by colored workers and supervised by overseers. To the invader, the absence of the owner was seen as a sign of "disloyalty" and, since the overseer was a trusted supervisor, they too were under suspicion and often arrested. Those slaves remaining on abandoned farms then transitioned into an unsettled status of subsistence farming on small plots. Without direction they might leave to work on different plantations and properties, and sometimes left their work on a whim which would endanger an entire crop. The sudden shift into a new and "free" existence of lax discipline led to unruliness and a lack of faith regarding contracts, usually verbal. Many of these colored workers deserted their homes and often their families, believing "with the thoughtlessness of children" that they would be free from work and supported in "ease and freedom." Shortly after New Bern's occupation an anxious Burnside wrote his superiors that the town was now being inundated with refugees from surrounding towns and plantations. Like Butler previously, he reported that "contrabands" were better put to work on fortifications than producing agriculture for the South.[13] The same would be repeated at Plymouth as raiders returned with more and more "contrabands."

A chronicler of Company A, 25th Massachusetts Regiment, Samuel H. Putnam, wrote "*every returning expedition was accompanied by stalwart darkies who were glad to accept protection and rations by "toting" the arms and equipment of tired or lazy soldiers. Some remained with the troops but more drifted into the body of laborers employed and fed by the quartermaster.*"[14] One Connecticut soldier expressed a fascination with the black people he came in contact with and how his fellow enlisted men used the so-called "freed" slaves to serve them in their tents. They were put to work "cooking, laundering, blacking boots and polished guns," with the soldier in a discerning moment noting that though "no longer a slave, [he] was probably held in higher regard by his former Southern master."[15] There was always the possibility that the "contraband" was "sent in" as an enemy general suspected, to reconnoiter for several days and slip out undetected with information.[16]

---

13 Hill, p278
14 Putnam, p95
15 Fair, p70
16 Harris, p156

John Bernhard Thuersam

"Contrabands"

The availability of the "contrabands" and their usefulness as labor was utilized by the enemy authorities who could now obtain full rations for idle Negroes and recruit them into blue-uniformed "contraband" units for future raiding operations. This policy turned some formerly productive but now-abandoned plantations into army recruiting station for months, thus making any successful crop cultivation impossible.[17] But as "contrabands" were enlisted, uniformed and marched away, their wives and dependents were often left to their own devices or the vague promises of the enlistment sergeant. It logically followed that the ensuing problem of high desertions among colored troops was traced to concern for their families. Addressing this problem was Laura S. Haviland, a Canadian-born Quaker relief worker among black soldiers in 1864 Vicksburg who overheard one ex-slave say that "we are concluding to leave our regiment and build something to shelter and house our children."[18]

After his troops landed at Edenton in mid-October, the enemy commander was forced "to put guards on many private houses" and send out patrols "in order to arrest the pillage which was commenced by men employed in all capacities aboard US government transports and schooners" upon reaching the docks. He added that "the plundering was indiscriminate as to friend or foe … and the army is thus saddled with the stigma of vandalism …"[19]

---

17 Randall, p70
18 Haviland, p132
19 OR, XXIX, I, 478-480

The continuing outrages and terrorism against civilians prompted the Confederate States Senate to act and in early October 1862 passed the following resolution to catalogue the crimes:

"It is notorious that many and most flagrant acts violative of the usages of war, of the rights of humanity and even of common decency, have been and are still being perpetrated by the forces of the United States upon the persons and property of citizens of the Confederate States …"

The Senate then resolved to establish a committee of 13 Senators or one from each State to take testimony in relation to such outrages for the public record.[20] North Carolina was represented by Senator William T. Dortch.

Total war came to the peaceful town of Williamston in early November 1862 when enemy troops and artillery arrived on transports from New Bern, after first landing at occupied-Little Washington. Their intention was to defeat and capture the three regiments of North Carolina troops reported to be defending the eastern counties. Within six or so miles of Williamston this force of some 5,000 New Englanders, many of them raw recruits, encountered about 600 men of the 26th North Carolina Regiment led by Col. Henry Burgwyn, Jr. After a brief engagement Burgwyn's vastly-outnumbered force retreated across the bridge into town and beyond. The bridge was burned to prevent enemy pursuit.[21]

At noon the following day the pursuing enemy troops entered a nearly-deserted Williamston and immediately set to looting stores and homes, destroying whatever could not be carried away. Any residences found empty were set on fire and any "contrabands" found were led away. One Massachusetts soldier wrote home of the burning homes, stealing of whiskey, horses, mules and other contraband articles.[22] With the town still smoldering and reports of reinforced North Carolina troops now-nearing the town, the enemy precipitously returned to their stronghold at Plymouth. In their hasty retreat the enemy left behind wagons, baggage, camp equipage and uneaten food on plates.[23]

The devastation of Williamston was recorded by resident D. W. Bagley on November 13, 1862:

---

20 OR, II, IV, 906
21 McCallum, p100
22 Barrett, p139
23 Edmondston, p294

"The Yankees destroyed all the poultry, hogs, cattle, sheep, etc., they could find, leaving nothing; what they did not use were killed to rot. There are not enough horses, mules or oxen left to haul the carrion off, the Yankees having stolen all horses and mules within their reach." He added that "They stole and destroyed all the furniture, clothing, leather and every valuable article, or any and everything on which we placed any affection. They destroyed libraries, books, medicines and tools; many thousands of dollars in cash were robbed from the citizens, especially the ladies.

"Graveyards were desecrated and bodies disinterred, several newly-made graves were dug up in search of treasure. Churches were ransacked and even the ancient order of Masonry was robbed of its jewels; they destroyed what little widows with houses full of little children had and then robbed the blind, bedridden, the poorest poor and even the few possessions of the Negroes.

"They then threw filth into the wells, including carcasses and excrement. They would catch hogs and cattle, cut a quarter from them and leave the balance to die and rot. The atmosphere is strongly infected with the odor of carrion in spite of the efforts of citizens to remove it."

Diarist Bagley also noted that Lt. Col. Lamb's Williamston hotel was targeted by invading enemy troops who decided not to burn it but leave notice of their visit. They led cattle up to the second floor where they were butchered and left to decay inside. As a finale they knocked in all the masonry fireplaces in the building.[24]

On retreating, the enemy marched through the deserted town of Hamilton where they wantonly torched homes after being looted of their contents. They marched three miles from the burning town to an encampment for the night, their path illuminated by the flames behind them. The enemy commander contemplated a movement toward Tarboro on November 5th to destroy it as well but remained concerned about reports of several North Carolina regiments nearby and continued their march to Plymouth to board transports for a return to New Bern. The net result of this enemy raid to Williamston was the burning of many private homes, scores of livestock killed, the destruction of much private property as well as carrying off a large number of "contrabands."[25] Rather than attaining the intended goal of capturing three "rebel" regiments, the enemy netted a total of five prisoners.

---

24 McCallum, p107
25 Barrett, p139

Civilians Being Looted

This war upon civilians found its way into the *Boston Evening Traveller*, a copy of which was sent by Brig-Gen James G. Martin to the enemy's department commander for an explanation. The response stated that "draught animals, carriages, beeves, pigs and forage were taken by my order," but added "every other species of depredations … was … not done by my orders … the principal cause was that so many houses contained apple brandy."[26]

Only a week would pass before a larger expedition of 13,000 troops departed New Bern with the goal of destroying the railroad bridge across the Neuse River at Goldsboro. The march was synchronized with the Northern advance against General Robert E. Lee at Fredericksburg and an expectation of breaking Lee's critical Wilmington and Weldon railroad supply line from the port of Wilmington. The actions of passing enemy troops were recorded in the letter of Mrs. Kinchin Taylor in mid-November who wrote her brother of the outrages committed at her home:

"The (enemy) Zouaves swarmed in like Devils, yelling, whooping and screaming," she wrote. "Her Negro servant, Ness, drew a knife and told the soldiers he would kill the first man who laid a finger on her. Still, the soldiers sacked the house, threw the furniture out of it and chopped it to pieces. They built a fire out of the doors they removed, cut up the corn crop and threw in upon the fire, killed all the fattening hogs, sheep, cattle & cows and burned them as well. They took her carriage and horse, telling her they would have burned the house had she not been inside it." [27]

---

26 OR, XXII, II,446
27 Edmondston, p293

The enemy halted at Kinston on December 15th where he was opposed by General Nathan G. "Shanks" Evans small force of twenty-four hundred North and South Carolinians. During a spirited engagement the enemy sent a demand of surrender to which General Evans replied: "tell your general to go to Hell" and then withdrew his force to refit. Being now unopposed and before departing Kinston, the enemy troops went to work thoroughly looting the town. Relating the experience in a letter to her brother soon after the battle, a physician's wife wrote of the enemy soldiers "carrying on wholesale robbery ... taking every article of bed clothing, kitchen utensils, sugar, honey, preserves, tablecloths — in fact everything."[28] And then having learned of Lee's victory at Fredericksburg and fearing reinforcements on their way by rail to North Carolina, the enemy commander decided to divert his force to Goldsboro's railroad yards to inflict as much damage as possible.[29]

Advancing to White Hall Ferry on December 16th, the enemy found the bridge burned and decided on rebuilding it for their crossing. They were hampered by the devastating fire over the river from the 11th and 35th North Carolina Regiments and an artillery company, but the enemy eventually crossed in force. Continuing to Goldsboro's railroad yard they destroyed property and burned the targeted bridge despite the courageous efforts of North Carolina troops to extinguish the flames under intense enemy artillery fire.[30]

On their return march to New Bern the enemy troops believed themselves victorious after a long campaign of "sweeping away" so much private property, carrying off cattle, hogs, poultry, sweet potatoes and corn. Though the expedition's goal of destroying the railroad bridge at Goldsboro was accomplished, in truth the damage was superficial and repaired within a few days and back in operation within two weeks.[31] After returning to New Bern the enemy continued to plan destructive operations against targets like Kinston and Goldsboro in hopes of disrupting Lee's supply line to the port of Wilmington. This would help transform Plymouth into a fortified supply center for future operations to be conducted against the Wilmington & Weldon Railroad.

---

28 Letter of Mrs. Mary E. Miller to John Jameson, Dec. 18, 1862, NCHR, V, Oct. 1928, pp 452-457
29 Roe, p167
30 OR, XVIII, 1, p86
31 C.L. Price, MA Thesis, UNC 1951, p176

And the enemy did not disclaim nor disguise the devastation they wrought. A Connecticut soldier at New Bern wrote his wife in January 1863 of his regiment's work in the effort to restore North Carolina to the Union:

"If you could see the ruin, devastation and utter abandonment of villages, plantations and farms which just a short time ago was peopled, fenced and held livestock. Houses once comfortable that are now either burned or deserted, barns in ashes all along to roadside, fences destroyed for miles and over thousands of acres, no cows, horses, mules, sheep or poultry to be seen where the Union army advances, and you would see conclusively the destitution for the coming year is to be fourfold greater than the past year. If this war continues another twelve months this country will be little less than a howling wilderness and the abomination of desolation" will be written on every gate-post." [32]

The foregoing should cause the reader to pause and reflect upon just how this killing, wholesale robbery and devastation was in any way calculated to "save the Union." One introspective Northern officer recorded in his diary only two days into Sherman's infamous march toward Savannah: "In what way will the destruction of so much [civilian] property aid us with restoring peace, harmony and union in our distracted country?" [33]

Though retribution in kind against Northern civilians, farms and towns was certainly possible, one searches in vain for examples of Southern troops committing atrocities as in the preceding. Lee's march into enemy-occupied Maryland and Pennsylvania in late-June 1863 provides an example of this. Lee reminded his men at Chambersburg "that we make war only upon armed men and we cannot take vengeance for the wrongs our people have suffered without lowering ourselves in the eyes of all those whose abhorrence has been excited by the atrocities of our enemies, and offending Him to whom vengeance belongeth, without whose favor and support their efforts must all prove in vain." Lee additionally exhorted his troops "to abstain, with most scrupulous care, from unwanted and unnecessary and wanton injury to private property," and "ordering all officers to arrest and bring to summary punishment all who shall in any was offend against the orders on this subject."[34]

---

32 W.A. Willoughby, W.H. Noble Papers, Duke University
33 Glathaar, p146
34 Winston, p245

But the increased importance of Plymouth to the enemy was not going unnoticed and in late November 1862 a sixteen-man squad of the 3rd Cavalry's Company K, under the command of Sergeant Levi Fagan, were picketing Plymouth's outskirts to observe and report on enemy activity. However, during a stormy evening they were surprised, captured and held prisoner at New Bern. They fortunately were paroled a month later to await exchange before returning to their units.[35]

Other units came to picket the town once again and report on enemy strength and weaponry, as well as gunboat numbers, arrivals and departures. The time for retribution was soon to come.

"Fall upon the enemy like a whirlwind." — *Anonymous*

In the quiet pre-dawn hours of Wednesday, December 10, 1862, five companies of the 17th North Carolina Regiment, accompanied by a squadron of cavalry and battery of artillery, quickly overwhelmed sleeping enemy pickets on the southwest outskirts of town — capturing all but one who ran frantically toward Plymouth to alert his comrades. Leading the attack was Martin County-native Lt. Col. John C. Lamb, formerly captain of Company A, Pasquotank County's "Independent Guards." The 17th's Washington County men were detached elsewhere and did not participate in this action.[36]

---

35 McCallum, p28
36 Manarin, Vol VI, p201

Historian McCallum relates that as the 17th Regiment's men entered the town, the now-alerted enemy troops were hastily lined up on main street. Lamb immediately ordered a cavalry charge "rebel yell and all" which caused the enemy, for the most part 150 Massachusetts men and North Carolina deserters, "to break "in all directions" and toward the safety of a gunboat at the wharf. After Lamb's artillery blew a hole in the gunboat's boiler and caused her to drift downstream, the enemy soldiers either frantically paddled in skiffs downstream or broke into homes and fired at Lamb's men from windows and doors. Some of the enemy's 150 or so men fled into the Custom House while 17th Regiment sharpshooters targeted those fleeing to the wharf as well as ones barricaded within buildings.[37] At least one rifleman was positioned at a second-floor window of the Ausbon house at the corner of Third and Washington Streets. The evidence of enemy return fire at this marksman remains visible today in the house's siding[38]

Lt. Col. John C. Lamb

To forestall the enemy's escape, Lt. Col. Lamb positioned three pieces of Capt. Alexander Moore's Wilmington Light Artillery on the wharf to concentrate fire upon the enemy's sidewheel gunboat. The gunboat was hit several times as it moved off the wharf and drifted downstream, while its 100-pounder Parrott rifle and three 8" smoothbore cannon fired rapidly over and at the town during the engagement, demolishing and setting fire to several buildings, including the courthouse which was lost with its invaluable county records. Also set ablaze was the Masonic Lodge which the enemy had already looted of its jewels and regalia.[39]

Many enemy soldiers left behind had barricaded themselves within the town buildings while continuing to fire at Lamb's men, who were forced to use artillery fire to extricate them. While US Official Records state that Lamb's regiment "surprised the Federals at Plym-

---

37 Carolana, First Plymouth, Dec. 10, 1862. Lt. W.G. Lamb; Maj. J.M. Galloway; Pvt. P. Means. Clark Histories.
38 Another account claims this bullet damage as occurring in the Spring of 1862. (1990 Nat. Reg. Applic'n).
39 McCallum, p51

outh, routed the garrison and burned a portion of the town," it omits Northern responsibility in barricading themselves within buildings and the gunboat's destructive cannon fire upon the town.[40] Three months earlier a private of the 55th North Carolina Regiment wrote of the enemy at Little Washington "concealed in cellars from which they shot at our men." To extricate these snipers required blasting at the entire structure with artillery, often with the enemy's captured pieces.[41] The enemy commander, Capt. Barnabas Ewer, Jr. of the 3rd Massachusetts Infantry, was so terrified by the furious attack that he deserted his 150 men in battle and was later discovered a mile and a half downriver, hidden in a boat. He explained afterward that he expected his men to follow and seek refuge in the swamp.

Referring to this battle, diarist Edmondston's entry of December 12th, 1862 relates that *"our troops under Lt. Col. Lamb marched down and captured Plymouth with forty of the enemy, killing and wounding thirty more (an official report indicates 2 of the enemy killed, 3 wounded). The town was partially burned to prevent it affording shelter to Abolitionists and runaway Negroes in their train."* She added that it was Moore's Battery of the Third Battalion NC Artillery which crippled the enemy gunboat and sent it drifting downstream, as caused the destruction of the Washington County Court House. Moore's Artillery "nearly battered it down upon the heads" of enemy soldiers barricaded within, who "pierced [walls] for musket firing" at Lamb's men. Also inside were the enemy's colored laborers were killed as several shells exploded within", and Edmondston records that "about 50 Negroes belonging to Mr. Urquehart were captured who had either run away or were enticed by the enemy." Deploring the many dead colored men she "hoped "their brethren will hear of it and that it will be a lesson to them how they might leave home with their false friends."[42]

Three of Lamb's infantrymen were killed, and one of his seven wounded was Capt. (later Major) John M. Galloway of Rockingham County, who fell during the cavalry charge. Edmondston wrote of Galloway's brother visiting her on the way to care for John, while graciously offering her home for John's convalescence.[43]

---

40 OR, I, XVIII, 49
41 Clark, V, III, p287-312
42 Edmondston, p314
43 Ibid, p318

In his report dated December 12, 1862 and forwarded to Confederate States Adjutant General Samuel Cooper at Richmond, Maj. General Samuel G. French (Department of North Carolina & Southeastern Virginia) wrote from Petersburg, Virginia:

"Plymouth, N.C. was attacked by our forces under Lieut. Col. [John C.] Lamb, of the 17th North Carolina Regiment ... on the 10th instant at 5 a.m. The enemy's loss severe; 25 prisoners and 75 negroes taken. Town reduced to ashes. We had one captain and six men wounded; none killed. The gunboat protecting the enemy was driven away disabled.
"S. G. French,
  "Major-General."

It is certain that this devastation and ruin of the former town brought grief to any residents drifting back to their former home. To an enemy soldier the destruction was a "terrible sight but military necessity dictated its destruction. Such is war, he lamented."[44] To underscore the level of destruction wrought by the battle, the disgraced Capt. Ewer who abandoned his men would later write that "all the principal buildings on the street where the hotel [was] are gone and everything in headquarters was burned."

General French, a New Jersey-born Quaker, wrote afterward to the Northern commander that homes were only fired upon because enemy troops barricaded themselves within and fired upon the North Carolinians. Refuting a claim that "contraband" slaves held by the enemy at Plymouth were led away, French responded that this was a "fit and necessary war measure," paraphrasing Abraham Lincoln himself.[45] The once peaceful prewar town of some two-thousand souls had been "reduced to ashes," wrote General French.[46] Lt-Col. Lamb fulfilled his orders: end Plymouth's enemy occupation and use as a base for attacks up the Roanoke

Samuel G. French

---

44 *Napoleon Perkins Memoirs*, New Hampshire Historical Society
45 Durill, p139
46 Mahood, p136

River towards Weldon.[47]

After garrisoning the former town for a short period while burying the dead and sorting captured equipment, the victorious 17th Regiment departed for winter quarters near the town of Hamilton with their prisoners, arriving there on December 12th. The abundance of captured supplies made for a bountiful Christmas and here they remained until late-March 1863 when they joined General Daniel H. Hill in his attempt to liberate New Bern.[48]

This conflagration of December 10th effectively ended Plymouth's existence as a "town" as many families and people had fled to the interior and "refugeed" elsewhere. Some returned to Plymouth afterward, perhaps to see what had survived the conflagration. One noted that "there were no residences, no shops, no public buildings left standing save the federal customs house." An enemy attempt to retaliate for their rout at Plymouth was found in a mid-February diary entry noting:

"The Abolitionists came last week Friday to Hamilton in three gunboats and burned the hotel owned by Lt. Col. Lamb, then retired without doing further damage. This piece of petty personal spite is unworthy of the arms of a great nation." [49]

After the 17th Regiment departed for Hamilton what remained of Plymouth reverted to a quiet civilian existence except perhaps for a few troops left as sentries to warn of future enemy upriver incursions. This more peaceful period allowed area farmers to once again plant their fields and regain some normalcy in their lives.

After his impressive victory at Fredericksburg in December 1862, General Robert E. Lee remained concerned that his opponent's reinforcement would result in another Virginia offensive, thus felt unable to spare troops for defending eastern North Carolina. Lee remained under political pressure from North Carolina leaders clamoring for Richmond to do something to liberate the conquered region of their State.

Lee first assigned General James Longstreet to the south side of the James River to defend Richmond against enemy attack from that direction. In late February 1863, Longstreet created the Department

---

47 McCalllum, p51
48 Mahood, p131
49 Edmondston, p360. See Appendix B for Lt. Col. Lamb's action at Newport Barracks in early 1864.

of Virginia and North Carolina to oppose enemy operations southeast of Richmond and in northeastern North Carolina. General Daniel H. Hill was to command the new department. He was known as a spirited leader and fighter who would ably protect critical supply lines from eastern North Carolina, from which came immense amounts of corn, pork and bacon destined for Lee's army. Aware that farmers were reluctant to plant another crop until an adequate force for their protection was evident, Hill laid plans to attack and eliminate the enemy strongholds at Washington, Plymouth and New Bern.[50]

The distant booming of cannon was heard again as New Bern came under attack by Maj-General Daniel H. Hill in mid-March 1863. Failing to break through the fortifications there, Hill marched his force to Little Washington where he found the enemy behind strong fortifications. His commander, General Lee, advised against any assault as it would be too time-consuming, although his time would be well-spent bringing out as much in agricultural supplies as possible to feed his army.[51] Soon Hill's supply wagons would bring large quantities of potatoes, corn, lard and about 35,000 pounds of bacon out of the region.

Governor Zebulon Vance was being pressured by citizens to better defend the conquered northeastern part of the State, who also demanded that North Carolina troops be returned from Virginia for the liberation and defense of the region, including Plymouth. Washington County civilians were in line to experience the same confused question of allegiance and loyalty

Zebulon Vance

as the Outer Banks, Beaufort and New Bern had experienced as the enemy invasion swept over them. Any absent military-age men away in North Carolina units left their families liable to persecution or worse, which weighed heavily on the soldier in the field. Some simply walked back home.

The reasons for desertion become obvious when a man's family and property fell behind enemy lines, and felt powerless to protect his home and family. The enemy offered the attraction of remaining

---

50 Hill, p149
51 DH Hill Papers, p1007

at home in a blue-coated "volunteer" regiment while drawing Yankee greenbacks and rations instead of inflationary Confederate money, and having your family reasonably protected. The alternative was frightening. Those who went over to the enemy became known as "buffaloes" — a term "which had become synonymous with murder, thievery and desertion."[52]

A Vermont-born Northern colonel of New York troops was credited with a scheme to enlist those he termed North Carolina "loyalists" — or "Tories" — into Northern regiments, with the support of military governor Edward Stanly. The initial purpose was to make use of idle local men as stevedores at the docks as well as soldiers should they actually prove "loyal."[53] Two regiments of local men were organized, one at Plymouth, the other at Washington, the latter serving as a recruiting center for the region. Recording the presence of North Carolina men enlisting in enemy forces is diarist Catherine Edmondston, who wrote on November 2, 1862 that North Carolina forces captured a company of "buffaloes" so we hear, near Plymouth. What 'buffaloes' are does not appear but they are enemies and pilot the enemy through our country."[54]

Author Putnam of 25th Massachusetts regiment wrote in 1863 of "unionist men" at Plymouth being formed into a company of soldiers. He added that "we call them 'buffaloes.' The clear implication was that Southern men who espoused the Northern cause would be used as menials rather than as soldiers."[55] Nonetheless by November 1862 the enemy had enrolled a good number of men at Washington with promises of liberal bounty money and only serving in North Carolina.

The enemy was aware of the danger they exposed local men to when they enlisted in the so-called First and Second North Carolina "Volunteer" Regiments. The men themselves greatly feared the danger of capture and reprisals from their own people — and hanging for desertion or treason. They refused participation in combat situations and were used for construction, fortification labor and stevedores at docks. And being simple laborers, this released Northern soldiers from garrison labor and guard duty.[56]

---

[52] Correspondence: Edward Stanly to Charles Sumner, Feb. 1865
[53] Hill, p293
[54] Edmondston, p290
[55] Putnam, p123
[56] Hill, p294

According to some researchers the first known use of the term was a letter of July 25, 1862 reprinted in the *Wilmington Journal*. The author condemned Lincoln's proconsul Edward Stanly who encouraged "buffaloes" to vote in upcoming North Carolina elections. It seems that by then it had become a common term used by both invader and natives. General D. H. Hill wrote postwar that the name originated with the Northern soldiers as a mark of contempt for cowardice and recreancy to their own homes.[57]

Local planter John Poole wrote Governor Zebulon Vance of the problem caused by the State's inability to repel the enemy invasion and protect our loyal citizens, who were forced into enemy collaboration for their security. Poole argued that the enemy's gunboats travel unopposed past Plymouth daily and that only a show of force by the State will lead them to believe they have not been abandoned by their government. He recommended North Carolina cavalry be detailed there to enable swift opposition to the enemy occupation and local men made exempt from conscription to enable them to protect their families and homes.[58]

The result of the hangings for treason were immediately felt as a Northern colonel observed the "utterly demoralized" condition of the remaining "buffaloes" who now looked "to the swamps for protection they have so far failed of getting from our government." Should Maj.-General George Pickett liberate New Bern and the surrounding region he knew the "buffaloes" would become "panic stricken."[59]

An interesting parallel with desertion and treason less than 20 years earlier was the "San Patricio Battalion" of the Mexican army. Led by Irishman John Riley who deserted at Matamoros and given an officer's rank by General Pedro de Ampudia, it consisted of US Army deserters, many of them Irish Catholics refusing to fight against Roman Catholic Mexico. After deserting on the Rio Grande, they were later joined by disillusioned German immigrant-soldiers at Puebla. At Monterey, the "San Patricio's" rained artillery fire upon US troops led by Lt. Braxton Bragg, which helped repel several American assaults. At the Churubusco battle those captured were tried as traitors and desertion with fifty executed by hanging — the largest mass execution in US history. General Winfield Scott ordered the execution of thirty San

---

57 Ibid, p273
58 Ibid, p294
59 Delaney, p364

Patricio's captured during the Chapultepec battle, in full view of both armies as the battle raged.[60]

Not all men in eastern North Carolina deserted to protect their families. Some might have been escaping Confederate conscription and took their chances with the invader.[61] Many joined roving bands of deserters from both sides looting and burning homes, household goods and fences, plundering crops, stealing livestock, firewood and anything else of value.[62] And for their destructive nature, many were encouraged, armed and abetted by the enemy. Included in the mix of "buffaloes" were "armed Negroes, native unionist bushwhackers and criminally-intentioned local misfits" who preyed upon the prosperous and poor alike, relying upon brutality for their success."[63] They terrorized those who remained loyal to North Carolina, and few plantations and farms in the region were spared from the "unchecked rapine and pillage by Northern troops and lawless 'buffaloes.' Many of them were simply violent renegades, deserters from both sides who preyed upon civilians during the upheaval of war. They were said to have a headquarters of sorts at Wingfield Plantation north of Edenton on the Chowan River.

The former home of ardent secessionist Dr. Richard Dillard had been seized by an assortment of "fugitive Negroes, lawless white men, traitors and deserters" from both armies. In addition, the region was supportive of Northern troops who provided security to the 'buffaloes' — those who seemed possessed by the "spirit of anarchy and destruction." Despite their looting and terrorism being indiscriminate, a US Navy gunboat was stationed in the Chowan River behind the home to protect them from North Carolina forces. A Northern gunboat captain reported the attack of "a body of rebel troops" at Wingfield on November 19, 1862 and used his artillery to drive them off. Another 'rebel' attack near midnight drove the 'buffaloes' and 'contrabands' to the river where the gunboats took all on board and departed.[64]

As Wingfield was not fortified to resist attack a Northern officer was detailed to supervise construction of breastworks and a blockhouse of heavy timbers with embrasures. To provide the heavy labor

---

60 Wiki, accessed 10.27.23
61 Garren, p17
62 Bardolph, p173
63 Elliot, p51; 60
64 Dillard, p11

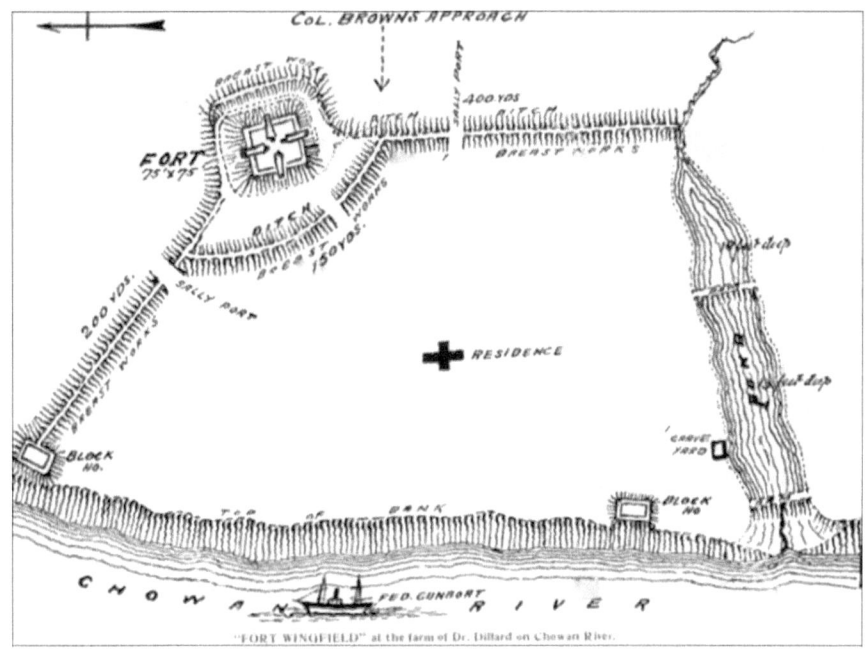

"FORT WINGFIELD" at the farm of Dr. Dillard on Chowan River.

for this project more raids on plantations resulted in more 'contrabands' available for the new fortifications. An expedition to destroy Wingfield was dispatched in March, 1863 with Col. John E. Brown and his 42nd North Carolina at Garysburg, stationed just north of Weldon. His attack accompanied by the "rebel yell" drove off enemy cavalry and marines landed by gunboats, and captured many 'buffaloes' Returning three weeks later with his command, Col. Brown's reconnaissance found no gunboats in the river and attacked Wingfield at dawn. A number of terrified 'buffaloes' and 'contrabands' fled into the swamps and others took to boats for safety at occupied Plymouth. Some twenty 'buffaloes' unable to escape barricaded themselves in a blockhouse and survived as Brown's regiment had no cannon. After three enemy gunboats from Plymouth appeared and began shelling Col. Brown's men, they set the Wingfield house on fire as they fell back.[65]

Nearby Edenton did not escape the enemy's attention as a force of 2,000 cavalry descended upon the town from Suffolk, Virginia. After a picket outside of town was shot by a sniper, the angered commander locked up all residents and threatened to set fire to the town. While civic leaders hurriedly conferred with the enemy commander, they

---

65 Wingfield, pp16-18

were able to dissuade him from penalizing all town inhabitants for the shooting and the enemy horsemen rode away.[66]

A Confederate scout wrote afterward of the occupation of New Bern and desolation of the countryside by Northern raids:

"If every person in the South could witness the useless ruin that the Yankees have caused in Jones and adjoining counties, the name and sight of the Yankee soldier would be hated throughout all eternity, and it would help to show what an abandoned and Godless foe we have to contend against."

When forty 'buffaloes' of the so-called First and Second "North Carolina" regiments were captured near Bachelor's Creek in February 1864 during General Pickett's advance toward New Bern, twenty-two were found to be deserters. They were court-martialed and sentenced to be hung in the presence of soldiers and civilians for their crime. Following the executions, a chaplain thought it appropriate to speak of this in a sermon, noting that though the dead "once marched under the same beautiful flag that waves above our heads, but in this evil hour they yielded to mischievous influences", sacrificing their patriotism and honor.[67]

When asked by one of the executed soldier's kin to release the body for burial in a blue uniform, General Robert F. Hoke expressed surprise and wondered why "so respectable a man would want to bury his brother-in-law in a Yankee uniform."[68]

---

66 Ibid, p22
67 Barefoot, p121
68 Hawkins, p19

Marauding Terrorists in North Carolina

"We must make old and young, rich and poor, feel the hard hand of war." — *General W. T. Sherman*

Civil strife between peoples and countries has existed throughout human history and seemingly always will. The creation of rules governing warfare helped mitigate inevitable hardships and the horror associated with it: i.e., protecting non-combatants, civilians and especially children caught between warring parties. Also considered was the humane treatment of prisoners, care for the sick and wounded, respect for private property — and avoidance of murder, rape, pillage, arson, torture, and robbery committed on civilians.[1]

The year 1862 saw a change in policy toward non-combatants, especially at the Outer Banks and New Bern. The peaceful homes, villages, farms and plantations surrounding New Bern now felt the hard hand of war from those who had forgotten Burnside's Proclamation. One author summed up the mindset of Northern commanders who now recognized "no innocents, no matter their age or occupation or station in life; nothing that could bring either aid or comfort to the enemy was to be left untouched. Entire towns were pillaged and burned. Chickens, cattle, pigs, grain, anything that could be consumed by man or horse was either taken or destroyed. Homes and barns, were burned; dreams were shattered."[2]

One Northern soldier recognized the destructive tendency of his

---

1 Addicott, p10
2 Walters, front jacket

John Bernhard Thuersam

army in late-1862 Mississippi, writing that he "*could scarcely believe the damage done to a country that so large an army passes through. All the fences are burned, mules and horses taken, fodder and corn taken in addition to many things confiscated. I would call it outright stealing back home. Many of these soldiers were prewar Democrats who justified the actions with the belief that secessionists had brought this war upon themselves.*" And in many, if not all cases, they admitted to be simply following the orders of superiors.[3]

Lincoln's tardy attempt at limiting atrocities against Americans resulted in the Lieber Code, aka "General Orders No. 100." Though puzzling in its creation, historian William A. Blair, noted that its enactment in late-April 1863 was by presidential fiat rather than congressional action as constitutionally required. The Constitution gives only Congress the power to declare war and "make rules for the regulation of land and naval forces."[4] This was simply another constitutional conundrum which joined Lincoln himself declaring war and raising an army without congressional sanction, as well as suspending the ancient writ of *habeas corpus*. In stark contrast, the Confederate States Congress formulated its own military code in May 1861, essentially copying the United States 1806 Articles of War.[5]

A German-immigrant appointed by Lincoln to formulate a guide for military commanders, Francis Lieber's own view was that the conflict was not technically a "civil war," that it was not between two contending sections, each claiming to be the legitimate government of both. The Confederate States had no intention of overthrowing the

---

3 Blair, p132
4 Ibid, p89
5 Addicott, p11

northern government and was in truth fighting in self-defense as were the American colonies in 1776.

The Lieber Code prohibited "all wanton violence committed against persons in the invaded country, all destruction of property, all robbery, pillage and sacking, all rape, wounding, maiming or killing of such inhabitants under penalty of death, or such other severe punishment as may seem adequate for the gravity of the offense." It further specified that "a soldier, officer or private, in the act of committing such violence, and disobeying a superior ordering him to abstain from it, may be lawfully killed on the spot by such superior." It is unknown if this last ever occurred.[6] Although the Code's language instructed officers "to keep good order among troops to the utmost of their power, as well as redress all abuses or disorders committed by any officer or soldier under their command," the pillaging and atrocities continued as if no new "code" existed. This also prescribed punishment for "those who commit waste and spoil, or who maliciously destroy any property whatsoever, belonging to the inhabitants of the United States." This begs the question of Lincoln's non-recognition of State secession and the South's people remaining "inhabitants of the United States."[7]

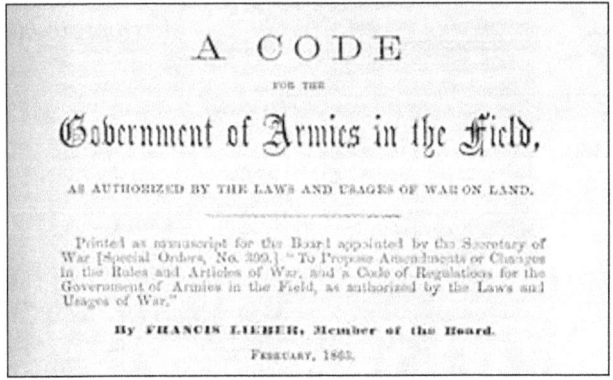

Already aware of the widespread depredations against American civilians preceding his Code, Lieber wrote General-in-Chief Henry Halleck shortly after its implementation that he "still fretted about crimes being committed against civilians by the US Army." He urged Halleck to issue a strong order to his generals after reading reports from "the West and South, written by men on our side of course, that the wanton destruction of property by our men is alarming and does

---

6 Lieber, p43
7 Addicott, p13

incalculable injury. It demoralizes our troops ... and makes a return to a state of peace more and more difficult."⁸ Halleck was fully aware that the very acts proscribed by Lieber's code had been regularly committed by his troops, "and after its adoption those crimes only increased in frequency and ferocity — with Halleck's approval and even encouragement." Without enforcement provisions and full of loopholes, the Code continued to allow wartime devastation and criminality if considered a "military necessity." If civilians were to flee a town surrounded and under siege, the Code made permissible driving them back into the town to hasten its surrender.⁹

Lieber stipulated that the confiscation of any "enemy" property could be based upon military necessity; the shelling of populated cities without warning if thought necessary; and forcing civilians into towns under siege should any try to escape, as their suffering would force surrender more quickly. Overall, Lieber's "code" changed nothing while giving wide latitude to field commanders who believed it merciful to bomb people into submission.¹⁰

"We are turning loose on the countryside a horde of pillagers and looters who would do their work systematically and well."
— *Sherman to Halleck, 1863*

---

8 Cisco, p99
9 Ibid, p101-103
10 Blair, p93

The depredations against North Carolinians were by no means singular or isolated events. The infamous sacking of Athens, Alabama by the 19th Illinois Infantry in early May 1862 was fully-sanctioned by their commander, General John B. Turchin, [Russian-born Ivan Vasilyevich Turchaninov]. After entering the town his soldiers stacked their arms and began looting stores and warehouses. While ransacking homes they tossed clothing into the streets, destroyed furniture and Bibles, fouled carpeting and curtains, rifled bureaus for watches, jewelry and family silver. Two Negro women were violated and none denied that the assaults had taken place. Turchin was afterward court-martialed, found guilty of not controlling his soldiers with a majority of the military tribunal requesting leniency. Though he afterward resigned his commission, Lincoln himself quickly reinstated Turchin to command.[11]

The increase of violence against civilians was of not confined to Sherman. It became common in eastern North Carolina as well as other parts of the South where the invading northern armies advanced. Sherman arrived at his brutal policies against civilians through his sense of federal government supremacy and an intolerance for any resistance to it; the proclamations of early 1862 were long forgotten as the looting began after Hatteras and New Bern's occupation. One can find empathy for Lincoln's proconsul Edward Stanly futile efforts to convince North Carolinians to remain in the Union, while Burnside's men looted New Bern and shipped stolen furniture, libraries, paintings and jewelry north on the transports they arrived on.

Historian Jeffrey Addicott writes that "by late 1863 the unwritten policy from Washington was to look the other way when it came to reports about its forces "living off the land, pillaging foodstuffs and livestock of country people."[12] Though large parts of the American South were occupied or under threat of invasion by early 1864, the South remained unbeaten and Lincoln knew his reelection chances were slim if the South was not brought quickly to heel. This vexation increasingly brought him to agree to the scorched-earth strategy of Sherman and Sheridan — as well as the bloody, hammer blows of Grant's conscripts and substitutes flailed against Lee's diminishing and hungry numbers in a war of attrition.

---

11 Ibid, p134
12 Addicott, p33

"Pledge allegiance to the flag, whatever flag they offer."
—*Silent Running, Mike and the Mechanics*

Martial Law is understood to be practically no law at all. Merely the unregulated will of a military commander, sanctioned by physical force and under it the whole machinery of civil justice disappears. Many were tried by military tribunals of the North's "reconstruction" acts though there was doubt as to whether the shifting status of any region was that of peace or war.[13] Though fighting a similar conflict between an established government versus those who had "seceded," it is noteworthy that General Washington fought the seven years of the Revolution to a successful end without once imposing martial law.[14] General Andrew Jackson later proclaimed martial law at New Orleans in 1814 and arrested those who denied he could lawfully do it. Jackson was later fined by a judge he had arrested.

Despite empty assurances that citizens' personal property would be safe from pillage and looting and that life would continue for peaceable Americans, General Ambrose Burnside issued a chilling general military order on April 28, 1862 reminding North Carolinians that they lived under martial law. The order read that *"whoever shall, within the limits to which the Union arms may extend in this department, utter one word against the government of the United States, will be at once arrested and closely confined. It must be distinctly understood that this department is under martial law, and treason, express or implied, will meet with a speedy punishment."*

Burnside's order was construed to cover almost any hearsay evidence of sympathy with North Carolina's defense and the Confederacy's cause of independence. Those judged in violation filled New Bern jail cells which even federal officers admitted were in "a most disgusting and filthy state and overcrowded, seriously endangering the health and lives of the prisoners; no efficient means are provided for heating or ventilation and the prisoners urinate into tubs which emit an intolerable odor."[15] Lincoln's proconsul Stanly tried to ameliorate the horrible conditions and cruelty, but was met with obstruction by military officers. They and other officers commanding expeditions emanating from New Bern were led by "inexperienced, ill-tempered

---

13 Dunning, p14
14 Fisher, p482
15 OR, 118, 7

and vindictive officers" who often arrested harmless citizens simply on the word of traitorous "buffaloes" or slaves.[16]

An early February 1863, the report of a Northern colonel states that "about 60 citizens were taken prisoner and released at Swan Quarter after taking an oath of allegiance to the Northern government."[17] The *Raleigh Standard* of February 4, 1863 reported on an official notice being posted at Elizabeth City that "every male inhabitant over sixteen years must take the oath of allegiance to the Lincoln government or leave the town."[18]

"The refugees suffer greatly … the women who support themselves and their families"

— *Wilmington Journal, 1863*

Rather than remain home to quietly accept a brutal fate, many fled their homes and farms during the war and eastern North Carolina was no exception. The fall of Fort Hatteras in August 1861 prompted many eastern North Carolinians to seek safety by moving inland; well-before the fall of New Bern in mid-March of 1862 its residents were already heading westward or planning to. Historian Mary Massey writes that the enemy occupation of New Bern caused some in far-off Raleigh to consider abandoning their homes and seeking a nomadic life preferable to "living under Yankee rule." Such is the work of hysteria.[19]

As reports of enemy depredations reached Plymouth, it caused

---

16 Hill, p294
17 OR, 26, 181 (Col. D.B. Morris)
18 Hill, p297
19 Massey, p12

residents to make preparations to flee or seek "refugee" inland with relatives of friends. Even those considered "unionist" feared soldiers with a penchant for looting and burning. When enemy gunboats were seen on the Roanoke in search of resistance, a mild evacuation became a contagious panic before armed troops landed at the town's wharf. Those in Plymouth fearing allegations of "treasonous" activities alleged by neighbors with prewar disagreements were often driven from their homes and forced into refugee life. There also were the infirm and aged who could had no place to go, as well as those with little desire to be uprooted who silently abided the invader's presence. Many who remained in Plymouth were merchants with inventory to protect and sell, regardless of loyalties, others were property owners who stayed in order to protect their homes, land and family.

At nearby Edenton some ladies fled to the safety of a distant plantation home rather than submit to an oath of allegiance to Lincoln. On their departure they witnessed a Yankee officer seizing bales of cotton as "contraband," most likely as personal income. What they had left behind was to become loot for the Yankees — "choice old wine & brandy, the books, the pictures, the linens and silver …"[20]

Rev. C. B. Haskell wrote that the infamous enemy raid of mid-November 1862, which occurred in Martin County, was perhaps the most destructive of the war in terms of wanton destruction of private property and wholesale robbery of non-combatants, male and female, rich and poor, slave and free. Though the raid caused the loss of some $2 million in civilian property, "perhaps not one dollar of Confederate military property was destroyed and perhaps only one grey-clad soldier killed." For those women managing a farm with young children, the greatest suffering was caused by the senseless slaughter of their cattle, hogs and poultry — the carcasses of which were strewn along roads for the buzzards to eat.[21] Historian Walter Brian Cisco wrote of one teenaged Tarheel girl being appalled by northerner's obsession with sparing no living thing, however insignificant. She saw them as "fiends incarnate."[22]

Another example in North Carolina was the invaders' slashing of family portraits with sabers, breaking up furniture and pouring molasses into pianos. Everything edible was destroyed, cattle and poultry

---

20 Edmondston, p118
21 McCallum, p106
22 Cisco, p164

driven off or shot; all granaries of corn and wheat were torn open, the contents carried off or ruined. During this carnival of destruction, it should be noted that despite the colored people of the area being encouraged to rise up and pillage what remained of the property of helpless women, they remained civil toward all.[23]

"Many civilians preferred the life of a nomad to living under Yankee rule."

Charleston Daily Mercury — March 19, 1862

Also encouraging residents to flee were newspaper editors who urged noncombatants to evacuate, especially on the approach of the enemy. The fate of New Orleans civilians under "Beast" Butler in early May 1862 made it clear what to expect in occupied North Carolina towns.[24] Most often non-military age men remained home in an attempt to safeguard their families, homes and household goods from Northern looters.

Amid this destruction and fear were the wives and children of North Carolina soldiers who often found themselves homeless and vulnerable to roving bands of lawless, marauding deserters from both sides. After Plymouth's fall to the enemy, heartsick wives who visited their husbands at their nearby camps often had little chance of returning home — and if his regiment moved, she was left in an extremely precarious position and especially if with children.

---

23 Andrews, p228
24 Massey, p17

Very often the soldier urged his wife to remain at home or with nearby relatives rather than "risk an insecure life as a refugee," which posed problems in conquered towns like New Bern, Plymouth and Washington. If discovered as the wife of a North Carolina soldier, she faced retribution and abuse from the occupier who viewed her as a traitor and spy.[25] If at home with children, the wife faced those they often referred to as Hessians "who came to search, plunder steal and burn in their barbaric campaigns of torch and torture — cowardly crews on pitiful business, brutally invading a lady's wardrobes & bureaus."[26] An added cruelty to those barely surviving at home enduring was the awful news of those close to them being killed and buried in shallow, far-off graves — "Poor fellows! Poor fellows! Oh, we are but just beginning to realize the terrors of this rain of anarchy much as we have hitherto suffered."

Not forgotten among those left homeless by the destruction of enemy troops are the colored women and children, the families of the men impressed into work gangs on enemy fortifications or general labor. All lived in shanties erected from scrap wood, with the women and children enrolled in daytime schools established and led by a Massachusetts woman.[27]

"We have the right to take every life, every acre of land, and every particle of property."

— *General W. T. Sherman*

One of the most destructive of the enemy's raids into the eastern counties from occupied New Bern began in mid-July 1863. The enemy force consisted mostly of a New York cavalry unit accompanied by colored troops of mostly contrabands. During the raid on the countryside, they burned bridges at Greenville, Tarboro and Rocky Mount, a cotton factory, railroad cars, engines and machine shops, storehouses and food stores. At plantations they overran, black workers were forced to plunder the owner's houses of valuables as well as leave with the horses, wagons and carriages. Pursued by North Carolina troops, the enemy column was intercepted at the "Burney Place" and barely escaped capture as they abandoned their contrabands and sped to-

---

25 Ibid, p27
26 Buck, p4
27 Lamphere, p1

ward safety at New Bern. The melee of battle forced many of the Negro women and children into nearby woods for safety, who afterward were saved by North Carolina troops that returned them to their homes. As enemy raiders fled this last engagement, they left their path strewn with broken carriages and stolen wearing apparel, tableware, fine China and quilts taken from the helpless women at the plantations. In their desperate flight, the enemy cut the throats of all horses to end their usefulness to the family.[28]

The depredations cited above were not isolated, nor ended when Northern authorities might have intervened to stop this war upon innocent Americans. The early-1865 entry of Sherman's marauders into North Carolina proved that this war upon American civilians had not ended. The towns of Monroe and Wadesboro were among the first of Sherman's targets as his cavalry threatened to kill an Episcopal bishop in Anson County if "he did not give up his watch, horse and possessions."[29] A nearby home had its furniture taken into the yard with the Yankees chopping it to pieces with an axe and scattering feathers from pillows on a bedroom floor before molasses was poured upon it.[30] Another resident, Esther Alden, wrote of the animals in agony at the invader's hands:

"The poor suffering horses! Some fortunately dead and out of their misery, others groaning in death pains, some with disabled limbs freely

---

28 Carolana.com, 50th NC Regt
29 Spencer, p64
30 Gibson, p189

John Bernhard Thuersam

hobbling about ... the cows and oxen slaughtered and left to rot! I counted eight dead calves lying dead in one pen; many times we saw two or three lying dead side by side." [31]

An eyewitness to the enemy's passing near Fayetteville was young Josephine Worth, who vividly recalled that "the sky was lurid with the flames from burning homesteads," adding that the enemy's route "could be traced by solitary chimneys where happy homes once stood." Josephine wrote also of her uncle's home four miles away where everything had been vandalized, "Even the family Bible was not sacred." One enemy soldier "opened it and spread it over a mule's back and rode upon it as a saddle." Another intentionally spat into cornbread cooking before the fire, "the bread intended to feed our four hungry children."[32]

In late-December 1863 the infamous Benjamin Butler detailed General Edward Wild with eighteen hundred colored troops to clear the northeastern counties of North Carolina of partisan and guerrilla forces harassing loyalist farmers. Wild's instructions were to "clear the country of slaves" which meant recruiting any able-bodied males, by force, if necessary, into his own brigade as recruits. Their dependents were taken as well to deny any usefulness to the farmers, and carried to Northern camps to serve as cooks and laundresses.[33]

Edward Wild

This pattern of "contraband" recruitment continued unabated due to slow if not stagnated enlistments of Northern men, draft resistance and riots in Northern cities, and the enlistment expirations of many existing white Northern troops. The enemy carried additional uniforms and accoutrements for those "recruited" during the raid and absorbed as soldiers into the black ranks. Wild afterward reported to his superior that "nine boatloads of Negroes were sent to Roanoke Island and two more to Norfolk, plus four long trains over land."

---

31 Jones, p262
32 Worth, p298
33 Barrett, p177

Described by inhabitants as a "monster of humanity" for leading black troops, Wild and his men occupied Elizabeth City from December 9 through 16th while keeping residents in a "perpetual panic." Wild then implemented a self-described "more rigorous style of warfare" by hanging a man he claimed was a "guerrilla," and forced women to watch his struggle for twenty minutes before he died of strangulation. Wild ordered the deceased, a private in a Georgia cavalry regiment, left hanging in the courthouse for two days. Wild justified his extreme actions by claiming that he found ordinary measures of warfare of little avail at Elizabeth City that he was forced to burn "their houses and barns, taking all livestock plus hostages from families."[34]

Col. Joel Griffin of the 8th Georgia Cavalry, expressed outrage to Wild at the summary execution of his soldier. He wrote that *"probably no expedition during the progress of the war, has been attended with more bitter disregard for the long-established usages of civilization and dictates of humanity than your late raid into the country bordering the Albemarle Sound."* The colonel further noted that although Wild's raid was of short duration, it was marked by crimes and enormities including looting and burning houses occupied by defenseless women and children, arresting "non-combatants, and imprisoning women in leg-irons." The colonel added that it was observed that surrendering Southern troops were fired upon by Wild's colored troops and "were only saved by the exertions of the more humane of your white officers." Colonel Griffin concluded his letter with his commanding officer's retaliatory execution of his northern prisoner from an Ohio regiment.[35]

---

34 OR, XXIX, I, I, 912
35 Barrett, p178

Fortress on the Roanoke

"This pretty little Southern town has been the scene of stirring operations during the year, and war's devastations have left it scarcely more than a mass of ruins. Bandied to and fro, like a shuttle-cock between two belligerents, having changed masters five times in two years, our army has built, theirs has burned. Its occupancy by the rebels, though brief, has left it in heaps."
— *Rev. Horace James, Supt. of Negro Affairs in North Carolina, 1864.*
pg. 34

This 1864 observation above disregards the peaceful and prosperous settlement on the Roanoke River which existed some 70 years before the arrival of Northern troops. That the town was a "shuttle-cock" in the reverend's words, was the result of the invader wanting a Roanoke River base from which to launch raids upon peaceful farms, plantations and towns.

The Northern re-occupation and fortification of Plymouth was to be two-fold: utilizing it as a base for more raids to Williamston, Tarboro, Kinston, Hamilton and Scotland Neck, Halifax and Weldon. Goldsboro, an important rail center bringing needed supplies from Wilmington to Lee's army in Virginia, was also within easy range.[1] The enemy marches to and from these targeted towns were opportunities to devastate the region by burning crops, killing livestock and destroying the homes of residents, while carrying off black farm workers which had a detrimental impact on agricultural production. The enemy presence had the dual purpose of tying down North Carolina troops who would otherwise be in Virginia, and also prevent valuable foodstuffs from reaching Lee's army in the field.

Both citizens and elected officials of the region loudly pressured Gov. Zebulon Vance to bring additional North Carolina troops back to the State to liberate those areas under enemy control like Plymouth in an effort to end the enemy's destructive raids.[2] Vance likewise pressured the Confederate government to release North Carolina troops to

---
1 Newsome, p62
2 Ibid, p32-33

better defend the State.³

While the 17th North Carolina remained in winter quarters near Hamilton, mounted patrols made periodic reconnaissance to the Plymouth area in case the enemy returned. In early March 1863, a Massachusetts regiment landed and a camp established amid the town remnants. In mid-afternoon on the 10th of March, Lt. Col Lamb sent about 50 skirmishers forward to drive in the enemy's pickets. These were reinforced with troops from the town, and artillery fire came from gunboats in the river. The 17th Regiment advanced in force at 10PM to near the entrenched enemy and, after better ascertaining enemy strength, withdrew to avoid fire from the gunboats. The standoff continued to early morning on the 13th when Lamb's men fired three signal rockets, which were answered by two rockets fired several miles upriver. After this the enemy commander reported that the 17th Regiment had withdrawn.⁴

An enemy post-action report was unsure of his adversary's intentions though it may well have been Lamb's desire to force his enemy to retreat on his gunboats, fearing a possible land and river assault, hence the rockets to alert any river forces. At this time the enemy was aware of an ironclad under construction upriver, but its potential effectiveness was discounted.⁵

---

3 ORA, 52(2):740 Vance letter to Davis
4 Carolana.com, 17th NC?
5 Carolana.com, 17th NC

The enemy presence soon increased at Plymouth as a regiment of New York troops were landed from transports in early-May 1863. Their new post was little-changed from how it was described some six months earlier by the disgraced northern captain driven out by Lt. Colonel Lamb's 17th Regiment: "[All] the principal buildings on the street where the hotel was is gone, and all at headquarters was burned." Those buildings blasted by Lamb's artillery were those the enemy had barricaded themselves into, and the local civilian population was assessed by an arriving enemy soldier to be about 500 persons, the "majority of whom were negroes."[6] The minority white population were likely those whose loyalties lay with their business and inventory, as well as those believing their property was safer while remaining there and acting as Tories. This was later known as the "Stockholm Syndrome" where the captives began identifying with their captors.

The new arrivals now set up camp near some incomplete breastworks to the south of town and were set to work cutting timber for what would become the new fortress.[7] To house their troops the enemy began constructing rough barracks, supply and administrative buildings which did nothing to restore the small-town charm that once existed.

Little then remained of the former town's homes, stores and places of worship, and this being underscored by a Massachusetts soldier disembarking from a transport in some seven months later who described Plymouth as "dilapidated" and likely a remnant of what was a "quite a thriving village previously." Apparently informed of past contests over possession of the town, he wrote "rebel forces and our own had each a turn at attempting to burn it, and thus the best-built portion of Plymouth had been consumed" by fire. The writer added that "the town itself consisted of a few tumble-down houses that had escaped the flames," a few masonry stores and homes and the rest "a medley of Negro shanties" constructed of split pitch-pine logs, plus a number of rudely-framed buildings meant for government purposes.[8]

This artilleryman also noted the thriving town of some 2,000 people before the war had become a "general rendezvous for fugitive Negro men and families coming into our lines. Many were the ever-present colored and white refugees aware that they could obtain

---

6 Dickey, p255
7 Mahood, p136-138
8 Goss, p55

John Bernhard Thuersam

food in exchange for information, especially that of the movements of North Carolina troops. Added to this were deserters and those escaping North Carolina conscription officers.[9]

The human cost, in addition to death and maiming, was the breakup of families both white and colored. Mrs. Edmondston wrote in mid-1863 of a Virginia slave woman enticed away by emancipation and leaving behind her two young children. Faced with the care of these abandoned children, the plantation mistress then visited a northern general at his Norfolk headquarters. She told him that "these children have been deprived of their mother by your act and I come here to surrender them to you."[10]

In early 1863 the elaborate fortification began in and around Plymouth's remnants began "with all dispatch possible" after Connecticut-native Brig-General Henry Wessells was assigned to direct the work. An 1833 graduate of West Point, he ranked 29th in an undistinguished class, served in the Mexican War and compiled a middling Civil War record before assignment to Plymouth.[11] After the embarrassing rout of Northern infantry and their gunboat there only six months earlier, Wessells was anointed to transform the ruins of the former town into a formidable stronghold of breastworks, redoubts and earthen fortresses bristling with cannon and supported by four gunboats. In the process, the once-peaceful town of Plymouth became a formidable outpost of the enemy's military district.

Wessell's garrison troops were primarily Pennsylvanians and New Yorkers in infantry and artillery units, accompanied by companies of cavalry. They were put to garrison work stabilizing the town's war-damaged and dilapidated houses in which they and other incoming enemy troops would occupy. Afterward, simple wooden barracks and other necessary structures were built with scrap wood and newly-sawn lumber from the old river mill west of town. These troops formed the initial labor force which established a defensive perimeter of rifle pits, breastworks and rudimentary gun emplacements.

A sergeant of a New York regiment described the construction of earthen-walled bastions to be equipped with artillery emplacements and interior parapets for riflemen. Outside the walls were sunken moats to slow attackers, and into which hand grenades could

---

9 Goss, p55
10 Edmondston, p421
11 Wiki, accessed 1.24.24

be lobbed from within. Regiments from Massachusetts and Pennsylvania also occupied what remained of Plymouth. The earth-moving and lumber-cutting necessitated a large workforce to shovel, load, transport and unload dirt to be fashioned into high, thick walls with a sloped face to the outside. The inner side of the walls had stepped-up parapets for riflemen and those not fully-enclosed with earth had pine log stockades with rifle loop-holes. One northern soldier wrote of these forts being "well-constructed but were in many respects outsized rifle pits."[12]

Wessells and his officers supervised this extensive array of breastworks, forts, redoubts and bombproofs which occupied their time through the summer months. The incorporation of Fort Grey about two miles upriver was directed at the ironclad threat as well as the emplacement on the western edge of town.[13] In all, the defensive logic was to form a continuous fortified semicircle around the town remnants and extended to the river on both ends. This would follow the surrounding topography of swamps and creeks with the river defended by gunboats. The southwest approach from the Washington Road was the only feasible direction from which a land assault could be made.

In keeping with this logic, the 85th (New York Regiment) Redoubt, later named Fort Wessells, was erected a mile and a half to the southwest near a woody marsh at Welch's Creek. From this position its artillery commanded the intersection of the Jamesville and Washing-

---

12 Mahood, p140
13 Lamphere, p1

ton Roads to the south. As Second Street reached easterly edge of town it became the Columbia Road and here, near the Latham house, was located the small and partially-earthen Conaby Redoubt with only two cannons. The sides and rear were pine-log stockades with loop-holes to fire through.

A little further down the Columbia Road and near the river was the mostly earthen Fort Compher (aka, Comfort) with four-cannon emplacements facing east. About two-thirds of this fort was earthen and facing east, while the remaining sides and rear were stockaded. These two positions loosely anchored the long breastworks south of town as it turned toward the river at the former town limits. Both were somewhat light defenses as the woody swamp toward Conaby Creek was a natural barrier. The enemy also counted on their gunboat artillery to defeat any assault from the east.[14] Beyond Fort Compher was a grassy area and cattle pen to provide fresh meat for the garrison troops.[15]

The pine-log stockading of Fort Williams in-situ with the long line of breastworks a quarter mile south of town was completed in late-May, just to the east of the Little Washington Road. To the west of this line, with swampland in between, was another redoubt — an enclosed defensive emplacement outside a larger fort. These were in most cases earthwork "rifle pits" dug out of the ground with walls built up around the excavation, offering protection to those lying prone or crouching within. Within each were mounted four guns ranging from 24 to 100-pounders, and two more forts were in the line of works with similar armament. This extensive fortification is what Wessell's specifically deemed "to be held at all hazards."

From their initial contact with the "contrabands" it became common for northern commanders to impress "contrabands" for labor and fatigue troops, especially for the hard work on fortifications being thrown up at Plymouth. This was considered miserable work by white Northern soldiers whose enlistments would expire soon, and officers by mid-1863 were grooming their troops for reenlistment with attractive bounty money. Should insufficient laborers be available for heavy work then slave-catching raids on plantations could easily obtain "contrabands" for workers. But often the raiders left empty-handed as the colored men had wisely disappeared before the bluecoats arrived to

---

14 Felix Vinay Maps, NCDeptArchivesHistory
15 R.D. Graham, 1864 Map

"emancipate" them. The Northern troops then developed more sophisticated impressment techniques such as Sunday morning raids on colored churches, nor were they not above the use of violence and threats to obtain enlistments. In the end, the very hard labor that "contrabands" were put to seriously eroded their health and it is recorded that the high mortality rate among black men so-employed was caused by inadequate shelter and an insufficient diet provided by the US Army.[16]

Adding to the firepower of the earthen fortress were the enemy gunboats at the river wharf, varying in number between three to five. Their armament — commonly two 20-pounder Parrott rifles and often 150-pounders — were thought more than adequate to defeat any naval threat coming downriver. Additionally, their naval cannon could elevate sufficiently to provide an intense defensive fire upon the critical southwest approach to the fortress.

The gunboat flotilla commander himself broadcast supreme confidence that was accepted by nearly all — that should the "rebel ironclad" ever appear his force was more than adequate to defeat it. The 100-pounder Parrot gun of Fort Gray, a mile and a half upriver, was the first line of defense if it appeared, with another redoubt constructed on the western edge of town mounting a 200-pounder rifled gun — as an extra measure of defensive power.[17]

During this time the enemy's fortification-building progress was being observed by the 17th Regiment's scouting parties. One audacious officer desiring a closer look led a small detachment under flag of truce to the outer defenses on June 7th. He summarily demand-

---

16 Stearns, pp324-325
17 Reed, p36

ed the immediate surrender of the fortress — which was declined. Departing without an enemy capitulation, certainly the intelligence gathered was well-worth the effort expended.[18]

During this second enemy occupation of Plymouth at least two regiments designated "North Carolina Colored Troops" were organized from "contrabands" gathered from area farms and plantations. It was not until November 1863 that recruiting began locally for the 37th US Colored Troops — a more accurate designation as they were not "North Carolina" troops — and those recruited often bore the surname of their owner. One officer captured at Plymouth was Major Oliver McNary of the 103rd Pennsylvania regiment, the acting recruiting officer and superintendent of Negro affairs at Plymouth. When apprehended he was disguised as an enlisted man as he likely feared execution for his role in arming slaves for rebellion. At the capitulation, Hoke reportedly asked Wessells for "the whereabouts of Major Hiram Marvin" of the 85th New York regiment who Hoke believed was responsible for "stealing and drilling negroes" for military service.[19] Colored men later credited to the 37th and 10th were reportedly at Plymouth in April 1864 but still considered part of the so-called North Carolina "volunteers." Some were reported killed in battle, some captured and many fled to the swamps.

Satisfied that the strongholds of both New Bern and Plymouth were well-defended against any threat from North Carolina's forces, theater commander General Butler was dismissive of any ironclad threat on the Roanoke River and believed it a hoax.[20] There still remained a sense of insecurity among the rank and file as Wessell's nearest reinforcements were some 70 nautical miles away on Roanoke Island, and about the same distance southward to Little Washington.[21] In mid-April 1863 rumors circulated of North Carolina forces and the ironclad steaming toward Wessell's growing fortress at Plymouth. He asked for an additional 5,000 men from his superior, who had none to spare, as his department was already sending troops to Grant in Virginia.[22]

As the month of May 1863 closed, the troops within Plymouth's

---

18 Mahood, p140
19 McNary, p5
20 OR 9, 491
21 Lamphere, p1
22 OR, 33, 877

fortress learned of the rout at Chancellorsville after Stonewall Jackson's early-morning flank attack. Though very dispiriting news, one enemy soldier writing home in early June noted the recent visit of three North Carolina cavalrymen bearing a flag of truce. The officer among them "swore vengeance on this place unless it is surrendered", which Wessells quickly dismissed. The writer then confidently boasted of their position's "gunboats, forts and artillery, in addition to breastworks for all our troops to work behind," all sufficient to repel the attack of 15,000 soldiers.[23]

Occupied Plymouth in April 1864 (carolana.com)

The garrison soldiers grumbled when the "Sons of Massachusetts" arrived in late June — strutting, nine-month men in white dress gloves who ridiculed the dirty appearance of their new comrades.[24] These "Sons" were assigned light duty such as patrols and avoided combat, likely the result of Massachusetts Gov. John Andrew's shrewd agreement with Lincoln to meet the State's enlistment quota and maintain Republican party hegemony there. Lincoln agreed to accept the short-term service to avoid conscription riots, while providing generous federal bounty money along with State, county and municipality bounties paid to anyone enlisting.

The garrison soldiers at Wessell's fortress found ways to break the monotony of dodging mosquitoes, cleaning weapons and building fireplaces for officer quarters. Soldiers were regularly assigned picket duty and reconnaissance missions to maintain their readiness. When camp tedium overcame them, they practiced "sadistic" pranks on their "contraband" compatriots which included tossing cartridges into their campfires and "throwing cups of flour in the unsuspecting darkies faces."[25]

---

23 Letter of George D. Rogers, 85th NY, 6.18.1863
24 Mahood, p144
25 Mosher, CWJ, I, p396

Those "contrabands" not in blue uniforms were detailed as cooks, servants, laborers and very often with a wide latitude regarding compensation. There was often a price to be paid for a colored informant as in the case of Nelson Sheppard. He went over to the enemy in mid-May 1863 at Plymouth where he served as a cook in the 24th New York and acted as a guide for several enemy cavalry raids in the direction of Williamston. After his capture in mid-April 1864 at Plymouth, the inhabitants who had suffered at the hands of his friends "got an order to whip him, which was done in the most approved style; the next day they dished up another dose, and for several days poor Nelson had to undergo chastisement." It was said he became quite nervous when North Carolina troops were near and would take to the swamps to hide, fearing retribution for his disloyalty.[26]

In mid-July 1863 the fortress garrison read newspaper accounts of the epic battle at Gettysburg which announced a great Northern victory, as well as Grant's capture of Vicksburg. Though Gettysburg was hailed as a Northern triumph, on the fourth day Lee had disengaged with his army still a threat to Washington, Philadelphia and Baltimore, before heading southward to entice the enemy from his protective trenches. Lee's 72,000-man army had been on the offensive for all three days and accomplished his primary mission of living off northern farm produce while war-ravaged Virginia recovered, and helped strengthen the growing antiwar sentiment in the north. Little mentioned is that many Northern troops arrived in New York City from Gettysburg to battle civilians rioting against Lincoln's draft law, using musket and cannons to disperse the angry crowds. This included part of the 9th New York regiment formerly at Plymouth, now battling their fellow New Yorkers opposed to the war. Shortly after this Gov. Andrew of Massachusetts called out his 44th Regiment and other militia units to quell the Boston draft riot. There an angry mob of some 4,000 residents stormed the Cooper Street Armory where the troops fired into the crowd, killing eight and wounded an untold number.[27]

In early November 1863 the troops at Plymouth first read of financial inducements to reenlist, made necessary due to the high bounties paid for new enlistees. To avoid mass desertions of veterans the War Department needed incentives for existing troops.[28]

---

26 Merrill, p119-120
27 Harris, p30-31
28 *New York Times*, Nov. 4, 1863

Plymouth's "Veteran Volunteers"

The following month a New York soldier recorded in his diary that "those regiments whose time expires next fall are asked to reenlist for three years or the war's duration." He wrote that the men "were lured by money in sums not imagined earlier: payment of an unpaid original bounty of $100, a new bounty of $400 plus a $2 recruiting premium, paid in $50 installments every six months. This was at a time when the annual family income in New York may have been $350. In addition to the $402 financial incentive was a month-long furlough home to see loved ones while wearing the blue uniform adorned with a gold sleeve-chevron of the new "Veterans Corps." Once at home the soldier would also receive a $50 bounty from the State of New York; and whatever bounty money was offered from the soldier's home county and town. The total of some $750 or more in bounty money was said to be sufficient to "build a house on the little farm on the road up home."[29] As a town or county did not require residency to receive the bounty-paid credit, the soldier home on reenlistment furlough could shop area communities and counties for the highest amount and credit his reenlistment to them. Civilians unwilling to serve and employers not wanting to lose workers, both contributed to each town's bounty account to attract substitutes.[30] Some blowback occurred as "Veteran Volunteers" at home would credit themselves to another community so as to not allow those they considered "shirkers" in their hometowns to avoid the draft.[31]

In some Northern States the amount of the total bounty for one man rose to $1,500 — a very large sum at that time. But despite these bounty-enriched men and their regiments being referred to as "Volun-

---

29 Mosher, CWJ, I, p442
30 Schmidt, p668
31 Ibid, p653

teers," they were in truth well-paid "mercenaries."[32] This was not lost on New York family men who had never before thought of enlisting but found it difficult to turn down invitations to serve as substitutes for $1000, for a one-year hitch.[33]

The dark side were those garrison troops tired of war and avoiding reenlistment who were assigned hard duty to encourage others to not make this mistake; officers were rewarded with money, promotions and furlough should their units achieve high or full reenlistment numbers. As the army leadership became increasingly Republican it became politically-expedient that soldiers be furloughed home to vote in State elections.[34] Another effect of the generous payments to veterans remaining in service was the case of a 24th New York wagoner, John Perry of the town of Perry. After his reenlistment at Plymouth in January 1864, payment and veteran furlough home, he was not heard from again.[35]

What had become "Wessell's Fortress" by early-April 1864 was vividly described by an arriving enemy artillerist. Greatly impressed by the fortification work accomplished in the previous 12 months, he wrote that "a small garrison could hold five times its strength and numbers at bay for a long time." Regarding the town's still-visible remnant, he saw the homes "had been mostly deserted by their original inhabitants, and the larger ones taken possession of by the troops for

---

32 Ford, p, ix
33 Marvel, p219
34 *New York Times*, Nov. 13, 1863
35 Merrill, p51

quarters. He further observed that "in its palmy days probably numbered fifteen hundred to two thousand inhabitants; streets regular and shade trees in abundance," though realizing that "in prior days many buildings had been burned to the ground" during an attack. Here he was referring to the December 1862 liberation of the town and destructive fire from both sides.[36]

At Plymouth the spring air was fresh. The enemy soldiers were enjoying fishing in the Roanoke and farmers were bringing in fresh meats, eggs, honey and poultry. The contrabands "were settled in their inferior huts about the suburbs and employed as cooks." It was admitted that the enemy soldiers were as comfortable as they could legitimately be allowed to be. The artillerist wrote also of scouting parties sent out, described as exciting and enjoyable, seldom failing to bring in anything labelled as "contrabands" or "contraband goods." The latter could be anything seized or stolen by the enemy at gunpoint, and furniture from "deserted" homes found its way into enemy barracks.[37]

Occupied Plymouth, Early 1864

A New Year 1864

The dawning of the third year of war found the American Confederacy as yet unbeaten and the possibility of European recognition remained. In April, four commissioners appointed by President Davis departed the port of Wilmington, North Carolina on a blockade runner to Canada with $1 million in gold with which to purchase weapons to arm Southern prisoners soon to be freed at Johnson's Island on Lake Erie. A detachment of Confederate Marines departed Wilmington earlier to capture the USS *Michigan* defending the prison. Should these succeed, the result might be a northern front in coordination with the South's Copperhead sympathizers.

The new American nation remained hopeful of independence despite enemy advances in the West with the Mississippi under northern

---

36 Ibid, p200
37 Ibid, p201

control. General Robert E. Lee was successfully defending Richmond and river defense ironclads were becoming available to resist destructive enemy inland incursions. This was the case on the Roanoke. Also, the important Wilmington and Weldon railroad remained a target for raids from occupied-Plymouth.

The enemy menace at Plymouth resulted in the construction of Fort Branch in 1862, located on the Roanoke at Rainbow Banks, southeast of Hamilton. Its twelve guns mounted on the high bluffs were a strong deterrent to enemy warships ascending the river. Gov. Zebulon Vance stressed to both Davis and Lee an immediate need to assign more North Carolina troops to eject the enemy from this region, which would release of desperately-needed foodstuffs to Lee's army. Davis was also advised that continued Northern control of the North Carolina sounds would eventually allow them to operate freely against the vital port of Wilmington.[38]

The enemy cavalry raids from Plymouth into nearby Martin County during the winter of 1863-1864 caused the detachment of the 35th North Carolina under Lt. Orinee Venters to regularly scout the region in between. Venters found there lived within a radius of fifteen or so miles surrounding Plymouth "a large element of disloyalists known as "buffaloes" who reported to the enemy. During this time of cold, snow and sleet Venter's men could have no fires, but did often surprise mounted enemy raiders leaving Plymouth and forced their retreat. On another occasion Venter's 40 men ambushed a force of 100 cavalry, "many killed and many more wounded, we captured eight, but some wounded made their escape." Lt. Venters quickly shouted commands of attack to imaginary regiments to his left and right, causing the enemy to retreat pell-mell as their captain exclaimed "these woods are full of Rebs."[39]

In January 1864 Maj-General George Pickett's attempt at liberating New Bern failed, and blamed on poor coordination and leadership. Afterward, an enemy admiral admitted had their forts been probed and attacked on their weak river flank, success would have crowned Pickett's men with victory. Despite the defeat, one of Pickett's subordinates, Brig-Gen Robert F. Hoke, was highly-praised by the *Raleigh Daily Confederate* for his "rout of the enemy and pursuit of the fugi-

---

38 Barefoot, p106
39 Wright, E. Arnold "On Scouting Duty in North Carolina" *Confederate Veteran*, July 1918, p303

tives. ..." General Lee wrote Hoke in early February complimenting he and his "gallant brigade accomplished their part of the work," while "regretting very much that success did attend the whole expedition." Lee recognized in the 27-year-old brigadier what a North Carolina major had astutely written of Hoke's demeanor: a "gravity beyond his years, conjoined with judgment, discretion and serenity amid danger, marked him for command and the conduct of great enterprises." Pickett's failure and Hoke's exemplary handling of his men had more than a few suggesting that New Bern would have been liberated had Hoke led the advance.[40]

This General Hoke was a native of Lincolnton, North Carolina, born in 1837 on the South Fork River tributary of the Catawba River. His ancestors were Palatines from Alsace-Lorriane who had migrated to North Carolina from New York and Pennsylvania. Hoke's early education was acquired at the Lincolnton Male Academy with a curriculum in "grammar, logic, mathematics, chemistry, Greek, Latin and the classics," and his grades were just above average. At age fifteen in 1852 Hoke was enrolled in the Kentucky Military Institute which boasted a faculty of West Point graduates, but withdrew after one year due to family business needs. (Barefoot, p9, 15)

Robert F. Hoke

1860 found Robert in Washington, DC studying law at night and working at the US Census Bureau by day. He attended Lincoln's inauguration on March 4, 1861 and with a friend was able to shake the new President's hand at an afterward reception. Robert was back in Lincolnton shortly afterward, and on April 22nd enrolled with ninety-six others in the Lincolnton's "Southern Stars" militia company. Robert's uncle, William J. Hoke was the captain, and Robert second lieutenant. His military career had begun.[41]

General Hoke and his North Carolinians were heartened by their assignment defending their native State rather than the Virginia theater of war. While back in the Tarheel State, Lee encouraged Hoke in a letter of January 29th to attract new recruits to swell his ranks.

---

40 *Raleigh Daily Confederate*, Feb. 14, 1864
41 Barefoot, pp9-21

10
"Three Cheers for North Carolina!"

"We must ... teach the enemy that he must get what he wants by attacking someone who will not resist; glory will always give battle for the liberty of their country ... and do not let him go without a struggle."
— *Thucydides*

An important naval development, contributing enormously to General Hoke's April 1864 victory at Plymouth, was begun by the innovative Secretary of the Navy Stephen R. Mallory of Florida. As the South began the war with no real warships, he presciently devised the ironclad program in 1862 as a means of defending important rivers along the Southern coastline. In North Carolina this plan would bear fruit in the construction of the ironclads *Albemarle, Neuse, North Carolina* and *Raleigh*. Mallory had been influenced by Mystic, Connecticut natives Nelson and Asa Tift who had lived in the South for many years and knew Mallory in Key West prior to the war. It was Nelson who produced a rude sketch of an armed, double-ended ironclad "barge" cheaply built for this purpose. Mallory reasoned while ironclads ably protected the rivers, a privateer fleet could devastate the northern merchant fleet at sea. The patriotic Tift brothers constructed the CSS *Mississippi* at New Orleans in 1862, asking only reimbursement for expenses.[1]

---

1 Fair, p61

A principal goal of Mallory's was freeing the coastal South of enemy warships as well as denying them access to the principal waterways for interior raids. For North Carolina specifically he asked Commander James W. Cooke, a former career-US Naval officer, to determine what important waterways in the State needed ironclad protection. The Albemarle Sound and Roanoke River were among those identified by Cooke. The contract and construction of what would become the CSS *Albemarle* began with 19-year-old Gilbert Elliot from nearby Elizabeth City. As a teenager he had learned the shipwright craft at his maternal grandfather's shipyard on the Pasquotank River shore. Though well-experienced in shipbuilding early in life, he was also reading law under Charles Kinney of Elizabeth City and acclaimed for his "fine legal mind."[2] Assigned as constructor of the ironclad was Peter Evans Smith, a Roanoke farmer with a mechanical bent, but better known as an inventor who devised several labor-saving and innovative tools during the ironclad's construction.[3] What was to follow was an unprecedented accomplishment of constructing a formidable warship in a virtual cornfield, under the most primitive conditions amid enemy raids. Few examples of American ingenuity match this.

The *Albemarle* and *Neuse* were not alone in North Carolina waters as the CSS *North Carolina* and CSS *Raleigh* had been under construction to the south on the Cape Fear River during 1863. The *North Carolina* was commissioned in July 1863, and the *Raleigh* in early 1864. Both were for some reason built with green timbers which caused leaks and hull warping after contact with seawater. Nonetheless, the *Raleigh* scattered the enemy blockading fleet on the evening of May 6, 1864, but she ran aground on an inlet sandbar the following morning causing her to break in two as the tide ran out.[4]

This ironclad's construction was supervised by Beaufort-native Commander Cooke, a very distinguished career US Navy officer who resigned his commission and initially assigned to the defense of Roanoke Island. He was captured in battle after his embarrassingly small ship was disabled and captured. He was soon exchanged and sent to Edward's Ferry to oversee construction and command the ram *Albemarle*. Cooke had already suffered greatly from war with the north, losing his farm in Fairfax, Virginia to the enemy. His neighbor there

---

2 Elliot, p11
3 Powell, p282
4 Campbell, p193-194

wrote his 500-tree peach orchard was cut down by the enemy and his prized piano taken into his yard, the keys and innards all ripped out and used as a horse water-trough."⁵

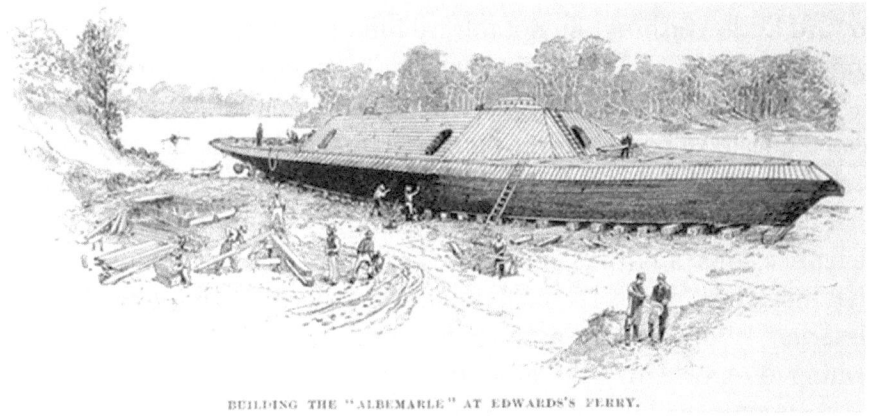

BUILDING THE "ALBEMARLE" AT EDWARDS'S FERRY.

What was dubbed the "Edwards Ferry Shipyard" on the Roanoke near today's Scotland Neck was in truth a cornfield when his skeleton crew of soldiers and engineers began work in January 1863. No facility, raw materials or anything existed there in the local countryside. Area residents generously donated metals to be smelted for armor; the ironclad's frame used local wood, and inventive metal drilling techniques sped construction. Though the *Albemarle* drew only nine feet of water, her negatives included only eight knots of speed, no armor plate more than four inches thick, and like the other North Carolina ironclads, she was built with green, unseasoned, i.e., kiln-dried lumber. This meant warping timbers as soon as the hull came in contact with water which required constant caulking and filling. Sheathing the hull with copper could have helped but was unavailable in the Confederate States.⁶

Few in the Northern high command saw an ironclad under construction on the Roanoke as posing a real threat. This was the subject of a report completed in early November 1862 by a Northern naval officer who traveled the 30-some miles from Plymouth upriver to Rainbow Bluff via gunboat. His report stated that no ironclad was in evidence on the Roanoke nor did he believe construction of one "of a formidable character" might be attempted above Williamston. He also wrote of northern gunboats being totally unfitted for service on the

---

5 Edmondston, p421
6 Still, p59

upper Roanoke given the often-swift currents as their decks would be exposed to sharpshooters and batteries concealed on the bluffs.[7]

General H. W. Wessells commanded the enemy's fortress at Plymouth was himself convinced that North Carolina forces were marching toward Little Washington, not toward him. But he was sufficiently concerned to officially-request 5,000 additional garrison troops from General John Peck at New Bern, and copied Burnside. In the letter he also requested a heavily-armed gunboat be sent in case the reported "rebel ironclad" appeared. Both Burnside and underling Peck believed that the four gunboats at Plymouth were more than sufficient flank defense against an ironclad if it ever appeared. It is worth considering that much of Wessells regional military intelligence was derived from deserters, refugees and contrabands coming into his camp and often willing to report anything for food, clothing and shelter.[8]

Security problems arose at Edward's Ferry shipyard as word of the ironclad spread. The construction site was plagued by enemy scouting parties and deserters feigning Southern allegiance. One worker, a former guard at Salisbury Prison plus an accomplice, absorbed information about the ram and disappeared in a boat to report construction progress to the enemy at Plymouth, who likely was rewarded for his duplicity.[9] Nonetheless, work continued unabated and soon the ram was under sufficient steam power for Cooke to sail her to Halifax and Hamilton for fitting out. There it was equipped with 6.4-inch Brooke guns front and rear, each pivot-mounted to fire in three directions.[10] As a further precaution, given the enemy's knowledge of the ironclad, a detachment from the 22nd North Carolina Regiment was detailed to guard the "shipyard."[11]

The ram's initial "Tarheel volunteer" crew were soldiers unfamiliar with naval vessels and tactics, but soon after getting underway for Plymouth the steamer *Cora* caught up bringing twenty experienced naval crewmen for the ironclad. The crew now numbered fifty. They helped finish final details and watched the river ahead to avoid grounding.[12] The fear of the ram's potential at Plymouth caused Wessells to instruct his engineers to mount a powerful 100-pounder

---

7 OR, 1, 8, pp180-183. See also McCallum, pp104-105
8 Mahood, p165
9 Edmondston, p439
10 *New Bern Daily Journal*, 12.31.1882
11 Edmondston, p395
12 Campbell, p144

Parrott gun and two 32-pounder naval guns at Fort Grey (aka, Gray), slightly west of town and up the Roanoke. It was hoped that these could either disable the ironclad or blow it to bits once it arrived. In addition, river obstructions above town at each end of the oblong Tabor Island and covered by the large caliber guns were also intended to prevent unwanted passage.

The confidence in Hoke's plan was rooted in *Albemarle's* anticipated completion and the high-level belief that Pickett's late-January 1864 New Bern campaign failed due to a lack of naval support. Though CSS *Neuse* at Kinston and CSS *Albemarle* at Edward's Ferry were then unable to assist in Pickett's campaign, the latter was now much closer to completion. Soon afterward Brig-General Robert F. Hoke, a Lt.-Colonel during New Bern's loss two years earlier, discussed with Lee a new offensive to liberate that town and both agreed a coordinated naval and land operation was necessary. The recently unsuccessful Pickett concurred.

It was with great confidence in Hoke's abilities as a leader and strategist that Lee assigned him as commander of the second New Bern operation with full supervision over both ironclads which were nearing completion in February and would hopefully be serviceable by March 1. Lee had earlier noted Col. Hoke's able handling of a brigade at Fredericksburg in December 1862 and complimented his "short and decisive charge" upon the enemy there. Stonewall Jackson had highly-praised Hoke's courage and patriotism; Jubal Early touted his "coolness, courage and intelligence."[13] Only three weeks after the Fredericksburg battle, Lee presented Col. Hoke with the three-stars and wreath insignia of a brigadier-general.

In early 1864 many voices were suggesting that had Hoke been in overall command of the earlier New Bern campaign, victory would have been achieved. In mid-February 1864, Major John W. Moore of the 3rd NC Artillery wrote of Hoke's unique talents, that he "was still in his youth, but a gravity beyond his years conjoined with judgment, discretion and serenity amid danger, marked him for command and the conduct of great enterprises."[14] For this new offensive which was ultimately aimed at liberating New Bern, Hoke's plan was a three-part strategy that would first neutralize enemy fortifications at Plymouth, which the enemy considered impregnable. He then would move

---

13 Early, p185
14 Barefoot, p118

southward to liberate Washington and lastly proceed against New Bern. With the ironclad *Albemarle* operational and wreaking havoc with enemy gunboats, Hoke's campaign, if victorious, would capture tons of badly-needed supplies and munitions for North Carolina's defense and Lee's hungry army. Success would also stop the destructive enemy attacks on the Wilmington & Weldon Railroad emanating from the enemy's Plymouth fortress. Additionally, time was of the essence as Lee expected Hoke's brigade back in Virginia before the muddy roads of spring rains dried and the enemy renewed his attacks on Richmond and Petersburg. There was absolutely no time for delays.

"Great deeds are usually wrought at great risks."

— *Herodotus*

All eyes were now on the completion of one of the two ironclads, deemed absolutely essential to Hoke's success. As of mid-March, the ram *Neuse* remained behind schedule, but the *Albemarle* was expected in mid-April. This news convinced Hoke that his advance upon Plymouth in coordination with the CSS *Albemarle* steaming down the Roanoke River would be the most feasible, and should the *Neuse* be operational after taking the Plymouth fortress, a liberation of Little Washington and New Bern would be quite likely. Lee advised Pickett, the departmental commander, to support Hoke who was familiar with the region and to communicate nothing regarding the operation via telegraph.[15]

Hoke requested the *Albemarle* to be subject to his authority and in early March was in Richmond conferring with President Davis on the operational plans. Expressing concern over the enemy's foothold in northeastern North Carolina, the President asked how Hoke would contend with the "buffaloe" element. Hoke's top recommendation was the arrest and deportation of renegade Raleigh newspaper editor William Woods Holden, who encouraged desertions by publicly advocating peace talks with the enemy. After Hoke's assurance of taking the fight to the enemy, Davis was delighted to know someone still thought something could be done.[16] With the President's full confidence in Hoke, Davis heartily-approved of him to lead of the expedition and dispatched his aide-de-camp Col. J. Taylor Wood to serve as an official observer.[17]

---

15 Barefoot, p109
16 Ibid, p125
17 Manarin, Vol VIII, p563

A May 14, 1905 article in the *Charlotte Observer* revealed that while Hoke returned to North Carolina by rail from Richmond, he overheard three Plymouth men discussing the many depredations committed by the occupation troops there. They spoke of area farmers losing their colored workers to the enemy at Plymouth and the detrimental effect on the South's essential agricultural economy. This was useful as Hoke would have certainly made it a point to know his adversary at Plymouth, the commander, his men and their battle experience and approximate strength. The men who occupied the enemy fortress of earthen redoubts were well-fed, well-equipped and well-paid men. Many had just received reenlistment-bounty money and few had actual combat experience beyond skirmishing. The men Hoke would lead against Plymouth's fortress were battle-tested, hard-driven veterans who had endured nearly three years of unrelenting, bloody warfare in Lee's Army of Northern Virginia.

"Let your plans be dark and impenetrable as night, and when you move, fall like a thunderbolt."   — *Sun Tzu*

General Hoke now launched his efforts to deceive the ever-present enemy spies and newspaper reporters on his brigade's movements. His artillery was loaded on rail cars headed north to Richmond while the movement of his brigade's southward were cloaked in great secrecy, and when marching all those witnessing the passage of his troops were arrested.[18] Additionally, a feint was launched from Wilmington

---

18 Barefoot, p112

John Bernhard Thuersam

by 4,000 troops under Maj-General James G. Martin marching north toward New Bern along the coast. This was a plan to deceive the enemy as to the actual target while disrupting rail traffic from enemy-held Morehead City.[19] So effective was Hoke's deception that Fortress Plymouth's commander was receiving intelligence reports of North Carolina regiments assembling near Edenton. A Northern surgeon at Plymouth recalled later that Hoke's "secrecy and celerity" led his commander to believe Washington to be the target.[20]

As it was a most important to the success of the operation, Hoke needed the absolute assurance of cooperation from Commander Cooke at Edward's Ferry. In late-March Hoke visited the *Albemarle* to view progress and confer with Cooke, ultimately persuading the apprehensive naval officer to bring his likely incomplete warship to Plymouth to ensure victory.[21] The captain warned that the vessel might be lacking some armor and armament, still receiving finishing touches as it departed its moorings on April 17th.

Among the *Albemarle*'s late-arriving sailors was enlistee Benjamin H. Gray, a capable colored 12-year-old when first assigned to Wilmington Squadron warships and detached in early 1864 to the ram.[22] His position aboard was carrying gunpowder bags to the two pivot-mounted 6.4-inch Brooke rifled cannons from the lower magazine. It was not uncommon to find free-black crewmen on Southern vessels during the war as the CSS *Chicora* had at least three serving as crew. Another was black ships carpenter Edward Walsh, a Bermudan who sailed with Capt. John Newland Maffitt who would later command the *Albemarle*. Dr. Edward Smith of American University has estimated that by February 1865, 1,150 free-black seamen served aboard Southern ships, amounting to some 20 percent of total naval personnel. After the war, Gray was a resident of Bertie County and Confederate pensioner; after his death in 1917, widow Margaret

Benjamin H. Gray

---

19 Clark,ed, Regts, 3:31-32
20 Wm. M. Smith; *Siege & Capture of Plymouth*. Mollus-NY, p344
21 Elliott, p166
22 Elliot, p183

continued to receive this in recognition of his patriotic service to his State.[23]

"Opportunities multiply as they are seized."   — *Sun Tzu*

The success of Hoke's elaborately well-timed plan depended on the *Albemarle* arriving as his troops were preparing their frontal assault on the earthen bastions of Fortress Plymouth. An unknown was whether the ram could pass the two river obstructions — perhaps blasting by them — while under fire from the enemy 100-pounder. Even if held at bay above the obstructions, the ram could still have bombarded the fortress with its 6.4-inch Brooke guns. But Providence was in Hoke's favor as a rainy spring brought rising water levels to assist the *Albemarle's* progress downstream and lift it above enemy obstructions. With their gunboats driven off or sunk, and the ironclad bombarding the enemy from the rear, success would be ensured. General Hoke and his men would not miss the opportunity arrayed before them.

General Hoke's Division included his old brigade and a regiment he formerly commanded, the 21st North Carolina. This unit was now under Col. William G. Lewis, and comprised of citizen-soldiers from Davidson, Yadkin, Surry, Forsyth, Stokes, Rockingham and Guilford counties. At Plymouth, Hoke entrusted Col. John T. Mercer of the 21st Georgia to command his old brigade.

Also in this brigade was the 6th NC Regiment, commanded by Col. Samuel McDowell Tate with his troops from Orange, Burke, Caswell, Alamance, Wake, Rowan, Catawba, Wake, Chatham, Mitchell and Yancy counties; and the 43rd NC Regiment, men who hailed from Mecklenburg, Wilson, Halifax, Edgecombe, Warren, Union and Anson counties; additionally, the 54th NC Regiment comprised of men from Rowan, Burke, Cumberland, Northampton, Iredell, Guilford, Wilkes, Yadkin, Polk and Granville counties; and lastly was the 21st Georgia Regiment of Col. John T. Mercer, with its soldiers drawn from the mostly western counties of Campbell, Floyd, Fulton, Polk, Gordon, Troup, Dale, Stewart and Chattooga.

"An agricultural people are the bravest men, most valiant soldiers, and citizens least given to evil designs."

  — *Cato*

---

23 Diechman, p000

The brigade of Brig-General Matt Ransom included his former regiment, the 35th NC Regiment, now under Col. John G. Jones with Capt. William Rand Kenan, adjutant. The men of this regiment were natives of Onslow, McDowell, Moore, Chatham, Person, Union, Henderson, Mecklenburg, Wayne, Burke and Catawba counties. Additional regiments in Ransom's brigade included the 8th North Carolina under Lt. Col. James W. Whitson whose men hailed from Pasquotank, Currituck, New Hanover, Granville, Pitt, Cabarrus and Rowan counties; the 24th North Carolina was recruited in Halifax, Onslow, Cumberland, Robeson, Person and Franklin counties; and the 25th North Carolina were mountain men recruited in Henderson, Jackson, Haywood, Cherokee, Transylvania, Clay, Macon and Buncombe counties.

In addition, Col. Stephen Dodson Ramseur's 49th North Carolina were men from Rutherford, Davidson, Cleveland, Rowan, Iredell, Gaston, Catawba and Lincoln counties; and the 56th North Carolina Regiment of Col. Paul F. Faison were of men from Camden, Northampton, Henderson, Mecklenburg and Orange counties.

Also under Hoke was Brig-General James L. Kemper's brigade, then-under Col. William T. Terry, which included the 1st, 3rd, 7th, 11th and 24th Virginia Regiments — all battle-hardened veterans of Lee's Army of Northern Virginia. Adding strength to Hoke's three brigades was the 12th North Carolina Cavalry, part of Col. James Dearing's Virginia cavalry and the Virginia Horse Artillery. The latter was augmented by the Wilmington Light Artillery and Lt. Col. Edgar F. Moseley's Alabama True Blues Artillery. Major JPW Read's Battalion was present and included the 38th Virginia Light Infantry, Fauquier Artillery's Company A; Richmond Fayette Artillery, Company B; and Company D of the Lynchburg Artillery.[24]

"Great battles are won with artillery" — *Napoleon*

Knowing much artillery would be needed to dislodge the enemy, Hoke had also summoned Branch's Battalion of Pegram's, Miller's and Bradford's Batteries, as well as several companies of Guion's Battalion, 1st NC Artillery. This small, veteran army under Hoke was an irresistible force.

The prelude to Hoke's assault was the yet-incomplete *Albemarle* being moved a few miles downstream to Hamilton at the end of

---

24 Carolana.com, NC Regts Civil War

March where final outfitting work could be accomplished as General Hoke finalized plans with Commander Cooke. Hoke's Division of three brigades and smaller commands moved and assembled with as much secrecy as possible so as to not alert the enemy of a threat to Plymouth. In mid-April, three regiments of North Carolina troops were sent to Brig. General Matt Ransom at Tarboro, and another regiment arrived from Edenton.

From Tarboro they marched through torrents of rain to Hamilton where they encamped two miles outside of town on April 16th. Writing his wife that night from camp, Col. Gaston Lewis of the 43rd NC Regiment reported his men "in good spirits" and holding no doubts of their success against the enemy." The growing column of troops wisely avoided Williamston which was infested with enemy patrols, and by Sunday morning Hoke's force had swollen to some 7,000 men with thirty-five artillery pieces. As Hoke remained mindful of enemy forces at New Bern, he wisely directed the 54th North Carolina to remain at Kinston to intercept reinforcements the enemy might dispatch to a beleaguered Plymouth.[25]

Hoke was cognizant of the terrain surrounding Plymouth which left but one feasible approach from the southwest on the Jamesville or Washington Roads, and both were commanded by the enemy's artillery in Fort Wessells (aka, 85th Redoubt) at the Sanderson Farm, bordered by woody marsh and swamp. The western side of the long breastworks in front of town continued toward the river, Battery Worth, a near pentagon of earthen walls with a stockaded rear, mounted the massive 200-pounder gun which was thought sufficient to blast the ironclad out of the water.

To the northwest were river obstructions above and below Warren's Neck intended to stop the *Albemarle*, guarded by the 100-pounder gun of nearby Fort Grey.[26] As indicated by Felix Vinay's drawings at the time, Forts Williams, Wessells and Grey were all stoutly-erected, raised-earth fortifications with parapets for cannon and rifles. To the east, both Fort Compher (aka, "Comfort") and the Conaby Redoubt were barely three-sided and their rear possibly enclosed with walls of stakes or palisade.[27] By the time of Ransom's assault, the enemy may have erected minor breastworks to augment the two forts.

---

25 Barefoot, pp129-130
26 See Graham Map, April 1864
27 Newsome, p211

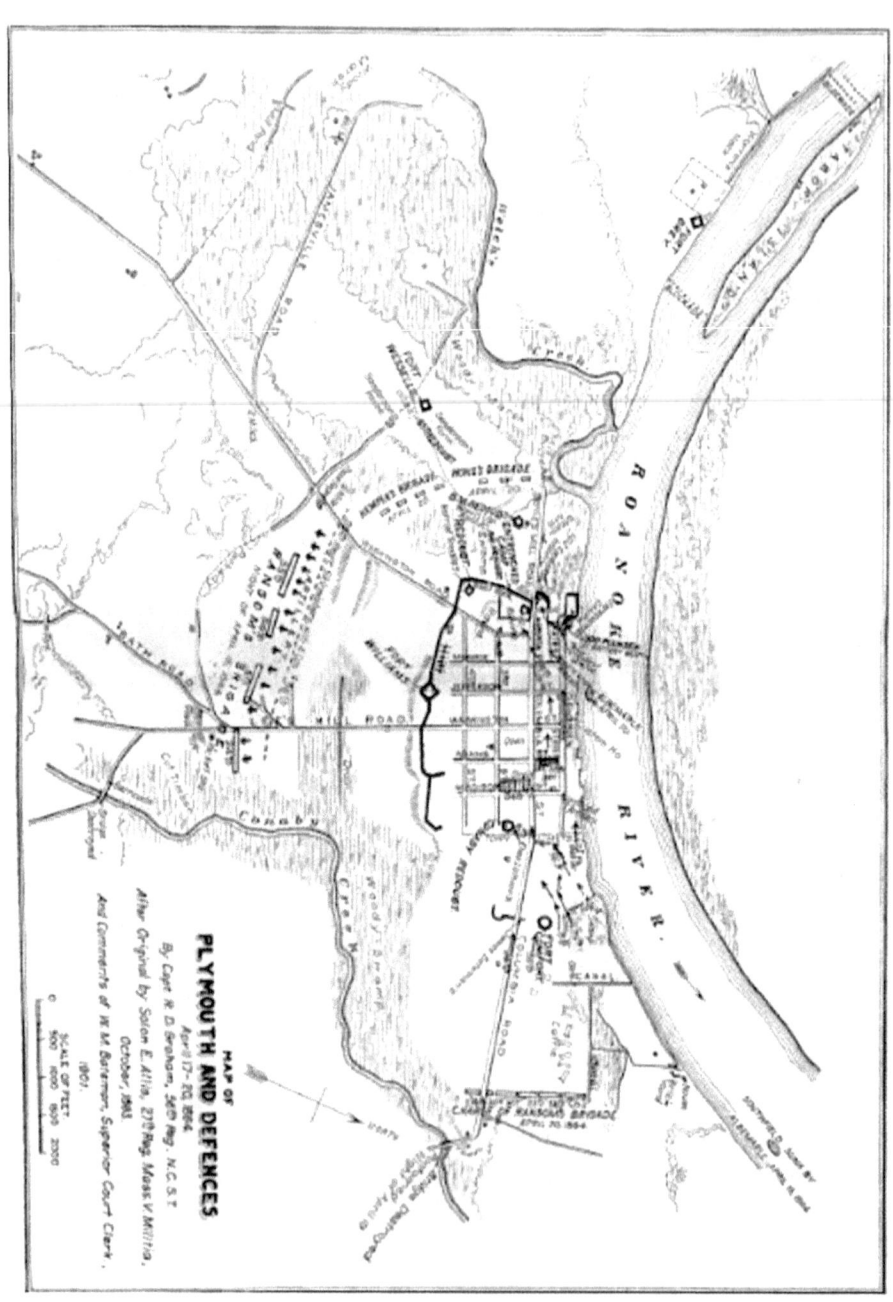

These latter defensive positions reflected a lesser concern of attack from this direction given the woody marshlands plus a deep and meandering Conaby Creek flowing from the south toward the Roanoke River east of Plymouth. A canal off the Roanoke near a livestock pen was located here. A long line of breastworks ran from Conaby Redoubt on the eastern edge of town, all along the southern-facing town limits flanking Washington Street as it became Lee's Mill Road heading southward. Just to the west of this road at the breastworks was the earthen Fort Williams, with additional redoubts just outside of town past Monroe Street.

Major John W. Graham of the 56th North Carolina wrote of 1864 Plymouth: "As the federal forces had occupied Plymouth for more than twelve months, every effort had been made to render the place secure from attack with the many forts and redoubts along the line of breastworks being protected by moats, palisades, *cheavaux de frise* (anti-cavalry stakes), and made as strong to resist bombardment or assault as engineering skill could devise."[28]

John W. Graham

A formerly small and prosperous community on the Roanoke in early 1861 had been nearly destroyed by the end of 1862. In 1863 and early 1864 it had become a staging area for destructive enemy raids to the interior which looted, burned and leveled farms and homes. When Hoke's force arrived in mid-April 1864 little remained of Plymouth except those homes and buildings which had escaped previous bombardments, subsequent fires and had become rickety shelters for homeless squatters. The North Carolina soldiers with Hoke could not restore the town to its former glory, but it could remove enemy troops in the region.

"Come back with your shield, or your body upon it."

— *Plutarch*

By 4PM on Sunday, April 17th the vanguard of Hoke's forces ap-

---

28 Graham, p177

proached to within five miles of Plymouth on the Jamesville Road. Before reaching Welch's Creek to the west of town Col. Dearing's cavalry and artillery were sent northward toward the enemy's Fort Grey, along with Terry's brigade of Virginian's. Hoke wanted this fort neutralized before *Albemarle's* arrival.

As Hoke's and Ransom's brigades advanced they discovered the Jamesville Road bridge at Welch's Creek was destroyed. Shifting southward to pass over a mill dam to reach the Washington Road about a mile below the Jamesville Road, all turned north toward the intersection. Hoke established his field headquarters in a nearby farmhouse while his cavalry pressed on first. At 4PM they surprised enemy pickets at the crossroads, capturing or killing all but two and scattering bluecoat cavalry sent to their rescue. The enemy was now aware of Hoke's presence and the long drum roll was sounded inside the fortress walls.

At twilight Hoke's brigade was advancing to the left of the Washington Road with Ransom's to the right and in front of Fort Williams. Both sides sent skirmishers forward amid intermittent rifle firing while enemy artillery shells Hoke's lines. By this time Hoke learned that noncombatants in the fortress were being evacuated to Roanoke Island on gunboats.[29] The river as well came alive with "buffaloes" who "floated down the river in canoes and took refuge in woods" in addition to many of the colored men from the area and employed by the enemy.[30] Historian Newsome points out that the colored troops were not a part of Wessells garrison and at that time North Carolina had no colored regiments, but did have colored soldiers within them. There were several officers from 4 different US Colored Troops (USCT) regiments recruiting from those at Plymouth.[31] All feared the result of capture for either treason or aiding the enemy, or enrolling slaves for rebellion. This can be seen as a counter-measure to curb the enemy spiriting away agricultural workers as noted previously.

In the early morning hours of Monday, April 18th enemy skirmishers formed on their southwest line as Hoke's artillery began firing "hissing, rushing and screeching" shells" which crashed into the fortress's guardhouses and barracks.[32] Soon after, Kemper's brigade ar-

---

29 Ibid, p178
30 Wright, p200
31 Newsome, p212
32 Mahood, p168

rayed itself in directly front of Fort Grey in preparation for an assault and Ransom's Brigade shifted eastward in front of Fort Williams. To cover the assault of Fort Wessells, Hoke directed an earthen redoubt erected by the 56th North Carolina near the Washington Road from which it could shell the fort with its 32-pounder. While it was being constructed the enemy in Fort Wessells soon began shelling this new battery, assisted by Fort Williams, but Hoke's guns nearly silenced the former. The rest of the day passed with intermittent shelling from both sides while Hoke's cavalry patrolled the Columbia Road to the east, monitoring any enemy movements there. The lack of strong fortifications and troops on this flank likely led Hoke to consider an assault there. To the west, Dearing's cavalry performed a reconnaissance in force of Fort Grey on the Roanoke which was two miles upstream from town, protected by the enemy gunboats. Dearing's artillery quickly crippled one craft and sent it drifting toward Plymouth's wharf where it sank.[33] As his sharpshooters targeted enemy cannoneers in the fort, Col. Dearing was anxiously looking upriver for signs of the *Albemarle*.

Before sundown General Hoke moved Ransom's brigade forward against the long breastworks flanking the Washington Road with Fort Williams near the center.[34] As sharpshooters and flying artillery advanced while firing rapidly, driving enemy skirmishers behind their breastworks, General Ransom rode conspicuously on his horse in the thick of fighting urging them onward. Hoke's intent was to have this assault draw the enemy's artillery fire to his right, or eastward side, while his own brigade under Col. Mercer overwhelmed Fort Wessells to the west of town.

A *Richmond Examiner* correspondent wrote the following account of Ransom's advance toward Fort Williams under artillery fire and a full moon: "*The enemy had now commenced a furious shelling when our artillery batteries advanced at a dashing gallop … the solid line of infantry pressing forward at a double quick to support our artillery. As they would get the range the batteries would limber up, dash forward and open a murderous fire upon the enemy. Again and again, they advance until within 800 yards of Fort Williams, the infantry pressing closely up, but reserving their fire.*" The same writer added: "*The sight was magnificent — the screaming, hissing shell, meeting and passing*

---

33 Graham, p178
34 Ibid, p179

each other through the sulphurous air, appeared as blazing comets with their burning fuses and would burst with frightful noise, scattering their fragments as thick as hail." [35]

Major Graham described the murderous barrage from Fort Williams being endured by Ransom's men coming "from more than twenty pieces of artillery and two gunboats, firing every grade of shell from the 200-pounder to the 12-pound Napoleon." After every infantry advance toward the enemy breastworks, Ransom's men quickly dropped to the ground "to avoid as far as possible the heavy shower of grape with which they are greeted." While Ransom's men drew the enemy's concentrated fire, Hoke's brigade under Col. Mercer charged the now-isolated Fort Wessells from Welch's Creek swamp as their artillery pounded the earthen redoubt surrounded by a stockade, deep moat and high parapet. This fort was stubbornly defended by about 45 of the enemy, including a few officers, firing a light 32-pounder and 6-pounder field piece. The assaulting force had to dodge the improvised "Hanes grenades" lobbed at them by those within. These were 2-inch diameter hollow iron spheres filled with gunpowder set off by a percussion cap upon impact, or a fuse. The men of the 6th North Carolina quickly surrounded the redoubt, into which they poured a deadly fire while poorly-directed shells from their own gunboats exploded within. Mercer's artillery was then brought to within 200 yards for virtual point-blank firing as sharpshooters targeted the defenders.[36]

Cut off from the main fortress, Fort Wessells was surrendered at 11PM that evening with its 52 survivors accepted by Col. Dearing as

---

35 Graham, p179. Writer described a "R", April 24, 1864
36 Iobst, p194

Col. Mercer had been killed leading the assault; his losses totaled 60 men killed and wounded. Hoke lost a courageous officer, a man who was the West Point classmate of Generals J.E.B. Stuart, John B. Hood, GWC Lee and William Dorsey Pender. Among the enemy dead at Fort Wessells was the redoubt's commander, who had led a stubborn defense of the earthen work.[37] General Ransom's assault athwart Washington Road was winding down by 10PM as his artillery ammunition became exhausted. He then ordered the guns withdrawn while leaving the infantry in place until 1AM, at which time they withdrew to their earlier position[38] General Ransom's diversionary assault had successfully focused the enemy's artillery away from those overwhelming Fort Wessells, leaving it now in Hoke's possession.

As a precautionary move while the previous attacks were in progress, Hoke sent the 24th and 56th North Carolina to the Columbia Road on his far right to close off any possibility of an enemy escape to the east. Hoke was satisfied that his left flank was now secure and Fortress Plymouth surrounded on three sides — hopefully with an ironclad soon behind it.[39] Though now isolated and but a minor threat to Hoke's main force, Fort Grey had fought off all assaults but Hoke rightly anticipated the *Albemarle's* Brooke naval-rifles would soon neutralize it.

With his namesake fort capitulating late Monday night, the enemy commander paced the floor uneasily while pondering his chances of survival amid such a furious attack leaving him now nearly isolated. Already a gunboat had been sunk by Hoke's artillery, Fort Grey was isolated and Fort Wessells lost. His superiors refused him any reinforcements and if the ironclad appeared it would decimate him from behind. Apprised of the ram nearing Plymouth late Monday night, the enemy naval commander had lashed his gunboat to another to form a river blockade, and assured his superiors that he would "whip the ram" if it did not stay under the cover of Hoke's new river battery near Fort Grey. He was also confident that his earlier delivery to the fort of 100 more projectiles for its 100-pounder rifle would stop the ram. To the enemy's chagrin, General Hoke received a welcome ally with the recent spring freshet whose rains provided the *Albemarle* with 10 feet clearance above enemy obstructions — sufficient for the ironclad

---

37 Graham, p180
38 Barrett, pp191-192
39 Barrett, p193-194

to safely glide above.⁴⁰ It was still making way for Plymouth as its 376 tons of weight and small powerplant allowed only five knots at top speed. The armed steamer CSS *Cotton Plant* followed close behind the slow ironclad with troops aboard, including sharpshooters.

In the early morning hours of Tuesday, April 19th, the ram was silently passing Fort Grey about 3:30AM when the 100-pounder crew fired a few projectiles at the dark shape passing them. A few hits bounced off the *Albemarle* like pebbles against an empty barrel.⁴¹ With its ports closed and no lights visible, the ram continued another mile and neared Battery Worth at the town's western limit. Strangely it drew no fire from this battery, which was established for the purpose of destroying the ram. Shortly afterward the ironclad was fully astride the town in the early light of morning, its gunports were opened and all cleared for action. To his immediate front Commander Cooke spotted two enemy steamers, the first of which he rammed at full speed and which caused it to sink rapidly. The second enemy gunboat fired ineffectively at the ram while taking on survivors of the sinking craft. By quarter-past 5AM the river battle was over with the lead enemy ship laying on the river bottom and its cohort fleeing downriver amid shots from the *Albemarle's* cannon.⁴² Throughout the day and into the evening the ram kept up a steady barrage from its Brooke guns on Battery Worth as the *Cotton Plant's* sharpshooters behind the ram targeted any visible enemy defenders. Halting and dropping anchor at the end of Jefferson Street, the *Albemarle* had a clearer view of Fort Williams on the west side of town and began "methodically shooting it to pieces" from the rear.⁴³

Satisfied that another direct attack of Ransom's men on the enemy's southern front would be too costly, Hoke began considering assaulting the flanks. The enemy left his eastern approach less-protected because of what they considered "an impassable swamp" and their faith in the artillery of the gunboats. With the *Albemarle* canceling the latter, it became clear to Hoke that an aggressive move on the weaker eastern flank would very likely produce success.

---

40 Elliot, p170
41 Ibid, p175
42 Ibid, p183
43 Campbell, p155

"Never interrupt your enemy while he is making a mistake."
— *Napoleon*

Ransom's men were marched eastward with a dense woodland screening the movement from enemy view and by sunset were at Conaby Creek, about a mile distant from town where the Columbia Road crosses. Skirmishers led by "Fighting Quartermaster" Capt. Cicero Durham of Cleveland County found the bridge destroyed and the enemy strongly positioned on the far side, but several pieces of artillery and sharpshooters covered a brave member of the 24th NC Regiment who swam across. He quickly returned with a skiff to load several more men who cross to the enemy's side.

Soon bridge pontoons arrived, a bridge constructed by Hoke's engineers in a mere quarter-hour allowed Ransom's men to cross and form a line nearly a mile in front of the enemy's two forts on that flank. With this movement completed by midnight and light breastworks established, they laid down on their arms to sleep. One soldier described mid-April's night air as "sharp and piercing" but "we need rest for the morrow and the terrible work ahead."[44]

Unaware of their fortress being encircled, the enemy within was reportedly in good spirits knowing Ransom "could not successfully take their works in front, but all knew it was only a question of time before they were completely surrounded." A Connecticut lieutenant wrote with trepidation that it was clear that "we must succumb sooner

---

44 Graham, p183

or later."⁴⁵ And with the *Albemarle* broadsiding the fortress at will after sinking and driving off their naval protection, the gloom of defeat affected all within.⁴⁶

Ransom's men were aroused at first light on Wednesday, April 20th and awaited the rocket signal to commence their attack on the enemy's eastern flank. To the town's west, Hoke's massed artillery opened fire as his and Kemper's brigade assembled directly in front of Fortress Plymouth threatening another assault. Additionally, the *Albemarle* unleashed a devastating enfilading fire along the former town's river front and behind the enemy's breastworks flanking Fort Williams and facing Hoke's men.

> "He will win whose army is animated by the same spirit throughout the ranks"
>
> — *Sun Tzu*

With the rocket signal received, Ransom's advance began with the order to "fix bayonets" and "Forward march" was heard throughout the brigade. The 56th North Carolina was on the right and flanked by sharpshooters, with the 25th, 35th, 8th and 24th Regiments to the left. They encountered the enemy's livestock pen near the river and drove the cattle forward as a living wall for a brief time, but soon after a 56th North Carolina soldier wrote: "they turned about dashed through our line and sought safety in flight."⁴⁷

At this time Hoke ordered his artillery to fire upon Fort Williams' breastworks to indicate preparation for attack, with his Virginians replacing Ransom's to the south of town shouting their "Rebel yells" which heralded a full-scale assault. This will draw fire away from Ransom's Brigade, freeze the enemy in position and preclude reinforcements being sent to the enemy's eastern flank.⁴⁸

Ransom's men advanced across very difficult terrain under fire, with one soldier writing that, after the cattle drove incident, "the next obstacle was a swamp, in places waist-deep, through which the regiment floundered as best it could, impeded by the mire and cypress tree "knees" with which it abounded. The 56th North Carolina was the first

---

45 Blakeslee, p57
46 Mahood, p180
47 Clark, ed. Vol III, p340
48 Ibid, Vol V, p184

through and immediately reformed under oblique enemy fire from the left, charged up a slight hill while routing the enemy sheltered behind a fence, here at the outer line of the town. This and adjacent houses blocked further advance in regimental line of battle."[49] This attack was supported by four artillery batteries under Col. James Read Branch, who galloped forward to open fire upon the forts and town on both sides of the Second Street, the Columbia Road.

Another North Carolina soldier offered this vivid account of this phase of the battle:

"*Our brigade, under General Ransom, crossed Conaby Creek on a pontoon bridge about midnight. When we had gotten fully over the brigade was deployed into a line, arranged just as Ransom wanted it to be, then came the order to us 'boys' the most pleasant of all commands: 'Stack arms; lie down and rest until daybreak.' Just before falling asleep next to Corporal James Council, he said to me: 'Lt. Wright … before tomorrow night I shall be sleeping my eternal sleep.' I said, 'Jimmy, don't talk that way. Let us go to sleep.'"*

On the morning of April 20, 1864, Ransom's Brigade took part in one of the grandest charges, heroic from start to finish, that were made in any battle during the war. The charge commenced at early sunrise when the signal was sent up by the *Albemarle*, and by 4PM the town of Plymouth was ours," along with the remnant of the enemy garrison. "*In this charge, for over a quarter of a mile on an open field in front of a six-gun enemy battery, raked with grape and cannister, we made good and captured the fort.*"

True to his prediction of the night before, Corporal Council was lying in that sleep that knows no waking, together with fifty gallant men of the Thirty-fifth Regiment of North Carolina Troops.

Major Simon B. Taylor of Lenoir County was severely wounded in his right knee while being the first of our men to mount the fort's parapet and receive the white surrender flag of the boys in blue. He waved it high so it might be seen by the gallant boys in gray who had made the charge, not surpassed by any that was made in the most heroic of wars." [50]

The 24th North Carolina pushed forward on the Columbia Road (Second Street) with the 25th and 56th Regiments alongside on the river side; the 35th and 8th Regiments to the left near Third Street. The

---

49 Ibid, Vol III, p340
50 Wright, *Confederate Veteran*, May 1916, p200.

latter kept to the left of Second Street as an enemy battery on the other side of town kept up a rapid fire through town.

An eyewitness account by a soldier of Ransom's 8th North Carolina described that after their artillery bombardment of the enemy forts on the eastern flank, "our men rushed forward with the Rebel yell while the enemy in the Conaby Redoubt poured a destructive fire into the ranks of our regiment." This redoubt was just south of Charles Latham's house and almost 300 yards from Fort Compher, which the 35th Regiment had captured. It is reported that civilians trapped within in the fortress huddled in Latham's basement while the battle raged outside.

"Victory belongs to the most persevering."

— *Napoleon*

As the regiment rushed up to the fort's stockade "the enemy pulled their guns out of the loop holes our men inserted theirs and fired at those within ... such deadly work could not last long." As the 8th Regiment poured around the fort's rear and its gate burst open, the fort immediately surrendered. "Three cheers for North Carolina" were given by the regiment to announce their triumph. Apparently thrilled with their victory, the 8th North Carolina continued toward Fort Williams where it found a protective ditch an uncrossable obstacle, and retreated amid a "fearful volley" of enemy fire which unnecessarily killed and wounded many of the men."[51] Wounded in the 8th Regiment's assault was color bearer Joseph Spence, a Pasquotank farmer who initially volunteered in the "State Guards of Pasquotank."[52]

The 8th North Carolina lost about a third of their number killed and wounded in the attack, one being color-bearer Perkins who was carried to the rear mortally-wounded. As he lay dying in a barn utilized as a makeshift hospital, he asked a fellow soldier what his comrades thought of his conduct that day. On being told this they all praised his gallantry and fearlessness, he said: "If that is so, if it were not for my sister alone at home, I would not mind dying."[53]

Major John W. Graham of the 56th North Carolina wrote: "After briefly halting to dress their lines, all pushed forward carefully, clearing the enemy from every street, yard and house, from the windows of which and from behind fences they poured an incessant fire." Major

---

51 Clark, ed. Vol V, pp186-187
52 Mast, p234
53 Clark, ed, Vol I, p164

Graham of the 56th Regiment added, "*But nothing could check our progress and within an hour they were driven into Fort Williams or into the entrenched camp at the west of the town.*"[54]

The 56th North Carolina swung left and formed a line of battle near the Plymouth jail, charging forward while flushing enemy soldiers out of underground holes and taking them prisoner. This regiment's arrival and intense musket firing demoralized the remaining enemy troops as they threw down their arms, waved white flags and surrendered to Capt. Joseph G. Lockhart.[55] During this time Capt. Graham had moved his men behind Fort Williams where he captured some 200 enemy soldiers on its western flank.[56]

"One long, wild, prolonged shout, went up from our army, and never was a flag of truce more eagerly and heartily greeted during the war."
— *43rd North Carolina Regiment Soldier*[57]

The former town of Plymouth was now back in North Carolina hands except for Fort Williams, within which the enemy commander had barricaded himself with a small remnant of his troops. Hoke's initial demand for surrender of this fort was refused which left him no option but to further bombard the fort. While showing no desire to continue the carnage, Hoke offered a personal interview with the enemy general, which was accepted, and during which he demanded unconditional surrender given the "untenable position and impossibility of relief," but was again refused. Hoke sadly departed the interview

---

54 Graham, p184-185
55 Ibid, p185
56 Iobst, p196
57 *Weekly Ansonian*, July 19, 1876

and ordered all artillery brought forward from the three land sides, along with the 6.4-inch Brooke guns of the *Albemarle*.

Within an hour Hoke's massed artillery began with devastating effect. After release from captivity, the enemy commander wrote a personal account of the living hell inside his fort:

"*This terrible fire had to be endured without reply as no man could live at the guns. The breast-height [stockade] was struck by solid-shot on every side, fragments of shells sought almost every interior angle of the work, the whole extent of the parapet was swept by musketry, and men were killed and wounded even on the banquette [protected interior] slope. ...*" [58]

At 10AM, Tuesday, April 20th, Wessells ordered the white flag of surrender hoisted. It was not until late Wednesday morning that a boat from Fort Grey, still in enemy hands, landed at the town wharf to surrender to General Hoke.[59] The remainder of Tuesday and all of Wednesday was spent collecting prisoners and weapons, securing the windfall of valuable supplies, cannon and ammunition, plus especially difficult to obtain medicines from the enemy infirmary. Hoke then sent the following message to his immediate superior officer:

"*April 22, 1864*
To: Lt.-General Braxton Bragg.
I have stormed and captured this place, capturing 1 brigadier, 1600 men, stores and 25 pieces of artillery.
R.F. Hoke. Brig.-General."

The following day President Davis telegraphed Hoke expressing his deep gratitude for this much-needed victory over the enemy. He wrote:

"Accept my thanks and congratulations for the brilliant success which has attended your attack and liberation of Plymouth. You are promoted to major-general from that date."

More accolades and official thanks were forthcoming for General Hoke and Commander Cooke from the Confederate States Congress and North Carolina's General Assembly. General Lee expressed approval of Hoke's promotion though "sorry to lose him to North Carolina operations."[60]

---

58 Ibid, p197
59 Morgan, p186
60 Barefoot, p150

In the aftermath of their hard-fought battle, Hoke praised his men for their valor and accomplishment at Plymouth, allowing them "to help themselves to [whatever enemy supplies] might please their fancy except the horses and wagons." The garrison flag of the defeated enemy commander was the only prize taken by Hoke.

The victory netted Hoke "2,500 prisoners along with 10,000 pounds of bacon, 1,000 barrels of flour, plus vast amounts of other stores." This included 500 horses, livestock, 28 pieces of artillery, 5,000 stands of small arms, clothing, socks, boots; the *Albemarle's* captain heartily welcomed the 200 tons of anthracite coal for his bunkers. This coal would prove invaluable in the later career of the *Albemarle* as it faced enemy squadrons in the Sound.[61]

Among Hoke's prisoners were found 25 deserters from North Carolina regiments gone over to the enemy, in blue uniform and under arms. They were carried to Kinston where a court martial provided a fair trial, convicted them of high treason, and all "duly executed by our brigade." In the early postwar the Northern secretary of war demanded that Hoke be held responsible for executing these so-called "US soldiers." But they were in fact North Carolina soldiers who deserted prior to becoming federal soldiers and committing treason. Hoke himself traveled to Washington to call upon Grant to end these proceedings. Grant agreed with Hoke.[62]

Williamston resident D. W. Bagley traveled to Plymouth just after the battle and identified the body of George Bunch among the slain soldiers in blue. Bunch was a fifteen-year-old Martin County farmer who enlisted in Company A of the 17th North Carolina in March 1863, but deserted to the enemy five months later.[63]

Both of Wessells superiors, Generals Peck and Butler, expressed surprise at his capitulation. Butler, who earlier dismissed concerns about the ironclad's existence, believed that with 2,500 men, numerous cannon behind strong earthen fortifications, and sixty days of rations, Wessells should have held out through a long siege.[64]

"For the courageous, nothing is unattainable"

— Alexander the Great

---

61 Campbell, p167
62 Clark, pp283-285
63 Bagley Diary, 11.9.1863; See McCallum, p185
64 Mahood, p184

11
Aftermath: Carnage & Ruination

"Where the battle rages, there the loyalty of the soldier is proven."
— *Martin Luther*

Several important factors enabled General Hoke's extraordinary victory over the enemy's Plymouth fortress, the foremost being his successful coordination between naval and land forces. Secondly, the enemy's higher-command level overconfidence — hubris — which led to their discounting of the abilities of their adversaries to construct a formidable warship without any necessary manufacturing facilities and materiel. This along with the ironclad's timely appearance at Plymouth was a miracle in itself. And on land, Hoke's veterans were battle-hardened from the Virginia theater where they had routinely fought and defeated numbers far greater than their own. Considering the enemy garrison numbered about 2,500 men, Hoke had barely 3-1 odds for success in attacking a strongly entrenched enemy with a very considerable artillery component. Though the initial land assault was not a complete surprise to the enemy within, the supreme effort and heroism of Hoke's North Carolinians — as well as that of the Virginians and Georgians with them — prevailed despite their significant casualties.

The bulk of the defenders were relatively untested men, backed by reserves of "buffaloes" and "contraband" conscripts fearing capture and/or execution for treason. Many of the white garrison soldiers were very recent "veteran volunteers" who received generous bounties for reenlisting with little inclination to die in battle. Some were awaiting their one-month furlough home to see family, others had just returned from their furlough home and many had pockets full of bounty money. This may reveal the meaning behind the vanquished enemy general requesting of General Hoke that his men "not be robbed."

Hoke's North Carolinians very likely viewed those behind the fortress's breastworks as those who had burned, looted and devastated homes, farms and towns — turning entire families into homeless refugees. Some no doubt viewed the enemy soldiers as the very face of the radicalism they believed was the cause of the war.[1] This immutable factor in Hoke's favor was a powerful motivation and desire to achieve victory at any cost. While within their earthen fortress the enemy soldiers performed as instructed, but as Hoke's motivated veterans methodically overwhelmed enemy defenses while the ironclad bombarded them from behind, resistance predictably collapsed. When the ironclad appeared and summarily sunk their gunboats, most became aware of the coming result.

Historian Newsome wrote that in his Plymouth campaign General Hoke "exhibited competence, clear thinking and resolve," and "by all accounts he planned matters thoroughly and acted decisively." Hoke had his plan but allowed flexibility, taking advantage of any developing opportunities and, most of all, trusted his most capable officers to carry out his directives. Rather "Stonewall-like" he stressed secrecy regarding his movements, favored surprise flank attacks and kept his rank and file unaware of the intended target. The latter greatly admired Hoke's leadership. This is underscored by Newsome's comment that "one strains to find a critical word from his men about his performance."[2]

There are of course a number of unknowns and luck involved in all things human and Hoke's approach and assault from the predictable direction should have been defeated. Wessells superiors felt confident he had sufficient men, artillery and gunboats to successfully defend his fortress. One of Wessells surgeons later wrote that Wessells had "been laboring under the mistaken impression" that North Carolina troops were concentrating at Edenton for a march to their real target, Little Washington. In addition, the surgeon opined that Wessels had

---

1 Trotter, p131
2 Newsome, p317

been grievously misled by the "secrecy and celerity of Hoke's three brigades."[3]

One might also conclude that any faulty intelligence Wessells received from his scouts and superiors were factors working against him. They and his naval arm assured him that the ironclad could be easily neutralized by the river obstructions, large caliber guns and gunboats. Again, the presence of the *Albemarle* at a pivotal point of the battle was enabled by chance as a dry spring would not have raised the river level well-above the obstructions, allowing the ram to pass. That the typical spring rains became the *Albemarle*'s ally was not necessarily due to luck, but very likely Hoke's knowledge of North Carolina's coastal weather patterns at that time of year. Given the local informants and allies, Wessells should have been aware of the river's rise and the naval commander as well, though the latter was vocally spoiling for a fight.

After the enemy's capitulation Hoke assigned a small garrison to Plymouth while his three brigades swung southward on April 25th to liberate Washington. This small force was relieved on April 30th by Lt. Col. George Wortham's 50th North Carolina who had marched from Virginia to serve as a more permanent garrison and to discourage the enemy's return. Part of this regiment would remain at Plymouth with the rest assigned to garrison Little Washington under Lt. Col. John C. Van Hook of Person County.

> "Dulce et decorum est pro patria mori
> It is sweet and fitting to die for one's country"
>
> — *Horace*

---

3 Mahood, p167

The liberation of Plymouth's fortified remains by Hoke's command was accomplished at significant human cost. His losses of men killed and wounded during the three-day engagement are uncertain, but best estimates were about 160 men killed and some 550 wounded. More than 50 percent of the latter number — 476 — were North Carolinians of General Ransom's Brigade who overwhelmed the enemy's right flank and swarmed into the middle of the enemy's works.

The enemy commander reported his loss as 2,834 men — mostly captives but including about 150 men killed, seriously wounded and missing, which may include colored men in the USCT and "buffaloes."[4] The colored and white North Carolinians in enemy service were aware of the penalty for treason and desertion so most fled to the swamps upon the arrival of Hoke's force. Some of these were afterward picked up in boats on the river and sound but undoubtedly many had fled to the safety of occupied New Bern.

Hoke's captives were assembled and marched about a mile distant where they were encamped with guards and four days rations drawn from their own quartermaster stores. Though complaints were heard about their small allowance of food for four days, Hoke's veterans considered it a daily feast given their usual meager subsistence.[5] In the early afternoon April 21st, the prisoners were marched to Tarboro where they boarded trains for the long ride into captivity at Andersonville in southwest Georgia. Wessells and other officers were sent to Richmond's Libby Prison to be held for exchange for Southern officers held by the enemy.[6]

With the enemy captives gone Hoke's provost marshal began sorting through property-damage and stolen property claims filed by residents who fled when the enemy returned and feared persecution for their political beliefs. The sorting became difficult as it was clouded by Wessells provost marshal who transferred land ownership to "loyal" citizens who submitted to an oath of allegiance to Lincoln's government. One property claim filed was that of local planter Charles Pettigrew, whose home was thoroughly looted of housewares and furniture by those professing "Unionism" in order to curry favor during the occupation.[7]

---

4 OR, I, XXXIII, 301
5 Mahood, p187
6 Barefoot, p152
7 J. W. Edmondston to Miss Bettie, Nov 5, 1864. Wright-Herring Papers, SHC

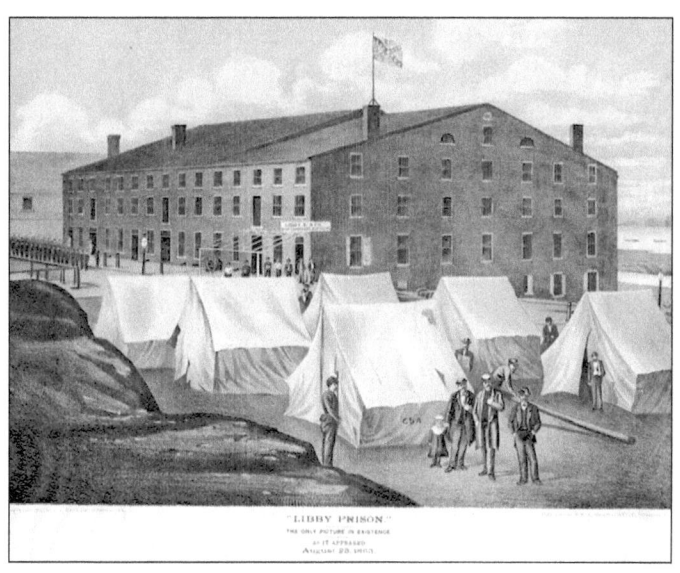

"LIBBY PRISON"

An echo from Revolutionary times was an enemy chaplain brought to Hoke who complained of being denied officer's privileges to retain his alleged personal library held in two wooden boxes. Noticing a break in the top of one box and spotting the name "Josiah Collins" of nearby Somerset Plantation on a bookplate, Hoke severely dressed him down for theft and stripped him of all privileges for looting civilian property.[8] It was during the Revolution that North Carolina's signer of the Declaration of Independence, William Hooper, found his books despoiled by invading British troops. He wrote: "My library … is shamefully injured and above 100 books taken away."[9] The enemy chaplain's thievery was a clear breach of the enemy's own Lieber Code, article 36 which prohibits the private appropriation of property; Article 46 also forbids officers from using their position and power in a hostile country for personal profit or gain, with the punishment for officers being cashiering.[10]

Those returning home were happy to find their colored farm hands greeting them with great affection and anxious for normal times to return. At Pettigrew plantation in particular, the workers familiar with cradle to grave health care, their own produce gardens and clothing allowances had refused to plant cash crops as lessees for "Unionist" farmers who had assumed control of "secessionist" proper-

---

8 Barefoot, p153
9 Colbourne, p16
10 Lieber, pp41

ties. These workers reported mistreatment from both enemy soldiers and the "Unionist" farmers controlling lands they had no title to.[11]

"Cowards die many times before their deaths; the valiant never taste death but once."

— *Julius Caesar*

Little Washington, the enemy-occupied town some 35 miles to the south was next targeted for liberation by now-Major-General Hoke. Upon news of his approach the enemy began evacuating the town on April 26th as it was not considered a strategic position worth holding. Its garrison consisted of some 500 New England and Pennsylvania troops along with "buffaloes" and colored troops commanded by Harvard law-graduate Brig. General Edward Harland of Connecticut. For three days before boarding transports to New Bern, Harland's troops ran riot while vandalizing and setting fire to homes and businesses. At least half of Little Washington — founded in 1776 and named for American patriot George Washington — was destroyed with many remaining inhabitants left homeless and destitute.[12] The *New York Times* of April 29, 1864 reported the movement while applauding Harland for "the evacuation with skill and deliberation becoming a brave and humane soldier."

This unnecessary atrocity committed by Harland's troops was roundly condemned by his district commander, Major-General Innis Palmer who wrote: "It is well-known that [Harland's] vandals did not even respect charitable institutions, but bursting open doors of the Masonic Order and Odd Fellows' lodge, pillaged them both and hawked about the streets the regalia and jewels. And this too, by Unit-

---

11 Charels Pettigrew to Caroline Pettigrew, April 24, 1864. Pettigrew Papers, SHC
12 See Newsome, pp285-287 for details of Little Washington's fate.

ed States troops! It is well-known that both public and private stores were entered and plundered, and that devastation and destruction ruled the hour." One other enemy officer saddened by the spectacle wrote: "… a portion of [our troops] have within a few days been guilty of an outrage against humanity, which brings the blush of shame to the cheek of every true man and soldier."[13] However, politicians in Washington were quick to criticize Palmer's low regard for their constituents, despite the obvious violations of Lieber's Code regarding civilians.

When General Hoke entered the smoking ruins of Little Washington he found "a ruined city … a sad scene — mostly chimneys and heaps of ashes to mark the place where fine homes once stood … the beautiful trees which shaded sidewalks were burnt, some almost to coal." Hoke left the 6th North Carolina to defend what remained of the town and assist its homeless citizens.

Prior to the 50th North Carolina marching to Washington County on April 30th, small detachments were assigned the job of collecting and bringing out provisions from eastern counties from New Bern to the Virginia line. While the 50th was enroute near the Albemarle & Chesapeake Canal locks, it was decided that a passing boat could be captured with the assistance of the lock-keeper. The boat selected was the US government mail boat plying between Norfolk and New Bern which was seized for valuables and then released except for the very dejected General Henry Wessells. He had been paroled by General Hoke after the former's defeat and was enroute to being exchanged for a Southern officer. Wessels strongly protested his arrest and detention, but was soon carried back to "the scene of his recent misfortune and humiliation."[14] Wessells was released once again on parole for exchange at Richmond.

To add further misery to Little Washington's residents, on May 2nd a Northern gunboat appeared and lobbed a shell into the town. Though not causing injury, it did succeed in terrifying the inhabitants trying to rebuild their lives and town.[15] Nonetheless, Hoke's liberation of both Plymouth and Washington enabled the crops, meats and grains of the region to make their way to General Lee's Army of Northern Virginia.

---

13 OR, 33, I, 310
14 Carolana.com, 50th, Major Wortham report.
15 Iobst, p199

The CSS *Albemarle's* long-awaited foray into the Albemarle Sound came nearly a month after the 50th NC Regiment's arrival as Plymouth's new garrison. On May 5th the *Albemarle* and CSS *Bombshell*, the latter a captured steamer, were escorting a transport down the Roanoke to the Albemarle Sound when they encountered eight enemy gunboats. Despite being outgunned by a total of 60 cannon, the *Albemarle* immediately steamed toward them while firing two point-blank shells into an enemy warship's boilers which disabled it, while some 500 enemy shells bounced harmlessly off her armor. After this engagement the smokestack-riddled *Albemarle* steamed back to the Plymouth wharf.[16]

The enemy spent the month of June imagining ways in which torpedoes could be secreted up to Plymouth, or to entice the ironclad out into the open water of the Sound once again to be attacked. But on June 17, Cooke, who was experiencing medical issues was replaced with the famed commander of CSS *Florida*, Commander John Newland Maffitt, whose very name "caused deep concern among those commanding the Union fleet in Albemarle Sound." The enemy was already painfully aware of Maffitt being a "wily, aggressive blockade runner" and redoubled their efforts to destroy the ironclad before it left the river.[17] Catherine Edmondston expressed pity for Maffitt's assignment to a river rather than sailing the open sea, writing of "how he will chafe cooped up in this narrow, crooked river after roaming at will the broad bosom of the sea in search of Yankee commerce."[18] But

---

16 Clark, p161
17 Elliot, p231
18 Edmondston, p578

despite Secretary Mallory's directive to Maffitt to destroy the enemy fleet in the Sound, Captain Cooke and others in higher authority considered *Albemarle's* presence at Plymouth to be a strong deterrent to enemy control of the region; Capt. Cooke himself feared *Albemarle's* capture or destruction if it ventured into the teeth of a waiting enemy fleet. Brig-General Laurence Baker, who commanded that district, wrote the Secretary of War in early July concerning Plymouth's small garrison of reserve troops and their very precarious position "if the ironclad came to harm." Baker lastly urged Maffitt to refrain from any engagements with the enemy unless certain of success.[19]

In an early July setback, the enemy learned that their five men setting torpedoes in the lower Roanoke had been captured. This likely led to their explosive devices being found and removed. To this unwelcome news, the enemy's spies returning from Halifax reported that two new ironclads and a floating battery were nearing completion there and would soon join *Albemarle*. The very thought of three formidable ironclads supported by a floating battery — all led by the audacious Commander John Newland Maffitt — caused the enemy navy great anxiety. Maffitt's navy barred their overland route to the Weldon's important railroad bridge and would threaten their dominance of the Sound.[20] Another voicing great concern was the enemy commander at occupied-New Bern who wrote his superiors on July 19th that should the *Albemarle* and company enter the Sounds "we have no naval force to cope with them … Captain Maffitt now commands the ram *Albemarle* and we all know that he is not a man to sit down at Plymouth … if he can get a fleet of these rams before we receive any iron vessels we must expect disaster."[21]

John Newland Maffitt

Maffitt was greatly respected by Northern naval officers with whom he had served earlier and well-known for his daring escapades few could emulate. As a prewar lieutenant he commanded the USS *Crusader* as part of the US Navy's anti-slavery squadron and captured

---

19 Elliot, p232
20 Ibid, p233
21 OR, I, XL, p3, 343

the slavers *Echo* in 1858, and *Bogota* in 1860 — both off Cuba, both with hundreds African slaves aboard, and both of New York registry. He afterward escorted them to Key West for adjudication and repatriation of the Africans to their homeland. Of his prewar efforts against the slave trade the *Wilmington* [North Carolina] *Daily Journal* of September 25, 1863 wrote:

> *"It is a curious fact for those who maintain that the civil war in America is founded upon the slave question, that Maffitt should be the very man who has distinguished himself actively against the slave trade."*

An enemy gunboat picket was stationed at the mouth of the Roanoke River should *Albemarle* decide to venture out, though a quiet, undetected night movement was possible such as the ironclad had performed the previous April at Plymouth. At 4AM on August 6th the ram steamed down to the Sound and halted while the wary pickets stood out slowly. The appearance was only temporary as by this time Navy Secretary Mallory had relented on his orders for Maffitt to engage the enemy in Albemarle Sound and well-understood General Baker's strategic reasoning. But Maffitt's adventurist nature soon emerged as he ordered his crew on a raid at the end of the month to capture the enemy mail boat *Fawn* while she made her routine trek from Norfolk to Roanoke with mail and paymaster funds. The expedition of twenty *Albemarle* crewmen in a small boat took backwaters to the Pamlico River and Sound, while intercepting and burning enemy sailing craft along the way. After a brisk fight to overpower the *Fawn* and with no casualties, the raiders held 29 prisoners including an enemy colonel, two majors, plus several soldiers, US government employees and civilians. As the raiders departed with their prisoners, the *Fawn* was left blocking the waterway as a blazing wreck. After reaching Plymouth the victorious raiders were saddened to learn that their commander, Maffitt, had received orders for Wilmington to command the blockade runner *Owl*.[22]

---

22 ORN, I, X, 736. See also Elliot, p243

Owl

On September 10, 1864 Lt. A. F. Warley CSN assumed command of the *Albemarle* at Plymouth and charged with thwarting enemy encroachments upriver. On October 22nd the 50th North Carolina was ordered to Tarboro and relieved by seven companies of the 67th North Carolina under Col. John N. Whitford. This regiment's men were Local Defense Troops under the Governor's authority and Confederate officers.

Plymouth's new garrison was aware of the enemy torpedo boat's presence near the mouth of the Roanoke and appropriately doubled the watch. An early evening "grand bacchanalian feast and dance" may account for sleepy sentries though the barking of a dog alerted them to the approaching enemy boats. Immediately the front-facing Brooke gun was loaded with grapeshot and depressed to fire. But at the same time came the enemy torpedo blast beneath the *Albemarle*.[23] The ironclad settled on the bottom in minutes while leaving its armored casemate with cannons above water. The enemy torpedo boat had been hit and sunk, its crew swimming to shore to escape. Unknown to the enemy, the *Albemarle* was already a defenseless hulk as Lt. Warley had wisely removed the two double-banded 6.4-inch Brooke guns from the *Albemarle* for use onshore in defense of Plymouth.[24] Its two naval guns joined the formidable array of cannon captured in Hoke's April assault.

In hindsight, Lt. Joseph Ellington of Company C, 50th North Carolina later wrote that the attack on the *Albemarle* "might easily have been prevented if our pickets had been as watchful as they should

---

23 Elliot, p256
24 Wiki, accessed 12.15.23

have been." He reported this same enemy officer already made several attempts during his regiment's garrison duty, but had failed each time with several of his men killed or captured. Also, the reason for the veteran 50th North Carolina's departure was an urgent appeal from General Lee to have them return to Virginia while the State replaced them at Plymouth and Washington with the less-experienced North Carolina Reserves. In the opinion of Lt. Ellington, this caused the loss of Plymouth once again to the enemy, writing that *"but for this change it is almost certain that the town would not have fallen at the time and under the circumstances it did, thus cutting off the chief source of supplies for our army in Virginia."*[25] Diarist Edmondston speaks disparagingly of those replacing the 50th North Carolina on October 31st to reinforce what remained of the garrison there "[which] must be weak indeed if these Home Guards now here are needed, undrilled, feeble and undisciplined as they are."[26]

On November 2nd Capt. Cooke sadly wrote Mr. Edmondston that Plymouth was once again ruled by the Yankees "with all our artillery captured and all guns and horses of the Montgomery Blues captured except for two guns and a few horses." This was the result of the enemy moving above Plymouth on the Middle River to avoid the town's batteries. As they approached Fort Williams from above town a furious cannon duel ensued with one of their ships suffering serious damage before an enemy shell ignited the fort's powder magazine. In this fight the defenders lost thirty-seven men captured along with twenty-two artillery pieces, and an abundance of ordnance stores — likely those captured during the town's second liberation the previous April. With the enemy now possessing the sunken remains of the *Albemarle* he now expected the enemy to advance upriver. Cooke then ordered the three regiments and remaining artillery taken from Plymouth to fall back upon Fort Branch. To strengthen the latter, he ordered all guns at Halifax brought downriver to the fort to oppose any enemy thrust.[27] Though not an official report of the action, Edmondston's diary entry asserts that the 67th Regiment's officers at Plymouth were responsible for posting "drunken, worthless pickets who let spar torpedo boats come up" the river undetected. She goes on to state that the loss was

---

25 Carolana.com, 50th, Lt. Ellington report
26 Edmondston, p630
27 Ibid, p632

three killed and fifty captured, with the garrison being recently-conscripted local men "who gave themselves up in hope of being released' on parole. Instead, the Yankees handcuffed them all as prisoners. For her the sad loss of Plymouth was only salved by news of Lee's repulses of Grant's often-suicidal attacks upon his lines in Virginia.

Fort Branch Battery

Being again in possession of the earthen fortress at Plymouth, the enemy received information in mid-December that Fort Branch at the upriver Rainbow Banks was being reinforced. Also, reports that additional ironclads like *Albemarle* were nearing completion at Hamilton led to the dispatch of 10,000 troops with gunboats in an effort to neutralize the fort and destroy the vessels. Just before Christmas two companies of the 70th North Carolina Regiment [First Junior Reserves] at Camp Baker, near Fort Branch, were sent to Poplar Point below the fort where they discovered enemy gunboats from Plymouth ascending the river. One had already been sunk by submerged torpedoes near Williamston with the others advancing slowly while dragging the river ahead for more explosives. To wreak havoc with gunboats the fort's defenders placed numerous "nests of 20 to 40 "submerged torpedoes in the river below the fort near Poplar Point, Williamston and Jamesville, the latter just above Plymouth. Just below Poplar Point was Dickson's Battery which shelled any gunboats coming into view while sharpshooters targeted anyone foolishly visible upon their decks. The enemy report stated that "as long as woods onshore continued full of sharpshooters, we could not dislodge them without a land force."[28] To further thwart the enemy's river advance, the following day another battery was placed just below the gunboats position, whose intense fire forced their return to Plymouth.

The enemy naval commander's report afterward stated that the infantry marching to Fort Branch had outpaced the gunboats slowly advancing while avoiding torpedoes. He was advised by the infantry commander nearing the fort that "being short on ammunition and provisions" and the lack of transports with supplies for his men, "it would not be prudent to risk an assault on the enemy's works, being ignorant of their force." The enemy then retreated to Jamesville where they arrived on January 15th.[29] Diarist Edmondston recorded on December 27th news of the fort having repulsed enemy gunboats by "sinking six and crippled some others. Three were blown up by Torpedoes, one got aground and blown up and two more were sunk by our batteries when the rest retreated to Plymouth."[30] The enemy reported the loss of six naval personnel killed and nine wounded during this foray to Fort Branch. It was further stated that the loss would have been heavier had the gunboats not had "improvised breastworks around their decks created from cotton bales, hammocks and clothing-filled bags, which afforded protection from the sharpshooters' balls."[31]

"Nothing except a battle lost can be half so melancholy as a battle won." — *Duke of Wellington, 1815*

---

28 McCallum, p119
29 Ibid, p121
30 Edmondston, p648
31 OR, I, 11, p177

EPILOGUE

The Debris of Battle

"Only the dead have seen the end of war." — *Plato*

During April 1864's latter weeks a peaceful calm descended upon the lower Roanoke River as the last of the combatants departed, but there was but little for former residents of Plymouth to return to. The Tarboro *Southerner* of April 30, 1864 expressed the feeling of many residents of Washington County:

"The people of eastern North Carolina now breathe more freely and hope the time is near at hand when that lovely portion of the State will be rid of the insolent threat of an insidious foe."

The Remnants of War

What remained of the formerly-prosperous river town in latter April 1864 was in shambles with little left habitable. One "J. H. Broadwell" wrote in 1974 of "houses in town having one to ten cannon balls shot through them" and "200-pound shells from river gunboats filling the town" after the epic April 1864 battle. The initial destruction of the town came in mid-December 1862 when enemy troops occupying Plymouth were furiously attack by the 17th North Carolina Regiment which drove them to the wharf and into the river with many captured.

A June 11, 1909 Raleigh *News & Observer* account of that engagement by Edward L. Conn notes the enemy "gunboats in the river opened fire on the town at short range, setting fire to the buildings, and when the conflict had terminated scarcely a dozen were left standing within the corporate limits."[1]

It is believed eleven prewar structures in Plymouth remained intact in early April 1864, and that four of those were lost during General Hoke's liberation of Plymouth April 17-19. Only five buildings from that last period exist today and the following architectural survey data is sourced from the town's 1990 National Register of Historic Places application.[2] That application cited the Roanoke Beacon as the most reliable source for its exact dating the buildings.

The Methodists were the oldest religious congregation in Plymouth but one finds only the cemetery remaining at 109 East Third Street. The likely-damaged wood church building was demolished after the 1864 battle and its lumber used for coffins.

1. Episcopal Church, ca.1837 at 106 Madison Street survived both battles, as well as looting and destruction by the occupation troops who vandalized the religious edifice. It is reported that postwar a Northern chaplain formerly serving at Plymouth raised funds to replace stolen articles. It was rebuilt postwar in the Gothic Revival style. (Beacon, Aug 1968).
2. Windley-Ausbon House, ca.1832 Windley-Ausbon house at Third and Washington Streets still bears the marks of fleeing enemy troops who fired at North Carolina sharpshooters in December 1862. The upper windows or roofs were utilized for shooting positions, and targeted those in blue scrambling to escape on skiffs or to their disabled gunboat.
3. David Clark House, ca.1810 at 219 Jefferson Street is a two-story frame home in the Federal style and likely the oldest surviving in Plymouth. It was purchased in 1833 by mill owner Elijah Cornell; after 1880 the home of Joseph and Sadie Chesson who completed additions to the house.
4. Charles Latham House, ca.1850 Greek Revival, high-basement home on the eastern edge of old town which survived the battle. The lower level is said to have been a civilian shelter during the 1864 battle and the men of the 8th NC Regiment would have come

---

1 Dickey, p256
2 Application.

upon it after neutralizing Fort Compher and the Conaby Redoubt. While the father, Charles, opposed State independence his sons, Louis Charles and Julian A. both joined the "Washington Volunteers" after Fort Sumter.[3]

5. Picot-Armistead House, ca.1832 at 302 West Main Street. A Federal-style residence, which except for a small hole caused by a cannon ball, miraculously escaped any war-damage. The loss of a wide front porch may have been unrepaired war damage. In 1840 Dr. Robert Armistead purchased the home; in 1857 brother Thomas Armistead lived there. The latter served as Sgt. Major of the 3rd NC Cavalry along with fellow Plymouth-natives Color Sgt. Levi Fagan and Regimental Surgeon Dr. Benjamin M. Walker. Their unit was known as the "omnipresent guardian of the people" protecting villages and settlements from enemy raids along the coast.[4]

"False words are not only evil in themselves, but they infect the soul with evil." — *Plato*

There exists a persistent legend of a "massacre" of colored northern troops which is likely traced to a colored soldier first captured by Hoke's men, then who escaped and returned to his friends in blue. It is further likely that his "massacre" story was amplified by northern newspaper and political sensationalism. As with Fort Pillow's story of a "massacre" as well as Andersonville, the Lincoln government — primarily the Radicals within it — sought to inflame hatred toward the South by alleging Southern atrocities against Northern soldiers which gained in intensity during the 1864 election year. This waving of the "bloody shirt" continued postwar to help ensure the Republican party's political victories and national hegemony. In his official report of Plymouth's surrender, General Wessells writes that the 85th Redoubt (Fort Wessells) capitulated "under threat of no quarter," yet later states that "no report has been received in regard to this."[5]

The "massacre" story originates with an orderly sergeant named Samuel Johnson, a member of a colored US cavalry unit at Plymouth during Hoke's attack. He was captured and attached to the 6th NC Regiment as a servant to a Lt. Johnson at Richmond, then escaped to enemy lines. Perhaps eager to find favor with his new friends,

---

3 NCDOAH, State Troops and Volunteers, p94
4 Carolana.com, 41st NC Regiment, 3rd Cavalry
5 OR, I, V33, XLV, pp295-302

he sought General Benjamin Butler who favored the use of colored troops. Johnson claimed that:

"After the "capture of Plymouth by the rebel forces all the negroes found in blue uniforms or with any outward marks of a Union soldier upon him, was killed. I saw some taken into the woods and hung. Others I saw stripped of their clothing and then stood on the bank of the river where they were shot in the back. Still others were killed by having their brains beaten out by the butt end of the muskets in the hands of the rebels. All were not killed the day of the capture. Those that were not were placed in a room with their [white] officers, they [the officers] having previously been dragged through the town with ropes around their necks, where they were kept confined until the following morning, when the remainder of the black soldiers were killed."

Without evidence of the story being truthful, Butler wrote his superior, Grant, of the alleged atrocity. Grant did not act on this accusation, but Butler was a news-hound and spread the story to reporters eager to report or invent shocking stories for their northern audience. As noted previously, "contrabands" entering Northern camps were quick to learn that information regarding Southern troops in the vicinity, however truthful, was greatly valued by eager Northern commanders who rewarded them with food and shelter. These reports were also valuable to gullible newspaper reporters seeking "atrocity" stories with which to shock their Northern readership. There was also the possibility that the colored informant was to slip out of camp a few days later to relay intelligence to his friends in grey.

The most damning evidence against a "massacre" came at a later meeting of veterans of the 101st and 103rd Pennsylvania Regiments, who were all present at the April 1864 battle and capitulation. It seemed odd to all that such a mass execution could have occurred without being observed, or protestations made at the time.[6]

Authors Richard Iobst (*The Bloody Sixth*); William Trotter (*Ironclads & Columbiads*) and Luther Dickey (*History of the 103rd Pennsylvania Regiment*) all concluded that according to their painstaking research, no "massacre" took place after General Hoke's victory.[7] Historian Iobst closes discussion of this allegation thusly:

---

6 Trotter, pp417-419
7 Barefoot, p390

"A thorough study of all available regimental correspondence does nothing to substantiate [claims of any post-battle massacre]. Until authentic evidence is uncovered, it is impossible to arrive at any other conclusion than that the entire statement [of the black soldier/servant of a northern Lt. Johnson] is a biased opinion of someone with a vivid imagination." [8]

Also, the "Buffaloes" with the enemy force at Plymouth were certainly terrified of capture by North Carolina forces they had deserted from. Once Hoke's force was near the Roanoke River was alive with nighttime activity as these deserters "floated down the river in canoes and took refuge in the woods."[9]

Lastly, Plymouth's historic ca.1832 Federal-style Armistead house is often mentioned in reference to an "underground railroad" connection in Plymouth, best described as a prewar mixture of fact and fiction generated by northern abolitionists, reformers and politicians. Perhaps the most accurate definition of the legend comes from General Samuel G. French, a New Jersey-born Quaker serving with the Confederate States army. He wrote of it as 'a term used to express how negro slaves were conveyed under cover of night to the North when enticed from their owners.'[10] Certainly fugitives of any race may have been harbored anywhere by a sympathetic people unaware of their reason for fleeing but no Northern utopia of personal freedom awaited slaves. Lincoln's own Republican party encouraged the containment of the black race to the South so as to fill the West with European immigrants who wanted no cheap labor competition. Frederick Douglass said of one northern city, which in 1860 held the most colored people of any in the north: "There is not, perhaps, anywhere to be found a city in which prejudice against color is more rampant than in Philadelphia." The ever-present racial discrimination of the north often drove emancipated slaves to return South.[11]

Northern States like Ohio were not receptive to the immigration of colored people in 1847 when "an aroused populace forcibly thwarted an attempt by John Randolph of Virginia to settle 518 colored people he had voluntarily emancipated.[12]

---

8 Iobst, p199
9 Wright, p200
10 French, p356
11 Gara, p xxi
12 Litwack, pp69-70

And dispelling the romantic myth of a better life in Canada, an 1851 Toronto newspaper editorial noted that Canadians desired "more restrictive immigration measures to check the influx of Negroes ..." and suggested the laying of a poll tax. The editorial further stated that Canadians "abhor slavery ... but patriotism induces us to exclaim against having our country overrun with blacks, any of whom are woefully depraved by their previous mode of life."[13] In addition, the *New York Herald* of March 23, 1860 wrote of settlements of colored people in Ontario: "The fugitive slaves go into Canada as beggars and the mass of them commit larceny and lay in jail until they become lowered and debased and ready for worse crimes." Many of these impoverished blacks returned to the US in 1863 to collect generous enlistment bounties.

Additionally, the Harriet Tubman legend of shepherding 300 slaves to Canada was dwarfed by Southern manumission efforts prior to the War. Those include Virginians John Randolph and George Custis who together freed more than 800 of their bondsmen in 1833 and 1857, respectively. The federal census of 1850 counted 434,495 free blacks in the US and this growing by nearly 50,000 by the 1860 census, and the vast majority living in the South.

A Tennessee unionist who identified the true reason behind slavery in America was Parson William G. Brownlow, editor of the *Knoxville Whig*. In a fall 1858 editorial he virulently chastised New England abolitionists for the country's troubles and held the North responsible for "that vile traffic." He wrote: "*The States of this union, commonly called the New England States, alias the free States, were never, to any great extent, slaveholding. No-siree, their virtuous and pious minds were chiefly exercised in slave-stealing and slave selling. They stole the African from his native land and sold him into bondage for the sake of gain.*"[14]

---

13 Gara, p66
14 Wiki, Brownlow, accessed 12.13.23

H. W. Wessells

Appendix A — Following General H. W. Wessells

After first refusing surrender despite being isolated in his Fort Williams redoubt and then experiencing a convincing bombardment from Hoke's massed artillery to reconsider, Wessells surrendered his entire command within the Plymouth fortress. It is said his reluctance was due to his ire at being a West Point graduate defeated by a mere brigadier of volunteer troops.

Once his defeated command was marched off to captivity at Andersonville prison in Georgia, Wessells was sent first to Richmond's Libby Prison for enemy officers, and eventually to Charleston. There the captive officers' quarters in town came under fire from his own artillery which was indiscriminately bombarding the city. On August 3, 1864 he was released in a prisoner exchange and three months later was overseeing a New York conscription center.[15] It was not until mid-March of 1865 that he was promoted to brevet rank of brigadier in recognition of "gallant and meritorious services" at the Plymouth battle.[16]

Wessells defeat and surrender of his command was not destined to undergo scrutiny by a court of inquiry nor court martial. As noted above, after several months captivity he returned to military service with no penalty for his actions or inaction at Plymouth. Considering this treatment, it is worth examining several other cases of Northern commanders in similar circumstances.

---

15 Warner, p551
16 Wiki, accessed 1.29.24. Brevet rank was honorary and with no authority or pay than his permanent rank.

After his disaster at Second Manassas, General John Pope was relegated to the obscurity of the northwest and likely escaped more serious consequences due to his political connections. Another example is General Don Carlos Buell who was harassed into retreat by John Hunt Morgan's cavalry in mid-1862 and who later failed to pursue General Braxton Bragg in Kentucky. Accused of "dilatory tactics" by an investigating military commission, Buell was eventually mustered out of volunteer service and resigned his regular army commission in 1864.

But in a case most similar to Wessells defeat was General Robert Milroy who in June of 1863 was "outmaneuvered, outfought and virtually gobbled up" by General Richard Ewell's 2nd Corps of Lee's army. Milroy's command lost 3,400 as prisoners and all of his artillery, as well as many dead and wounded. Milroy cheated capture only by escaping with several hundred of his horsemen. Afterward a court of inquiry formally "exonerated" him of culpability with no punishment or loss of rank.[17]

---

17 Warner, p326

Appendix B — Andersonville Prison

The Andersonville Stockade

Once the Plymouth fortress had been surrendered the surviving garrison troops were made prisoners of war and prepared for their long journey to the Andersonville prison stockade in Georgia. Many of them would perish there and for a more complete understanding of this aftermath of the battle the following is very useful.

This prison stockade was located in southwest Georgia, about 50 miles south-southwest of Macon. When questioned postwar regarding alleged ill-treatment of prisoners at Andersonville, former Vice-President Alexander Stephens first laid blame on Lincoln's government for refusing to allow prisoner exchanges and the delivery of medicines. He also noted that the prison site was selected for its mild climate far from the more "malarial" sections of the State, and surrounded by farms for food. Stephens also pointed to the cold, northern locations of Camp Douglas, Rock Island and Johnson's Island which Southern prisoners were subject to, and that despite being surrounded by plentiful harvests the mortality rate of northern prisons far exceeded that of the Southern prison camps.[18] In early 1863 Stephens traveled to Washington on a humanitarian mission to negotiate a prisoner exchange. While awaiting a reply from the Lincoln government he was informed:

---

18 Stevenson, p233

"No special commissioner on the subjects embraced in the proposed conference would be received."[19] It should be noted that the South had little access to medicines considered modern at the time due to the northern blockade and the US government declaring medicines "contraband of war." Because of this the South had to rely upon the use of indigenous remedies of old, such as roots and herb teas.

The only real northern response to offers of exchange were alleged reports of prisoner mistreatment by Richmond authorities released to newspapers eager for sensational stories. Lincoln's Secretary of War Stanton promoted a "Report No. 67" containing testimony from eight "emaciated and mistreated" Northern soldiers, allegedly escapees from Richmond's Libby Prison. Stanton wrote that "the enormity of the crime committed by the rebels toward our prisoners for the last several months, is not known or realized by our people and cannot but fill the civilized world with horror, when the facts are fully revealed. There appears to have been a deliberate system of savage and barbarous treatment & starvation."[20] But no offers of exchange of prisoners.

In January 1864, Robert Gould, Confederate agent of exchange wrote his northern counterpart proposing that surgeons of both armies be allowed to attend their own soldiers with provisions and medicines. This proposition was also rejected by northern authorities.

To allay unfounded Northern criticism and reach the humanity within Lincoln and Grant, a delegation of Northern prisoners from Andersonville were released by President Davis in the summer of 1864 to plead for their exchange. Despite their first-hand description of the sickness and malnutrition within the overcrowded stockade there was no offers of remedy. One of that delegation, Henry M. Brennan later wrote: "In my opinion and that of a good many others, a good part of the responsibility for the horrors of Andersonville rests with General U.S. Grant, who refused to make a fair exchange of prisoners." The unnamed chairman of that delegation reported that "he was more contemptuously treated by Secretary of War Stanton than he ever was at Andersonville."

The pardoned prisoners brought with them photographs of the conditions at Andersonville to stimulate exchanges. One northerner who was eyewitness to the taking of these photographs wrote: "I was

---

19 Ibid, p240
20 Stevenson, p243

a prisoner of war in that place during the summer of 1864 and I well remember seeing a photographer with his camera in one of the sentinel boxes near the south gate during July or August … I have often wondered in later years what success this photographer had and why the [northern] public never had the opportunity of seeing a genuine photograph of Andersonville."[21] The images of Andersonville did indeed reach Washington authorities but their official receipt was never officially acknowledged and there is no record of them in Northern journals. Jefferson Davis wrote of the attempt at humanitarian exchange:

"The photographs were terrible indeed, but the misery they portrayed was surpassed by some of the prisoners from northern camps we received in exchange in Savannah. Why was this delay between summer and November in sending vessels for sick and wounded, for whom no equivalents were asked? Were the Federal prisoners left to suffer, and afterward photographed to aid in firing the popular heart of the North?"

Responding to the allegation of nine percent of northern men in Southern prisons were starved to death by Jefferson Davis, Benjamin Hill of Georgia asked then "who tortured to death the twelve percent of the Southern men held in Northern prisons?"[22]

Finally, Grant had earned the nickname "butcher" for the often-futile and relentless assaults ordered of his men, as well as for the appalling and well-documented lack of concern for his own men lying wounded on the battlefield. An example is after the bloody Cold Harbor battle in June 1864, Grant delayed his approval of a truce requested by General Lee to attend to the dead and wounded, especially latter with their cries of agony.

One northern colonel said of Grant: 'If it be asked why so simple a duty as the rescue of the wounded and burial of the dead had thus been neglected … it was due to an unnecessary scruple on the part of … Grant … who delayed sending a flag of truce to Lee for this purpose because it would amount to an admission that he had been beaten …" Another, a Vermont soldier wrote of Grant's *"shameful and criminal negligence … for ordering a charge, and for "permitting wounded heroes of that charge to suffer and die as they did"* with no post-battle medical attention.[23]

---

21 Meredith, p187
22 Rutherford, p100
23 Furguson, p212-213

After finally approving the truce with Lee, soldiers from both sides emerged to bring in their dead and wounded while chasing away the flies and vultures. The number of northern dead far outnumbered the handful still alive. Author Ernest B. Furguson writes of Cold Harbor's aftermath that many of the Yankee's "whose wounds would have been non-fatal had died from lack of treatment, food and water." Many bodies were unrecognizable being black and swollen, but some had sewn their names on their tunics given their probable death in the assault. Hundreds simply had soil shoveled upon their bodies, others were dragged to mass graves.[24]

---

24 Ibid, p214

About the Author

John Bernhard Thuersam is a native of the Niagara Falls area and a resident of the southeastern US since 1977.

He authored *Key West's Civil War: Rather Unsafe for a Southern Man to Live Here* and edits the online blog www.Circa1865.org.

Bibliography — Master (2.8.24)
Primary Sources:

Abbott. Richard H. *Cotton & Capital: Boston Businessmen and Antislavery Reform.* University of Massachusetts Press. 1991.

Blakeslee. Bernard F. *History of the 16th Connecticut Volunteers.* Case, Lockwood and Brainard. 1875.

Browning. Orville H. *OHB Diary.* Theodore C. Pease & James G. Randall, editors. Illinois State Historical Library. 1933.

Clark. Walter. *Histories of the Several Regiments & Battalions from North Carolina. 1861-1865.* Nash Brothers. 1901.

Cox. Samuel S. *Eight Years in Congress: Memoir and Speeches of Samuel S. Cox.* D. Appleton and Company. 1865.

Davis. Jefferson. *Rise and Fall of the Confederate Government.* D. Appleton and Company. 1881

Dickey. Luther S. *History of the 103d Pennsylvania Regiment.* L.S. Dickey. 1910.

Early. Jubal A. *Jubal Early's Memoirs: Autobiographical Sketch & Narrative of the WBTS.* JB Lippencott, 1912.

Edmondston. Catherine Ann Devereaux. *Journal of a Secesh Lady.* Crabtree & Patton, editors. NCDAH, 1979.

Fox. Gustavus. *Confidential Correspondence.* Richard Wainwright, editor. De Vinne. 1920.

French. Samuel G. Two Wars: An Autobiography of Gen. Samuel G. French. *Confederate Veteran.* 1901.

Goss. Warren Lee. *The Soldier's Story of His Captivity at Andersonville,* Belle Isle. L.N. Richardson. 1873.

Grady. Benjamin Franklin. *The Case of the South Against the North.* Edwards & Broughton. 1899.

Graham, John W. *The Capture of Plymouth. Several Regiments and Battalions*; Vol V. (Walter Clark, ed.) Nash Bros. 1901.

Haviland. Laura S. *A Woman's Life-Work, Labors and Experiences.* Waldron and Stowe. 1882.

James. Rev. Horace. Annual Report of Sup't-General of Negro Affairs. Dept. of VA & NC. W.F. Brown & Co., 1865.

McNary. Oliver R. *What I Saw & Did Inside & Outside of Rebel Prisons.* Self-Published, 1891.

Merrill. Julian Whedon. *Records of the 24th Independent Battery, NY Light Artillery.* Ladies Cemetery Association, Perry, NY. 1870.

Moore, George Henry. *Notes on the History of Slavery in Massachu-*

setts. D. Appleton & Company, 1866.

Morgan. W. H. *Personal Reminiscences of the War. 1861-1865*. J.P. Bell Company. 1911.

Mosher, Charles C. (85th New York Regiment). *Civil War Journal*. Vol I & II. 1916

Official Records of the Union and Confederate Armies. Washington, DC.1881-1901.

Pettigrew Papers. Southern Historical Collection, University of North Carolina.

Putnam. Samuel H. *Story of Company A, Twenty-fifth Massachusetts Regiment*. Putnam, Davis and Company. 1886.

Reed. John A. *History of the 101st Massachusetts Veteran Volunteer Infantry, 1861-1865*. L.S. Dickey & Company. 1910.

Roe. Alfred S. *The Twenty-Fourth Massachusetts*. Twenty-Fourth Veteran Association. 1907.

Spencer. Cornelia Phillips. *The Last Ninety Days of the War in North Carolina*. Watchman Publishing Company. 1866.

Stevenson. Dr. Randolph. *The Southern Side; or, Andersonville Prison*. Turnbull Brothers, 1876.

Tolbert. Noble J., ed. *Papers of John W. Ellis*. Volumes 1 & 2. North Carolina Department of Archives and History. 1964

Worth. Josephine Bryan. *Sherman's Raid. United Daughters of the Confederacy Recollections*, Vol. 4.

Wright, J. Reminiscences of Plymouth, *Confederate Veteran*, May 1916, p200.

Secondary Sources:

Addicott. Jeffrey F. *Union Terror. Debunking False Justifications for Terror Against Civilians*. Shotwell Publishing. 2023.

Anderson. Lucy London. *North Carolina Women of the Confederacy*. Winoca Press. 1926.

Andrews. Matthew Page. *Women of the South in War Times*. The Norman, Remington Company. 1920

Auchampaugh. Philip Gerard. *James Buchanan and His Cabinet on the Eve of Secession*. 1926.

Bancroft. A.C. *The Life and Death of Jefferson Davis*. A.C. Bancroft. J.S. Ogilvie. 1889.

Barefoot, Daniel. *General Robert F. Hoke: Lee's Modest Warrior*. John F. Blair. 1996.

Bensel. Richard Franklin. *The American Ballot Box in the Mid-Nine-*

teenth Century. Cambridge University Press, 2004.

Blair. William A. *With Malice Toward Some: Treason and Loyalty in the Civil War Era*. UNC Press, 2014.

Boynton. Charles D. *History of the Navy During the Rebellion*, Vol. 2, D. Appleton and Company, 1868

Buck. Lucy Rebecca. *The Diary of Rebecca Lucy Buck During the War Between the States*. Buck Publishing Co., 1973.

Burgess. John W. *The Civil War and the Constitution*. Charles Scribner's Sons. 1910.

Campbell. R. Thomas. *Storm Over Carolina: The Confederate Navy's Struggle for Eastern North Carolina*. Cumberland House. 2005.

Christian. George L.; McGuire. Hunter. *The Confederate Cause & Conduct*. 1907. Christian & McGuire. 1907.

Cisco. Walter Brian. *War Crimes Against Southern Civilians*. Pelican Publishing Company. 2007.

Colbourne. Trevor. *Lamp of Experience: Whig History & the Intellectual Origins of the American Revolution*. 1965. Liberty Fund, Inc.

Conrad. Henry Clay. *History of Delaware*. Volume I. Self-published. 1908.

Crabtree & Patton, editors. *Journal of a Secesh Lady. Diary of Catherine Edmondston, 1860-66*. NC Dept of Archives & History, 1979.

Diechman. Catherine. *Rogues & Runners: Bermuda and the American Civil War*. Bermuda National Trust. 2003

Dodd. William E. *Life of Nathaniel Macon*. Edwards & Broughton. 1903

Dow. George Francis. *Slave Ships and Slaving*. Cornell Maritime Press. 1968.

Dowd. Clement. *Life of Zebulon Vance*. Observer Printing Company. 1897.

Dumond. Dwight L. *The Secession Movement: 1860-1861*. MacMillan Company. 1931.

Dunning. William A. The Constitution of the United States in Civil War. *Political Science Quarterly*. June 1886. Vol. 1.

Durrill, Wayne K. *War of Another Kind: A Southern Community in the Civil War*. Oxford University Press, 1990.

Elliott. Robert G.. *A Tarheel Confederate and His Family*. RGE Publications. 1989.

Elliott. Robert G. *Ironclad of the Roanoke. Gilbert Elliott's Albemarle*. White Mane Publishing. 1994

Fair, John D. *The Tifts of Georgia: Connecticut Yankees in King Cotton's Court*. Mercer University Press. 2010.

Fenn. Elizabeth; Wood. Peter. *Natives & Newcomers. The Way We Lived in North Carolina Before 1770*. UNC Press. 1983.

Foley. John P. *The Jeffersonian Cyclopedia*. Funk & Wagnalls Company. 1900

Ford. (conscription, desertion?

Franklin. John Hope. *The Free Negro in North Carolina: 1790-1860*. UNC Press, 1943.

Furguson. Ernest B. *Not War, But Murder: Cold Harbor 1864*. Vintage Books, 2000.

Gara. Larry. *The Liberty Line: The Legend of the Underground Railroad*. University Press of Kentucky. 1961.

Garren. Terrell T. *Mountain Myth: Unionism in Western North Carolina*. Reprint Company. 2006.

Gibson. John M. *Those 163 Days*. Bramhall House. 1961

Gilpatrick. Delbert H. *Jeffersonian Democracy in North Carolina, 1789-1816*. Columbia University Press. 1931.

Glatthaar. Joseph T. *Sherman's March to the Sea and Beyond*. New York University Press. 1985

Graham. Matthew J. *The Ninth Regiment New York Volunteers*. E.P. Coby & Company. 1900.

Gunther. John. *Inside Africa; Nigeria: Its History in Brief*. Harper & Brothers, 1955.

Hamilton. Joseph G. DeR. *Reconstruction in North Carolina*. Edwards & Broughton. 1906

Harris, William C. (editor). *In the Country of the Enemy*. University Press of Florida. 1999.

Hemming. John. *Red Gold: The Conquest of the Brazilian Indians, 1500-1760*. Harvard University Press. 1978.

Hesseltine, William P. *Lincoln and the War Governors*, Alfred A. Knopf, 1955.

Hill, Daniel H. *North Carolina During the War Between the States: Bethel to Sharpsburg*. Edwards & Broughton, 1926.

Hollandsworth. John G. *The Louisiana Native Guards*. LSU Press. 1995.

von Holst. Hermann. *Constitutional and Political History of the United States*. Vol. 1. Callaghan and Company. 1889.

Hummel. Jeffrey Rogers. *Emancipating Slaves, Enslaving Free Men*.

Jeffrey Rogers Hummel. Open Court Publishing, 1996

Hundley. Daniel R. Social *Relations in Our Southern States. 1860*. Henry B. Price Publisher. 1860.

Jardin. Andre. *Tocqueville: A Biography*. Farrar, Straus & Farrar. 1988

Jensen. Merrill. *The Articles of Confederation: An Interpretation*. University of Wisconsin Press. 1963.

Johnson, Guion Griffis. *Ante-Bellum North Carolina, A Social History*. UNC-Chapel Hill. 1937.

Jones. JP. McDonough. JL. *War So Terrible: Sherman and Atlanta*. W.W. Norton & Company. 1987.

Jones. Howard Mumford. *O Strange New World. American Culture: The Formative Years*. Viking Press. 1964.

Kelin. Herbert S. *Slavery in the Americas. A Comparative Study of Virginian and Cuba*. Quadrangle Books, 1967.

Kruman. Marc W. *Parties and Politics in North Carolina: 1836-1865*. LSU Press. 1983.

Lefler, Hugh; Newsome, Albert. *North Carolina: History of a Southern State*. UNC Press. 1954.

Leiber, Francis. *The 1863 Laws of War*. Stackpole Books, 2005.

Levy, Andrew. *The Frist Emancipator: Slavery, Religion and the Quiet Revolution of Robert Carter*. Random House. 2005.

Lindblade. Eric A. *Fight As Long As Possible. Battle of Newport Barracks*. Ten Roads Publishing. 2014.

Lindsey. David. *Irrepressible Democrat: "Sunset" Cox*. Wayne State University Press. 1959.

Litwack. Leon. *North of Slavery: The Negro in the Free States, 1790-1860*. University of Chicago Press. 1961.

Mahon. John K. *The War of 1812*. University of Florida Press. 1972.

McKay. Ernest A. *The Civil War and New York City*. Syracuse University Press. 1990.

McKean. Brenda. *Blood and War at My Doorstep*. Volume 1. Xlibris. 2011.

McPherson. James. *Battle Cry of Freedom*. Oxford University Press. 1988.

McRee. Griffith J. *Life and Correspondence of James Iredell*. Volume I. D. Appleton. 1859.

Mahood, Wayne. *The Plymouth Pilgrims, The Eighty-first New York Infantry in the Civil War*. Longstreet House. 1989.

Manarin, *North Carolina Troops 1861-1865*, NC Office of Archives &

History. 1977.

Mannix. Daniel P. *Black Cargoes: A History of the Atlantic Slave Trade, 1518-1865*. Viking Press. 1962.

Marvel. Willam. *Lincoln's Darkest Year: The War in 1862*. Houghton-Mifflin Company. 2008.

Maslowski. Peter. *Treason Must Be Made Odious: Military Occupation & Reconstruction in Tennessee, 1862-1865*. KTO Press. 1978.

Massey. Mary Elizabeth. *Refugee Life in the Confederacy*. Louisiana State University Press. 1964.

Mast. Greg. *State Troops and Volunteers: A Photographic Record of North Carolina's Civil War Soldiers*. NCDOAH. 1995.

Maugham. Robin. *The Slaves of Timbuktu*. Harper & Sons. 1961.

Meredith. Roy. *Mr. Lincoln's Camera Man: Mathew Brady*. Dover Publications. 1974

Mitcham, Jr. Samuel W. *It Wasn't About Slavery: Exposing the Great Lie of the Civil War*. Regnery History, 2020.

Montgomery. David. *Beyond Equality: Labor and the Radical Republicans, 1862-1872*. University of Illinois Press. 1981.

Moss, Juanita P. *The Battle of Plymouth, North Carolina*. Heritage Books, 2009.

Newsome, Hampton. *The Fight for the Old North State: Civil War in North Carolia, January-May 1864*. University of Kansas, 2019.

Powell. William S. *North Carolina: A History*. W.W. Norton, 1977.

Powell. William S. *Dictionary of North Carolina Biography*, Vol. 5. 1979. UNC Press.

Priest. John Michael. *Capt. Wren's Civil War Diary: From New Bern to Fredericksburg*. Berkley Books. 1990.

Randall. James G. *The Civil War and Reconstruction*. D.C. Heath and Company. 1937.

Rhodes. James Ford. *History of the Civil War: 1861-1865*. Dover Books. 1999.

Rogers. Henry M. *Memories of Ninety Years*. Houghton-Mifflin Company. 1928.

Rutherford. Mildred Lewis. *Truths of History*. Southern Lion Books. 1998.

Seward. Frederick W. *William H. Seward*; Volume II. Derby & Miller Publishers. 1891.

Scrugham. Mary. *Peaceable Americans of 1860-61: A Study in Public Opinion*. Columbia University. 1921.

Shy. John. *A People Numerous and Armed*. University of Michigan Press, 1990.

Sideman, Belle; Friedman, Lillian. *Europe Looks at the Civil War*. Collier Books. 1962

Sitterson. Joseph Carlyle. *The Secession Movement in North Carolina*. UNC Press, 1939.

Stammp. Kenneth M. *And the War Came: The North and the Secession Crisis, 1860-1861*. LSU Press. 1950.

Stearns. Frank P. *Life and Public Services of Goerge Luther Stearns*, J.B. Lippencott & Co. 1907.

Still, Jr. William N. *Iron Afloat: The Story of the Confederate Ironclads*. University of South Carolina Press. 1985.

Tarbell. Ida. *Life of Abraham Lincoln*. MacMillan. 1917.

Taylor. John M. *William Henry Seward: Lincoln's Right-Hand Man*. Harper Collins. 1991.

Taylor. Rosser Howard. *Slaveholding in North Carolina: An Economic View*. James Sprunt Historical Publications. UNC Press. 1926.

Thomas. Hugh. *The Slave Trade. The Story of the Atlantic Slave Trade: 1440-1870*. Touchstone. 1997.

Thuersam. John Bernhard. *Key West's Civil War: Rather Unsafe for a Southern Man to Live Here*. Shotwell Publishing. 2022.

Trotter. Jack. *Last Train to Dixie*. Shotwell Publishing. 2021

Trotter. William R. *Ironclads and Columbiads: The Civil War in North Carolina. The Coast*. John F. Blair, 1989.

Tucker. Glenn. *Zeb Vance: Champion of Personal Freedom*. Bobbs-Merrill Company. 1965.

Wagstaff, Henry McGilbert. *State Rights and Political Parties in North Carolina, 1776-1861*. Johns-Hopkins Press, 1906.

Walters. John B. *Merchant of Terror: General Sherman and Total War*. Bobbs-Merrill Company, Inc. 1973.

Warner. Ezra J. *Generals in Blue: Lives of the Union Commanders*. LSU Press. 1964.

West, Jr. Richard S. *Lincoln's Scapegoat General: A Life of Benjamin F. Butler, 1818-1893*. Houghton-Mifflin Company. 1965.

White, James Edward. *New Bern and the Civil War*. History Press, 2018.

White. Jonathan W. *Emancipation, the Union Army and the Reelection of Abraham Lincoln*. LSU Press. 2014

Winston. Robert. *Robert E. Lee: A Biography*. William Morrow &

Company. 1934.

Wilson, Clyde N. *Carolina Cavalier: The Life and Mind of James Johnston Pettigrew*. Chronicles Press, 2002.

Wolfe, Reese. *Yankee Ships: An Informal History of the American Merchant Marine*. Bobbs-Merrill Company, 1953.

Wood. W. Kirk. *Nullification, A Constitutional History, 1776-1833*. Volume 1. University Press of America. 2008.

Washington County Gen'l Society, Marriages, preface. (NHC library)

Manuscripts and Papers:

Bardolph. Richard. Inconstant Rebels: Desertion of NC Troops in the Civil War. *NC Historical Review*. Vol. XLI, No. 2., Spring 1964.

Barnes. John H. Early Blockade & Capture of Hatteras Forts, July 9-Sept. 1, 1861. *NY Hist Society Quarterly*, Vol. XLVI, No. 1, Jan. '62.

Beard. Charles A. Some Economic Origins of Jeffersonian Democracy. *American Historical Review*. Vol. XIX, No. 2. January 1914.

Bell. Herbert C. The West India Trade Before the American Revolution. *American Historical Review*, Vol. XXII, No. 2. January 1917.

Bonner. Macon. *Macon Bonner Papers, 1862-1864*. UNC Wilson Special Collections. Collection Number 03758-z.

Browning. Judkin. Removing the Mask of Nationality in NC, 1862-1865. *Journal of Southern History*, Vol. LXXI, No. 3, Aug 2005.

Carney. George J. 1864 Annual Report of the Superintendent General of Negro Affairs, Department of Virginia & North Carolina.

Dease Jared; Putt. Alyssa. *Buffaloes*. North Carolina Government and Heritage Library. 2022.

Delaney. Norman C. Charles H. Foster and the Unionists of North Carolina. *NC Historical Review*, Vol. XXXVII, No. 3. July 1960.

Dillard. Dr. Richard. *Civil War in Chowan County, North Carolina*. Self-published, 1916.

Douma & Rasmussen, A. *The Danish St. Croix Project: Revisiting the Lincoln Colonization. American 19th Century History*, 2014.

Dunning. William A. The Constitution of the United States in the Civil War. *Political Science Quarterly*, June 1886. .

Elliott, Jr. Robert N. James Davis and the Beginnings of the Newspaper in NC. *NCH Review*, Vol. XLII, No. 1, Winter 1965.

Fisher. Sydney G. Suspension of *Habeas Corpus* During the Civil War. *Political Science Qtrly*, Vol 3, No. 3, Sept. 1888, pp. 482-485.

Ford, Oren. *A History of the Bounty System Used During the Civil War*.

Thesis, University of the Pacific, 1933.

Hawkins. Rush. *An Account of the Assassination of Loyal Citizens of North Carolina.* New York. 1897.

Hoffmann. William S. John Branch and the Origins of the Whig Party in NC. *NC Historical Review*, Vol. XXXV, No. 3, July 1958.

Jacocks. W.P. *Federal Operations in Eastern North Carolina During the Civil War.* MA Thesis, UNC, 1905, pg. 8; OR, XVIII, Sr. I, 1.

Lamphere. Nathan. Civil War Plymouth Pilgrim Descendants Society. Sergeant, 85th NYS Vols. Online. Accessed 4.29.23.

Livingston. Donald. Is America a Republic? *Chronicles Magazine of American Culture.* May, 2009.

McCormick. John G. Personnel of the North Carolina Convention of 1861. UNC Chapel Hill, James Sprunt Monographs. 1900.

Moser. Harold D. Reaction in North Carolina to the Emancipation Proclamation. *NC Hist'l Review*, Vol. XLIV, No. 1, Winter 1967.

National Register of Historic Places Application for Plymouth, NC, 1990.

Parramore. Thomas C. A Year in Hertford County with Elkanah Watson. *NC Historical Review*, Vol. XLI, No. 4, Autumn 1964.

Pettigrew Papers, Southern Historical Collection. UNC Chapel Hill.

Randall. James G. Captured & Abandoned Property During the Civil War. *American Historical Review*, Vol. XIX, No. 1, Oct. 1913.

Stanly, Edward. A Military Governor Among Abolitionists. Letter to Charles Sumner from Edward Stanly. New York, 1865.

Tucker. Glenn. Some Aspects of North Carolina's Participation at Gettysburg. *NC Historical Review*, Vol. XXXV, No. 2, 1958.

Wagstaff. Henry McGilbert. *State Rights and Political Parties in North Carolina – 1776-1861.* Johns Hopkins Press, July-August 1906

Wright. Rev. E.A. Capture of Plymouth, N.C. *Confederate Veteran* magazine. Vol. XXIV, No. 5. May 1916. Pg. 200.

Maps: Map of Plymouth and Defenses, April 17-20, 1864. Capt. R. D. Graham, 56th NCST. 1901.

Newspapers:

Roanoke Beacon., Plymouth North Carolina. August 15, 1968.

Whitford. John D. *New Bern Daily Journal.* 31 December 1882.

Internet:

Clark. Walter. Fiftieth NC Regt. Lt. Joseph C. Ellington. *Histories of the Several Regiments & Battalions.* Vol III 1901. Accessed 5.12/23

Gray. Benjamin. *Under Both Flags* - North Carolina Department of Cultural Resources (NCDNR). Accessed 3.11.23.

Harper. Douglas. Slavery in Pennsylvania. www.SlaveryNorth.com; 2003. Accessed 12.3.23.

thecivilwarintheeast.com: 17th North Carolina Regiment, accessed 3.13.22

Macombs. Report on Capture of Plymouth, Oct. 1864. https://ironbrigader.com/2022/10/18/commander-william-h-macombs-report-on-the-recapture-of-plymouth-north-carolina-by-union-forces-october-31st-1864/. Accessed 7.17.23

41st North Carolina Regiment, 3rd Cavalry; www.carolana.com accessed 10.9.23.

Index

Adams, John 31, 38, 39, 47, 71
Africa 6, 13, 19, 20, 21, 25, 27, 51, 109, 224
Andersonville, Georgia 196, 209, 213, 215, 216, 217, 221
Andrew, Gov. John ... 108. 109, 159
Articles of War 81, 91, 138
Bagley, D.W. 191
Battery Worth 177, 183, 184
Blount, Thomas 37, 40
Biggs, Asa 59, 70, 94
Bounty 4, 11, 109, 106, 107, 110, 111, 132, 156, 159, 161, 162, 173, 194, 228
Brennan, Henry M. 216
Brick House Plantation 14, 16
Bownlow, Parson 212
Buchanan, President James 58, 61, 63, 64, 65, 66, 67, 72, 73, 75, 97
Buffaloes 84, 96, 117, 118, 132, 133, 134, 135, 136, 143, 164, 179, 196, 198, 211, 228
Burnside, Gen. Ambrose 82, 84, 88, 90, 91, 119, 141, 142, 170
Butler, Gen. Benjamin 90, 100, 112, 113, 119, 145, 158, 191, 210, 227
Calhoun, John C. 32, 55, 71
Canada 41, 102, 109, 163, 212
Caribbean colonization 102, 107
Chambersburg, Pennsylvania .. 125
Clark, David 208
Collins, Josiah 8, 9, 25, 197
Columbia Road 156, 180, 182, 184, 186, 187
Conaby Creek 14, 156, 179, 184, 186
Confederation, Articles of 8, 32, 34, 71, 225

Confederate States 71, 79, 85, 98, 100, 111, 114, 121, 129, 138, 169, 190, 211
Conscription 42, 103, 104, 106, 107, 108, 110, 111, 113
Constitution, US 8, 33, 61, 97
"Contrabands" 82, 86, 89, 90, 93, 102, 106, 107, 108, 109, 111, 113, 115, 117, 119, 120, 121, 122, 134, 135, 146, 156, 157, 158, 160, 163, 170, 210
Cooke, Commander James W. 168, 170, 174, 177, 183, 190, 200, 201, 204
Cox, Samuel S. 99, 101, 114, 221, 225
Croatoan 1
CSS *Albemarle* 167, 168, 169, 171, 172, 174, 175, 176, 177, 179, 180, 182, 183, 184, 185, 187, 189, 190, 195, 200, 201, 202, 203, 204, 223
CSS *Bombshell* 200
CSS *Chicora* 174
CSS *Cotton Plant* 183, 184
CSS *Florida* 200
CSS *Neuse* 167, 168, 171, 172
Davie, Gov. William R. 30, 43
Davis, George 66
Davis, President Jefferson .... vi, 64, 75, 103, 217, 222
Depredations 24, 85, 123, 139, 141, 143, 147, 173
Draft 104, 105, 106, 108, 109, 110, 113, 117, 148, 160, 161
Draft Riots 103, 160
Democracy 29, 35, 41, 49, 224, 228
Desertion 104, 107, 118, 120, 131, 132, 133, 160, 172, 196, 224, 228
Echo, slave ship 27, 202

Edenton, NC 5, 7, 8, 9, 10, 13, 14, 15, 17, 21, 25, 26, 30, 34, 38, 39, 41, 42, 45, 94, 120, 134, 135, 144, 174, 177, 194
Edmondston, Catherine Ann.... 95, 117, 118, 128, 132, 154, 200, 204, 206, 221, 223
Edward's Ferry .. 168, 170, 171, 174
Elliot, Gilbert........................ 168, 223
Ellis, Gov. John W. 56, 94, 222
Episcopal............................ 147, 208
Ewer, Jr., Capt. Barnabas... 128, 129
Forbes, John Murray 109
Fort Branch......... 164, 204, 205, 206
Fort Compher .... vii, 156, 177, 187, 209
Fort Grey............ 155, 171, 177, 179, 180, 182, 183, 189
Fort Wessells.............. 155, 177, 181, 182, 183, 209
Fort Williams 156, 178, 179, 180, 181, 184, 185, 186, 188, 189, 204, 213
French, Gen. Samuel G. 129, 211 221
Giddings, Joshua............................ 26
Goldsboro, NC.......... 58, 67, 82, 85, 88, 123, 124, 151
Graham, Maj. John W. 179, 181, 182, 188, 221
Grant, Gen. Ulysses........... 105, 114, 141, 158, 160, 191, 205, 210, 216, 217
Gray, Benjamin 174, 230
Greeley, Horace............ 73, 89, 106
Halifax, NC.......... 14, 15, 19, 26, 30, 33, 34, 38, 40, 43, 47, 56, 70, 95, 118, 151, 170, 175, 176, 201, 204,
Halleck, Gen. Henry.........105, 139, 140
Hamilton, Alexander......32, 36, 37, 38, 49, 62
Harland, Gen. Edward 198

Hartford Convention 39, 42, 43, 71
Hatteras forts........................ 94, 228
Hill, Gen. Daniel H. 130, 131, 133, 224
Hoke, Gen. Robert F......... v, vi, 136, 158, 165, 166, 167, 171, 172, 173, 174, 175, 176, 177, 179, 180, 181, 182, 183, 184, 185, 186, 189, 190, 191, 193, 194, 195, 196, 197, 198, 199, 205
Indentured Servants.............. 3, 4, 5
Jefferson, Thomas 37, 38, 39, 40, 41, 74, 93
Jones, Willie............................ 30, 33
Johnson, Samuel 209
Kemper, Gen. James L...... 176, 180, 185
Kentucky Resolutions 36, 39, 40
Lamb, Lt-Col. John C........... 76, 94, 122, 126, 127, 128, 129, 130, 152, 153
Latham, Charles................. 59, 156, 187, 208
Lawrence, Amos 108, 109
Lee, Richard Henry 31
Lee, Gen. Robert E. 31, 88, 97, 123, 164, 227
Lieber Code.......... 91, 138,139, 197
Lincoln, Abraham........... 37, 43, 53, 56, 58, 59, 60, 62, 63, 66, 68, 69, 70, 72, 73, 75, 76, 80, 81, 85, 88, 89, 90, 91, 93, 97, 98, 99, 100, 102, 103, 104, 105, 107, 108, 109, 110, 111, 113, 114, 117, 129, 132, 138, 139, 141, 142, 143, 144, 159, 160, 165, 196, 209, 211, 215, 216, 224, 226, 227
Little Washington, NC ... 17, 18, 37, 44, 45, 67, 88, 94, 95, 115, 121, 128, 131, 156, 158, 170, 172, 194, 195, 198, 199
Louisiana Native Guards ..111, 224
Phelps, Lake................. 9, 25, 26, 51

Pickett, Gen. George 133, 136, 164, 165, 171, 172
Picot-Armistead House 209
Macon, Nathaniel 29, 37, 40, 41, 44, 56, 59, 223
Maffitt, Capt. John Newland ...174, 200, 201, 202
Mallory, Stephen R. 167, 168, 201, 202
Martin, Gen. James G. 123, 174
Martin, Royal Gov. Josiah...........29
Massachusetts 7, 13, 16, 21, 22, 23, 24, 31, 39, 40, 42, 45, 82, 84, 86, 88, 91, 101, 104, 108, 109, 115, 119, 121, 127, 128, 132, 136, 152, 153, 155, 159, 160, 222
Massacre Legend....... 209, 210, 211
Mercer, Col. John T. . . 175, 181, 182
Methodists...............................7, 208
Morris, Col. Ellwood.............93, 94
"Morris Guards" 93, 94, 95
Murfree, Hardy 8, 14
Murphey, Archibald 43, 44
Naval Brigade...............................77
Negro Troops 83, 101
New Bern 10, 94, 96, 111, 115, 117, 119, 121, 122, 123, 124, 125, 126, 130, 131, 133, 136, 137, 141, 142, 143, 146, 147, 158, 164, 165, 170, 171, 172, 174, 177, 196, 198, 199, 201, 226, 227, 229
New England..... vi, 1, 2, 5, 6, 8, 14, 15, 16, 20, 21, 22, 23, 24, 27, 39, 40, 42, 43, 47, 52, 71, 76, 110, 198, 212
Newport Barracks, NC 130, 225
Nullification 39, 43, 46, 47, 53, 228
Pettigrew, Ebenezer.......8, 9, 10, 48
Pettigrew, James Johnston 26, 51, 228
Pettigrew, William S. 58, 70
Philadelphia..3, 29, 33, 50,160, 211

Poplar Point................................208
Portuguese.................. 19, 20, 21, 27
Quakers...........................2, 3, 7, 22
Ransom, Gen. Matt ... vii, 176, 177, 179, 180, 181, 182, 184, 185, 186, 187, 196
San Domingue 26, 27, 46, 101
San Patricio Battalion................133
Seward, William H. 23, 60, 80, 102, 226, 227
Smith, Peter Evans.....................168
South Carolina 12, 26, 40, 41, 46, 47, 52, 56, 63, 64, 65, 68, 69, 71, 80, 87, 97, 105, 106, 109
South Mills, Battle of.................117
Stanly, Edward.......... 48, 88, 89, 90, 91, 132, 141, 142, 229
Substitutes..104, 106, 141, 161, 162
Tarboro, NC 42, 58, 67, 96, 122, 146, 151, 177, 196, 203, 207
Tarleton...................................... v, 80
Taylor, Zachary 50
Tift Brothers 167, 224
Tories.......24, 29, 79, 83, 89, 95, 96, 97, 132, 153
Toronto 212
Treason.........61, 93, 96, 97, 98, 118, 132, 133, 142, 180, 190, 191, 193, 196, 223, 226
Turchin, Gen. John....................141
Tuscarora 1, 3, 4, 6
Underground Railroad 211, 224
US Colored Troops... 112, 158, 180
USS *Crusader*............................ 201
Vance, Gov. Zebulon 22, 89, 100, 131, 133, 151, 164, 223, 227
Veteran Volunteers.............161, 194
Virginia .... vi, 2, 4, 5, 7, 8, 12, 22, 23, 25, 27, 31, 36, 40, 41, 46, 52, 56, 62, 64, 66, 76, 87, 88, 96, 97, 100, 101, 102, 109, 111, 112, 129, 130, 131, 135, 151, 154, 158, 160, 165,

168, 172, 173, 176, 183, 195, 199, 204, 205, 211, 212
Washington, George.. 7, 14, 15, 37, 53, 97, 115, 198
Watson, Elkanah 13, 14, 16, 228
West Indies ... v, 5, 6, 13, 16, 17, 21, 25, 34, 37, 41, 76
Wessells, Gen. Henry 154, 155, 158, 159, 170, 108, 182, 189, 191, 194, 195, 196, 199, 209, 213, 214
Whigs 37, 48, 50, 51, 52, 56, 60
Wild, Gen. Edward 148, 149
Williamson, Hugh 13, 30, 35
Williamston, NC 116, 121, 122, 151, 160, 169, 177, 191, 205
Wilmington & Weldon Railroad ... 124, 172
Windley-Ausbon House 208
Wingfield Plantation 134
Worth, Josephine 148, 222

www.ingramcontent.com/pod-product-compliance
Lightning Source LLC
Chambersburg PA
CBHW060519080526
44586CB00012B/538